BRIGHT COLLEGE YEARS

ALSO BY ANNE MATTHEWS

Where the Buffalo Roam

BRIGHT
COLLEGE YEARS

Inside the American Campus Today

ANNE MATTHEWS

THE UNIVERSITY OF CHICAGO PRESS

Published by arrangement with Simon & Schuster, Inc.

The University of Chicago Press, Chicago 60637
Copyright © 1997 by Anne Matthews
All rights reserved.
Originally published 1997 by Simon & Schuster, Inc.
University of Chicago Press Edition 1998
Printed in the United States of America

04 03 02 01 00 99 98   6 5 4 3 2 1

Library of Congress Cataloging-in-Publication Data

Matthews, Anne, 1957–
    Bright college years : inside the American campus
today / Anne Matthews. — University of Chicago
Press ed.
        p.   cm.
    Includes index.
    ISBN 0-226-51092-1 (pbk. : alk. paper)
    1. Universities and colleges—United States—Case
studies.   2. College students—United States—Case
studies.   3. College students—United States—Attitudes—
Case studies.   4. College environment—United States—
Case studies.   I. Title.
[LA227.4.M38   1998]
378.73—dc21   98-20987
                                              CIP

♾ The paper used in this publication meets the minimum
requirements of the American National Standard for
Information Sciences—Permanence of Paper for Printed
Library Materials, ANSI Z39.48-1992.

Acknowledgments

Four years of research and over four hundred campus interviews went into this book's preparation. All statistics and findings cited come from published studies in the professional literature of higher education and the social sciences (or from discussions with the researchers involved); from fact-checked publications such as the *Atlantic Monthly, The Wall Street Journal,* and *The New York Times;* and from scholarly journals or higher-education trade periodicals, particularly *The Chronicle of Higher Education, Academe* (the magazine of the American Association of University Professors), *Dædalus* (a quarterly publication of the American Academy of Arts and Sciences), and *Change* (edited by the American Association for Higher Education).

Research sponsored by foundations with an interest in the condition of American campuses proved invaluable, too, especially the many reports, conference proceedings, and roundtables that have been or continue to be underwritten by the Carnegie, Spencer, Rockefeller, Johnson, and Ford Foundations, and by the Pew Charitable Trusts. Professional publications of the National Association of College and University Attorneys, the Council for the Advancement and Support of Education, and the National Center for the Study and Prevention of Campus Violence proved very useful, as did articles and reports issued under the auspices of the Institute for Research on Higher Education at the University of Pennsylvania and the Institute for Higher Education at Stanford University. Staff members at the library of the American Council on Education in Washington, D.C., the Columbia University libraries, the New York Public Library, Princeton University's Firestone Library, the Harvard Seminar for New Presidents, the University of Wisconsin Archives, the Library of Congress, and Phi Beta Kappa were all helpful in confirming historical and contemporary details of campus life.

I would like to thank the late Carl Wartenburg of Swarthmore College and the late Ernest Boyer of the Carnegie Foundation for insights into student and faculty issues nationwide; thanks go also to a dozen college and university presidents, current and emeritus, for firsthand accounts of an increasingly difficult job. For anyone interested in the physical history of the campus, I recommend Paul Venable Turner's *Campus: An American Planning Tradition* (The Architectural History Foundation/MIT Press, 1984); for its spiritual adventures, George Marsden's *The Soul of the American University* (Oxford University Press, 1994); and for an overview of late twentieth-century trends and developments, *Higher Learning in America, 1980–2000* (Arthur Levine, ed., Johns Hopkins University Press, 1994).

All the voices in this book are real people at real schools. Those at the edges of conventional academic power (from mid-level employees in development and campus services to office workers, graduate students, and adjunct instructors) often proved to be thoughtful backstage observers of the campus year. Some of the undergraduates were students in my own classes, some friends of their friends at colleges around the country, some serendipitously met; each proved kind and helpful to an inquisitive stranger. A few under the age of twenty-one requested pseudonyms, fearing their parents might recognize them in print; I agreed. Some campus adults—especially professors—asked for anonymity, too, but all very much wanted to help describe the daily rewards and pressures of a world behind walls to those who underwrite it.

My thanks to every one, especially faculty, administrators, staff, students, and alumni associated with the following institutions: Adelphi, Arizona State, Arizona, Bates, Berkeley, Bowdoin, Brandeis, Brown, Bryn Mawr, Carleton College, Case Western, The Claremont Colleges, The College of Charleston, Columbia, Cornell, Denison, Drake, Duke, Edgewood, Florida State, George Mason, Georgetown, Guelph, Harvard, Haverford, Hunter, Indiana, Lafayette, Lawrence, Middlebury, Mills, Mind Extension University, Minnesota, New York University, Northwestern, Notre Dame, Oklahoma, Oregon, Penn State, Princeton, Rice, Rollins, Rutgers, Seton Hall, Sinte Gleska, Spelman, Stanford, SUNY-Cortland, Texas Tech, Towson State, Tufts, Virginia, Texas (Austin and El Paso), Wells, Wesleyan, Wisconsin, Wofford, and Yale.

My special thanks, as well, to Cynthia Cannell of Janklow & Nesbit; to Rebecca Saletan and Denise Roy of Simon & Schuster; to friends and family in Madison, Princeton, Highland Park, Herrontown, Sussex, Vermont, Boston, and New York for advice and support; and to the Freedom Forum Media Studies Center for its generous fellowship program.

For many of my teachers,
and all my students.

Bright college years, with pleasure rife,
The shortest, gladdest years of life.

—nineteenth-century
American college song,
originating at Yale

BRIGHT COLLEGE YEARS

Contents

Foreword

A handful of American places enjoy powerful double lives, one daily and real, another conducted largely in the national imagination. Manhattan, like California, is such a place; so are Alaska and the Mississippi Delta, the frontier West, and the inner city. Oldest and strongest of these common dreamscapes is the campus. We have argued about its aims and ways since the summer of 1638, when Harvard became the first college in the New World to open north of the Rio Grande. *Bright College Years* is an informal portrait of today's American campus and the forces that shape it: the weight of tradition, the tangles of ego, the empty pocket, the shock of the new.

Higher education is a remarkably unwatched industry. Pundits and reformers attack its more public absurdities; legislatures and applicants bemoan the rising cost of degrees. Few decision-makers, consumers, or citizens know what life is actually like inside the first-year dorm, the faculty meeting, the president's waiting room—or why it is that way.

Because I was born on a campus and raised in the academic habitat of library and lab, I have had the good fortune to

17

watch an American institution adapting to market pressures and knowledge explosions over four difficult decades. In addition to reporting on higher education for *The New York Times* and other publications, I have been a faculty member and a university administrator, an adjunct instructor and a research fellow. I like to write about U.S. places facing immense change, where history lies very close to the surface, whose residents passionately believe they are exceptions to any rule. One such locale is the Great Plains, those dry demanding lands west of the 98th meridian that I describe in my last book, *Where the Buffalo Roam.* Another is the college and university world, just as mortgaged to the past, struggling even harder to evolve. Unlike the Plains, the American campus is not a geopolitical whole. It is an archipelago nation-within-a-nation, two thousand islands in the social sea, some splendidly fortified, some emerging, some subsiding, with common problems and a common tongue but no clear capital or sound economy.

As participant and observer—a rare crossed wire—I have combined social history, narrative, memoir, and reportage to offer a native daughter's field notes, trying to suggest points of entry to an ancient and not always welcoming society, to investigate the tensions and riddles all schools face at century's end. Does this nation want the campus to be a counterworld or a social mirror? How much are we truly willing to invest to produce college graduates able to cope with, and compete with, the rest of the planet? Our answers, like our silences, will shape twenty-first–century America in direct and often disconcerting ways.

The book's chapters are excursional and seasonal, as are its interludes on campus history and college teaching; the book runs from summer to summer, one year implying many. The first section explores the campus of ambition and desire. Next come the darkening weeks of a campus autumn, when students often learn most intensely, in and out of class. Each winter, faculty assess research and teaching, selfishness and self-lessness, failure and fame. The spring section chronicles the campus as administrators see it. In the final chapter, we arrive again at the first days of summer, and explore the alumni campus of money and memory. (Though community colleges, like graduate and professional programs, are worth a volume in themselves, *Bright College Years* treats only the life of the four-year institution, higher education's traditional core.)

The college campus is not an easy mechanism for social change, nor a particularly cooperative one. Campuses often look pastoral but act commercial, struggle to maintain serene facades even though questioning and conflict are their natural condition, frequently prefer to say A but do B. And yet the campus is home to the most serious work in the world, as beneath academe's surface silliness, built-in waste, and seeming irrelevance is a hardy, unkillable core of transcendent purpose. When smart people live at close quarters with the great mysteries (natural and human, present and past) the cost is often high; joining the knowledge business can be as risky as staring into the sun. But even in its least cost-efficient aspects—the dead ends and last stands, the instants of insight as unpredictable as earthquakes, the challenges and dissections that must follow every one—real value lies, and honor, too.

SUMMER:
The Price of Passage

On May weekend mornings of soft sun and river wind, the homeless of Manhattan will often gather to beg and smoke beside the Eighth Avenue entrance to Madison Square Garden. But on this clear warm Sunday, they only back against its grey tile walls and stare. By car and bus and subway, on bikes, on foot, twenty thousand high school juniors are descending upon New York's annual college fair to find a future. By eleven o'clock, the sports arena's escalators and corridors swim with faces. I stop a few and ask their names. Shatel Javeed, raised in Bangladesh. Amparo Lopez, parents Cuban and Senegalese. Umpas Ninvanichkul, born in Tashkent. Diallo Momadou, from Haiti by way of the Bronx.

They are the new America, arriving at their Ellis Island. In the Garden's upstairs exhibition hall the noise is tremendous, a rising roar like a jet warming up, as anxious adolescents translate campus brochures into Spanish, Arabic, Creole, or North Jersey for the watchful parents and grandparents and small cousins trailing every step. In hundreds of college booths, slick catalogues pile and spill. Earn your B.A. in Pastry Arts at the

Culinary Institute of America. Major in meditation at Naropa, America's only Buddhist campus. Videos of trees and stone towers play and replay. Campus recruiters in business suits, hoarse, smiling, watchful, line every aisle: yes, we're looking for strong B students, yes, we have lots of sports, oh, no no no, financial aid is never a problem.

The American collegiate mosaic forms and reforms each year, but today some pieces are clearly missing. African Americans with academic talent are now recruited in middle school, wooed and fought over; the last thing they want are more brochures. Alumni children, like male athletes, remain a protected group. Well-off suburbanites, any sort, need not waste a fine warm Sunday. With adequate grades plus open-handed parents, college doors everywhere will swing wide.

Overachievers can sleep in, too. A public information fair like this, run by the national association of college-guidance counselors, is of no real use to the 100,000 students trying for places at the nation's thirty or forty most competitive schools, the trophy colleges with apply/admit ratios of twelve or fifteen or eighteen to one. For the supremely ambitious, prepped to exhaustion by vocabulary trainers and interview coaches, junior-year summer is a marathon's final lap. Imperial domains like Harvard and Stanford, name-brand enclaves like Wellesley and Oberlin, will often skip these open events, too. If they chose, they could sell every seat many times over, at any price. But 95 percent of American colleges are not at all selective, cannot luxuriate in debates over admitting smart versus talented versus energetic students. For the struggling middle ranks, especially—the obscure rural campuses and the big dull universities, the genteel church institutions stranded by time and change—a college fair is a good way to corral warm bodies.

Beside the show floor is a roped-off advising area. At its long tables sit two dozen counselors from area high schools. All are volunteers, giving up a Sunday to start would-be collegians through the campus maze. I slip into a chair between two of the most experienced. At my left is Paul Hecht, a lean man with curly grey-brown hair and a Wesleyan College T-shirt ("That's the Macon, Georgia, Wesleyan, you understand; the *complete* Southern-belle finishing school"). He heads the college office at Randolph High, on upper Manhattan's 135th Street. To my right labors Jeffrey Spielvogel, a calm, slow-voiced college counselor from Lewis High, in the suburban borough of Queens. The sleeves of his salmon-striped dress shirt are rolled high, to no avail; the Garden's air-conditioning surrendered long ago. But high-schoolers wait half an hour and more for an opening at the advising tables, and a stranger's interrogation: Grade-point average? Extracurriculars? Field of study? What do you want from life?

A self-assured blonde with splendid biceps plops into the metal folding chair across from Hecht. "I like volleyball and nursing, in that order," she informs him, sitting back expectantly. Her mother hovers, plucking at the girl's candy-pink blouse till her daughter backhands her, a swift, practiced blow. Hecht is deep in a battered *Peterson's Guide to Colleges*.

"Are you *good* at volleyball?" he demands, nose to index.

"Very," she says simply.

"NCAA Division One, then. Indiana. You'll love it," Hecht pronounces. Dazzled, she heads for the Indiana University booth and is replaced by a slender, anxious Hispanic girl from middle-class Forest Hills High, grade-point 3.5, wants to be a physicist, will consider only large East Coast cities.

"Not even Chicago?" Hecht asks. Her father pulls at her arm, whispers violently in Spanish. "No," she says softly, "my family doesn't even like it that I'm—sorry, I mean, Boston is my limit."

"Boston is a fine idea," says Hecht meaningfully. "Boston University, Boston College. Think twice about UMass-Amherst, their budget cuts have been shocking. *Si su padre tiene preguntas, llameme.*" He offers his card with a smile and bow. A sallow, acne-plagued boy next slips into the chair: C average, no activities, no clear ambitions, no points for interesting ethnicity, no apparent personality (except for a wrist tattoo reading "Abdul + Betty").

"What about SUNY?" howls Hecht, above the crowd roar, meaning the vast State University of New York system. "Okay," yells the kid obediently, "but I really wanna go outstate." "Louisiana, you'll love it." "I been there already." "So, you don't need me! Go see the SUNY people. Go, go, you heard me." The patient slouches off, gnawing on his Walkman cord, just as a heavyset mother and daughter in matching beige warm-up suits arrive, gold hoop earrings swinging against their coffee-dark cheeks. Even before they sit down, the mother is talking.

"We're Jamaican, money is not a concern, she's pre-med, probably radiology but maybe pediatrics, from Brooklyn, we're getting tons of unsolicited recruiting videos, I hear that's always a good sign, what about the Ivy League, are there any Ivy schools she can commute to?"

Hecht, nodding cordially, makes an instant decision. "Columbia. Barnard. Possibly Penn. The better the university, the better it looks when you apply to med school. Take the financial aid if you can get it. What about Howard?"

They've never heard of it. "What are your outside interests?" he gently asks the silent daughter; she fingers her silky sleeve and shrugs. We wait. A furrow deepens between Hecht's brows. She shrugs again. They depart, a liner and its dinghy.

"A pity. No killer instinct, and she's been watching much too much TV," comments Hecht, leaning back to scan the faces surging past our alcove, intent, impassive, terrified. "Frankly, they've *all* been watching much too much TV."

A black pre-pharmacy candidate and a redheaded field hockey forward present themselves, giggling. "This is like going to a 1-900 psychic!" Hecht's chair legs hit the floor. In two minutes and thirty seconds ("My personal land-speed record for deciding a life, ladies") he points them toward Syracuse, Tennessee, Old Dominion, maybe the University of Connecticut. "Do they have cosmetology at any of those schools?" the redhead demands. "Certainly not," says Hecht, miming a glove-slap. "But yes, I love your hair. And consider a Kaplan study course before taking the SATs."

Hecht has been advising college applicants since 1976. His East Harlem High school—"as inner-city as you can get"—has an aviation club, a fine student newspaper, and a touring Renaissance music choir. He sends 94 percent of its students to college, 87 percent to four-year schools. "The good campuses come to us because we have a product," he explains. "For every dollar they give you, I tell the kids, any college gets three to five dollars back in state and federal funds without ever touching their endowment. You're cost-efficient. So sell yourselves. With care. This is a business transaction. Don't forget it."

An immensely pregnant girl in a red leather jacket bends over our table, peace medallion swinging. Her round brown face is shadowed with fatigue, but she will not sit.

"How do I write a good college application essay?" she demands. Hecht considers. "Keep it fresh, creative, literate, grab their attention for no more than one page, get out gracefully."

She snorts, and stalks away. Many of the college-application brochures she clutches above the rounded shelf of her belly are full of personal questions, designed to provoke good essays: What would you do if you found a lion in the backyard? Given six inches of string, what would you create? If you could form a new political party, demands DePauw, what issues would it confront, and why? Life is filled with embarrassing and uncomfortable moments; please describe one of yours: Babson College wants to know. If you were to come upon a drowning child, inquires Guilford, would you feel compelled to save that child, even at great risk to yourself? Jeffrey Spielvogel watches sadly as the expectant mother vanishes into the crowds. I ask about the demographics at the high school where he teaches.

"Even five years ago, very WASP, but now we're strongly Asian. Korean, Chinese, Vietnamese, Filipino, Indonesian. A third of our students need extensive, *extensive,* help with English. Their SAT verbal scores get very, very low. Nor are they, um, sophisticated about what will be asked of them in college, even why they should be there at all. They only know they must go." He used to counsel kids to try for prestige campuses. Now he favors the best fit between applicant and campus.

"Their greatest fear is rejection," he explains. "I spend every spring stopping suicides, breakdowns, hysteria. Half I'll get into the New York State system, somewhere, somehow; the rest go all over, Georgia, Texas, California, and, yes, the Ivies. But the parents! Parents from hell. Parents who second-guess and short-circuit. Parents who won't come in for conferences unless they get a letter from a social worker. Parents who burst in to inform me, 'My child comes from greatness and will do great things.' Not with a 64 average and 380 math SATs, she won't."

Not all the prospectives wandering Madison Square Garden are seventeen. A quarter of U.S. undergraduates now are twenty-five and over: grown-ups reach for campus admissions packets, too, then hurry away to scan them in restrooms and stairwells. "For a son or daughter?" a Fordham rep asks kindly, smiling. "No," the middle-aged man murmurs, as he sidles off, "no, actually, for me." Women going back to school are happy and excited, the reps say, direct with their questions, even aggressive. The men are furtive and ashamed. Many have been out of work for months, or years; they know they must retool, learn computing, finish the degree abandoned in flush times, but they have knocked at too many closed doors lately, and this one comes especially hard. Whatever program they choose, the instructors may be their children's age, or their grandchildren's.

After an hour I walk the show floor, gathering great glossy sheaves of promotional brochures. Come to warm and caring Coker. Ohio University, you'll want to stay. It's easy to fit in, at Westbrook. "New York City: You Gotta Do It Once," Columbia pronounces. Alfred University ups the ante: "Your professors will know your name and your nuances; you will know their home phone numbers and their home cooking. . . . You'll never be bored here."

Run through our water sculpture on sunny days, invites Purdue. Join our surfing team, counters Pepperdine. "All dorms have free cable TV service," whispers Utica College of Syracuse University, "and students enjoy expanded personal fitness facilities." Food is a recurring motif. Sushi bars, waffle bars, made-to-order omelettes and fireside snack lounges crowd the catalogues. Graze our health food café, pleads Sarah Lawrence. Arizona urges "gorging on hot dogs at the Spring Fling." Swarthmore's brochure features a glowing, if cryptic, close-up of racially diverse students devouring chocolates while reading *National Geographic*.

Leafing through these splendid albums, with their heavy-coated stock of scarlet and jade and copper, their dazzling pop-ups and cutouts and wraparounds, would make anyone crave college. The copy is as soothing as Muzak in a mall, as sweetly urgent as the Shopping Channel. The same adjectives star page after page. Profound. Excellent. Life-enhancing. Personal. College will be fun, intimate, entertaining, fun, improving but nonthreatening. You will be painlessly prepared for a high-paying career. Hope, comfort, magic, all are here, whether you major in mall management at the University of Connecticut–Storrs, in astrophysics at MIT, in winemaking at the University of California–Davis.

"Mention us on the Veneto or the Ginza, and you'll likely receive a nod of recognition," claims Temple. Don't miss our lectures by Doctor Julius Erving, urges the University of Toledo, plus hot concerts "by Def Leppard, Michael Bolton, Cher and Boyz II Men." We recommend hot buttered popcorn and a fast game of backgammon in the student union, counters Iona, wanly. "Learn sophisticated research skills," Skidmore offers, but the next brochure in the pile is from Northwood University of West Palm Beach, carefully explaining that "even our English and art classes are taught from a business perspective," and reminding potential students not to miss the university's famous annual auto and fashion shows. The University of Central Florida is even more direct: "Our longest walk between buildings is ten minutes. . . . Disney World and great beaches are an hour away." "When a little retail therapy is in order," admits Franklin and Marshall, "shop till you drop at the nearby mall's 190 stores."

The American college and university world employs some 2.5 million people, more workers than the auto, steel, and textile industries combined. Even its own professors of economics cannot agree on higher education's size. Some call it a $200 billion enterprise, others $300 billion; it's a little larger than the computer business, a lot smaller than the restaurant industry. The health of America's campuses rests on the undergraduate head count, a million freshmen in the door each year, a million or so bachelor's degrees annually granted. The cycle is not as neat as it sounds. About nine million attend four-year schools full-time. Several million more float within the baccalaureate process, somewhere: taking a year off, transferring, going part-time, waiting out hard times. Taking one course, for the cheap student health insurance. Traveling for independent-study credit. Enrolling, quitting in three weeks, then living till next term on the cash refund of a government scholarship. Far more, eager to finish, are squeezed out of required courses semester after semester. Many schools cannot afford to expand sections or hire more instructors; many students work full-time and cannot make regular-day classes. College registrars report that the average time to degree is expanding from four years to six and more.

We practice precision guesswork, say college admissions officers, and their applicants do the same. How students decide on campuses is a great mystery of higher education. They wander the aisles of college fairs like this one; surf the Internet's campus Web sites; study the special college issues of *U.S. News & World Report* or *Money;* rely on the grapevine ("My brother's cousin swears that Santa Cruz is a *clothing-optional campus!*"); or else wait for the admissions officers who rush each fall through five and six high schools a day, some where BMWs fill the student lot, others where recruiters are led to student interviews by security officers in bulletproof vests. Today's traveling campus rep may be tomorrow's vice president; like college students, campus administrators learn their trade by trial and error. One former University of Virginia dean remembers the Eighties as a frantic statewide round of high school pep talks that clearly failed to thrill.

> "So, what are you going to do with your fine young minds?"
>
> "Work in the *coal* mine." [A voice from the back of the room.]
>
> "But college means a marvelous chance to expand your horizons!"
>
> "For that, we grow mari*juana*."

That was 1985. Today the earnings gap between a worker with a high school diploma and one with a four-year college degree has grown into a schism; survive the contemporary campus and your paycheck may nearly double. In France or Japan now, perhaps one secondary-school graduate in ten goes on to the elite preserve of higher education. On the eve of Pearl Harbor, America sent about the same percentage to college. By 1970, it was one in four. In the postindustrial economy, one U.S. high school graduate in two may attempt some form of campus life.

The immigrants and the first-generation applicants, the iron-willed working-class kids, the older learners who wander Madison Square Garden this early-summer morning form a partial glimpse of the new century's admissions pool. Ambition, hunger, a sense of closing doors bring them in, and exposure to any campus will often do the rest. Yet to retain funding and maintain prestige, the industry needs more raw material. For the first time since the 1930s, campuses are looking toward those for whom push is greater than pull: the marginal, the unprepared, the undertrained. Sometimes it works out. In lecture, in lab, a mind comes joyously alive. You never know who will take to education, or when. America is not only the world's campus superpower but the great home of second- and third- and seventh-chance learning. But 29 percent of today's first-time freshmen require remedial courses, usually in math or writing or both. The campus life-support machine of tutors and counselors saves some, loses more. Over one first-year in four quits before sophomore year. Nearly half those who enter college these days withdraw before finishing, defeated by strangeness, "thrown in the tank and left to flounder," as their instructors, exhausted or pitying, say.

For students fresh from high school, parental income is a strong predictor of college failure. If family earnings are in the bottom 25 percent, a student has only a one in ten chance of earning a bachelor's degree by age twenty-four. Children of divorce are much less likely to enroll at selective campuses, though no one yet knows why—perhaps emotional fragility, perhaps because one parent can't pay for college or the other won't. But for most schools, bringing in a class, any class, remains the central goal. For the next five months the most sought-after people in American higher education will be this vast second tier, "not dumb, just different," as admissions industry briefing books purr.

Viewed as a whole, the American college population is increasingly female, public, part-time, local, adult, and in debt. Fifty-five percent of current undergraduates are women. Eighty percent attend public institutions. Just one in five now fits the traditional profile (attending full-time, living on campus, under twenty-two). More and more, the choice of a campus rests on income, not merit. To attend a private school with no help from grants or loans takes more than a third of a typical family's income; nearly two-thirds, if you are among the working poor. Four college students in five choose schools in their home states, often to save money, a relative concept: on graduation day, over half will walk away with debts—$10,000, $30,000, $50,000—that may endure till their own children enter higher education. Outstanding federal college loans alone are $26 billion, and rising.

Yet a campus can fill every seat and still go broke. Smart, rich applicants (in industry terms, high-ability, low-need candidates) are rare. Need-blind admissions, the great campus leveler for forty years, make financial planners very nervous now, even at high-endowment schools. Campus work-study funding, like aid for the poorest would-be collegians, is shrinking fast. Full-time undergraduates are expensive creatures: the average per-student expenditure (counting salaries, construction and maintenance costs, and operation of campus research facilities) is close to $17,000 a year. To harvest a profitable class, over half of private four-year campuses use yield-management techniques learned from hotels and airlines; computerized programs signal which anxious or mediocre applicant will pay top price, which student with musical or athletic talent should be given a signing bonus—a half-price computer, a special fellowship. Discounting reigns. Some private liberal arts colleges now quietly offer price reductions of up to 40 percent. They have no choice. Every year, more and more college consumers simply declare sticker shock and bargain, hard. It works when buying cars, and campus customers know it. If schools do not offer price breaks, they will turn back into havens for the rich. Or they will die.

Of the 2,125 four-year campuses in the United States (595 public, 1,530 private), most believe they face a buyer's market, uneven, unpredictable. Some small colleges, like Muskingum, Pine Manor, and North Carolina Wesleyan, are cutting tuitions outright. Others, like Pennsylvania's Moravian College, gratefully give up the race for national status and concentrate on a local clientele ("I dreamed of making this school another Middlebury," Moravian's president once said wistfully, but he settled for niche marketing, which suited his client pool just fine; they *wanted* "an affordable family-atmosphere college serving good but not outstanding students within a 150-mile radius.") Established state university powers like Minnesota and Michigan, the so-called Public Ivies, have floods of good applicants and are raising standards and tuitions. At flagship schools like Berkeley, where you could once get a fine education nearly free, tuition-room-and-board packages are topping $10,000 a year, close to the private university level. Their cash-strapped public cousins across the Southeast dread the next decades, when far too many state residents will turn college age and clamor for in-state tuitions. Virginia alone expects 65,000 additional college students by the turn of the century, the equivalent of three new campuses. California may be a state where the highest-paid public official is the UCLA football coach, but all its other higher-ed appropriations are falling, demand for campus access soaring.

Recruiters plot and plan, market and strategize. "It's an arms race," says Beaver's admissions chief. Foreign students add almost $10 billion a year to the U.S. campus economy, but their overall numbers have declined since the 1980s. So colleges fly recruiters now to Malaysia, Singapore, Hong Kong, Seoul. One or two hits underwrite the trip; these students will all pay full freight. Asians tend to have sound study habits, their checks rarely bounce, and their behavior problems surface later, when they break it to their parents that they want to be conceptual sculptors or Peace Studies majors, not chemical engineers or cardiologists. But that's two years in the future, every $50,000 counts, and it may never happen: this is why Congress runs a national debt. Meanwhile, sign them up, fill the class. A pulse in one hand, a check in the other, say the reps, matter-of-factly. You have to shoot a dean these days to get thrown out.

Some institutions—including Yale and Stanford, Dartmouth and Penn—insist that applicants accept binding campus offers soon after admission. Some colleges hire bounty hunters. Outsourcing admissions, it's called: an Atlanta sales company provides an admissions director, who manages recruiting teams with firm monthly quotas for their relentless follow-up calls and visits, as college is pushed like credit cards or long-distance phone service. Many schools flinch at commercializing admissions. Many have little choice. People can afford anything they really want, the bounty hunters' manual says quietly. Customers buy on emotion. Watch for body movements, like leaning forward, which may signal desire. Mention price last.

Some schools sign up applicants over the phone. In Lynchburg, Virginia, the Reverend Jerry Falwell runs a campus called Liberty University. Its commencement speakers since 1990 include George Bush, Newt Gingrich, Pat Buchanan, Clarence Thomas, and Jesse Helms. Liberty welcomes applications on its 800 line. The operators at the other end, soft-voiced and polite, have a very short list of questions: your marital status, your felony convictions and contagious diseases, why you believe in moral family values, your prayer requests, your sweatshirt size, and your Visa/MasterCard number.

By late afternoon, many of the teenagers in Madison Square Garden are hungry and dazed. Quite a few parents are looking grim, realizing a Sixties adolescence is not a sound touchstone for this new world. Families perch on plastic chairs along the rim of the show floor, recovering their self-possession, blinking at the mob. The Villanova booth is getting little traffic; its brochures ("Villanova: A Community of Scholars!") stress languages, history, physics. "I'm grossed," says a boy, dropping their material in the trash. A few booths away, a thin kid with a shaved head, two nose rings, and a sardonic, eager face reads an instructional catalogue aloud.

"'This course considers ways gendered identities are produced, repositioned, legislated, pathologized, theorized and contested. Topics to be addressed include impersonation, passing, cross-dressing, veiling, voguing, fantasy and fetishism.' Hey, sign me up!" His father, very red, whips the book from his son's hand, nods abruptly to the rep, and stalks off. The rep slips the boy an application. He stashes it in his backpack, grins engagingly in thanks, and hurries to catch up with Dad.

The overflow crowd at the Financial Aid session comes out sweating.

"Sell my house! They say I can sell my house."

"I know, I heard. Either that or a third mortgage."

All around me, adolescents are still translating activities brochures, looking for little brothers' lost sweaters, flirting with friends. One or two, heading for the exit with slow, wandering steps, clutch their mothers' hands. A stocky father in a neat plaid shirt stops in mid-aisle, swings around, and holds out one wide palm, like the traffic cop he is. His dreadlocked son, hauling three shopping bags of shiny brochures, freezes in mid-whine.

"College," says the father, meaning every syllable. "College, or die."

Trust us, the campus world has always said, we command secrets, we know best. And as a nation we do trust, touchingly so—though a few queries seem in order for the utopia glimpsed in the recruiting videos. What's going *on* in there? And while we're at it—what, exactly, is college *for?* To join the educated working poor? To make you rich? Decent? Wise? The answers, to date, satisfy almost no one. This is a public-service industry with complicated feelings about the public, and over the centuries higher education has become accustomed to doing all the questioning.

But the American campus is not a democracy. It never has been. It is hundreds of small intense worlds that touch but do not blend, the realms of carillonneurs and astrophysicists; of midnight roof-climbers and annotators of eighteenth-century sermons and beer-bong savants; of women's ice-hockey squads and robotics postdocs and of necrolexicographers, who coax dead tongues like Middle Hittite or Sumerian into convenient dictionary form. Allied, they make a campus; grow enough campuses, and you have the vigorous parallel universe called U.S. higher education: driven, noisy, fecund, the envy of the planet.

The campus world can also seem saturated with strangeness, like a familiar landscape glimpsed in a mirror. It is a place enormously knowing, but almost never reasonable, situated in the United States but not entirely of it. Laws, customs, language all run differently there. Time does, too. The contemporary campus, in very real ways, remains a chunk of the twelfth century dropped live and squabbling on the threshold of the twenty-first. From free speech to due process, constitutional rights change or vanish at the campus gate. A private institution can, if it wishes, shut itself up like a medieval fortress, barring the public from its roads and fields. A public university may issue a letter declaring any citizen *persona non grata,* should he or she persistently trespass or annoy. Even a small campus often has its own security force and power plant; in the Cold War years, many schools made quiet plans for keeping campus residents safe (and townies out) in case of thermonuclear attack.

Deans and presidents often enjoy telling new students, "Here is the campus. Take it . . . if you can." The world of academe is strongly territorial, but not very social. Its three tribes—those who learn, those who profess, and those who arrange—carry a great deal of baggage, visible and invisible. All are jealous of traditional boundaries. Except for a few sacrificial liaisons (freshman-writing instructors, assistant deans of student life), contact among the camps is often ritual, and brief. Fifty-minute lectures. Procedural memos. Office hours by appointment only. That the other two cultures exist is a perpetual surprise, especially when classes are changing: Who *are* all these people? And why are they on *my* campus? But for seven centuries, the basic alchemy of the venture has held. Learn, or leave. Be willing to be changed, or get out.

———————— ◆ ————————

Just after the New York college fair, I stop by the departmental office to retrieve my mail. The office staff has vanished on an end-of-term liberation lunch, leaving three senior faculty to peer accusingly into the bowels of the copy machine.

"It's so temperamental."

"Quite the diva."

"Perhaps a swig of toner?"

I get halfway down the stairs before the last final exam lets out. No adult can outrun four hundred undergraduates at semester's end, but I know that if I stand very still they will flood around me like a tide past a rock. When you encounter students mostly in seminar rooms, fifteen docile note-takers, or find them pacing outside your office nervous and alone, it is easy to forget how *large* they all are now, male and female both: twenty-two years of vitamins, seat belts, soccer practice, salad bars. I am tall for my generation, but as the wave goes past I see only backpacks and T-shirts: Rugby Players Eat Their Dead, Jägermeister Forever, Feels Like Oncoming Traffic to Me.

I turn to watch them spill onto the sunny lawn, leaping to touch low maple branches, slapping palms, vital with release. A dark-haired girl in a purple vest does cartwheels, crying, "Free forever, freefreefreefreefree!" Three strapping boys in baseball caps fall to their knees beside a tall bronze oval sculpture and wriggle through: "Rebirthing! Rebirthing!" Their roommate blocks the path of a high-schooler heading for an admissions interview, stiff and anxious in a painfully new suit. "It's true, my man! For a mere $28,000 a year, *you, too,* can have a brain the consistency of a lima bean!"

I move under a beech tree to inspect my mail. A jar of homemade jam from a Bay Area student headed for Singapore, then to Microsoft. A note from a senior, off to Chile to teach English and climb mountains. An extravagant thank-you for a law school recommendation from the kid least likely to thrive in wing-tips. ("Madam, you are a goddess of the first rank; bring your legal business to me in future and I can insure you of an excellent discount.")

By three o'clock, office assistants are stripping concert notices and cheap-airfare flyers from hallway bulletin boards, a year of staples tinkling like rain into the garbage cans; by four, cars crammed with plastic milk crates and footlockers are pulling away from residence-hall parking lots. Five o'clock, and the janitors have flung open all the doors and windows, freeing nine months of communal smells—chalk dust and dry rot, wet towels and stale beer—to float up over the trees, and away.

Six, and the campus wells with quiet. Late sun eases along the slate walkways, moves gently through moving leaves. Mourning doves coast low over hazy lawns. A solitary jogger rounds the corner by the student-services building and is gone. On the central green, western afterlight slips down the old foursquare buildings, cornice, lintel, balustrade, arch; their honey-colored sandstone will be warm to the hand an hour after sundown.

When school is in session, the modern perimeter of campus rouses at about this hour, computer building and science labs that are at noon grey drab concrete becoming great lanterns of tinted glass: rose, sea-blue, bronze, sea-green among the darkening trees. Today the whole campus dims, cools, and brims with silence, a stage set between performances. As late spring moves into early summer, until the short-term customers straggle in for banking institutes, biology courses, music camps, and Elderhostels, two thousand college campuses across America will lie drowsing like this one, resting and mute. Late August, when tailgates again disgorge the mountain bike, the laser printer, the grim-faced mothers armed with Tub & Tile, seems blissfully distant.

A campus summer is really for locals, not strangers. Scholars in this season catch up on unread journals and polish grant applications, true enough, but you also spot them on the lawn by the student union, running bare toes through June grass, the nation's best minds turning majestically toward starlight concerts and peach ice-cream.

I remember plenty of microbiologists and Byzantine historians doing just that at the University of Wisconsin-Madison when I was growing up; from the late Fifties until the summer of 1970, the UW managed to be both bucolic and bohemian. New Yorkers in particular adored Madison's offhand kindness to radicals and loners and international strays, its meditative Holsteins grazing beside the cyclotron, its lakeside student union stocked with 3.2 beer and relentlessly authentic folksingers. The rest of the state loathed Madison. Send a decently raised young person to school there and six months later you got back a discontented stranger, babbling about aesthetic imperatives and French-roast coffee. Mad City, they grumbled: twenty square miles surrounded by reality.

A grave immutable cycle—summer session, fall registration, exam week, spring term, commencement, students-gone-away—ruled the life of every faculty child. Our professorial parents, fathers especially, were expected to be sedentary and brilliant. Most sat in their home studies seven days a week and thought. Mathematicians read science fiction, then leapt up suddenly to scribble equations. Astronomers, batlike, slept most of the day. I loved living on a campus because all the grown-ups knew such useful things: that you can put a butter-fly in the freezer and revive it months later; that a kitchen floor is mostly random atoms; that Michelangelo liked herring sandwiches for lunch, and for fun made fancy snowmen. Sometimes faculty parents even diagnosed, defended, or instructed what we learned to call Non-University People, citizens who (we whispered, fascinated) *probably watched TV.* Except for election returns and nature films, few of us were allowed near a television set. "You can have one if you can build one," one physicist told his complaining children, and they did.

But as July turned to August, a single sentence ("Play qui-etly, your father's putting together his courses") could bring us instantly to heel. In academe, summer is also a season of sudden departures and falls from grace, a time when people disappear due to graduate examinations failed, manuscripts re-jected, tenure denied. Chairmen and senior faculty were god-like. At department parties, I curtsied to every full professor I could find, only to be upstaged by very well-rehearsed peers. ("Mummy, may we botanize near that lovely stand of *Canadensis?*" "Of course, darlings, you need fresh air after reading so much Ibsen.") The grande-dame senior wives were more terrifying still. ("Isn't it hot?" a new instructor's fiancée might timidly venture. "My dear, you don't know what heat *is* until you've given birth on sabbatical in Mogamba.")

I soon found sanctuary in the cool, dim lower reaches of the university's library school, half-hidden among elms in the heart of campus. Its children's literature room was a closed re-search collection, but after a taxing interview on theme and structure in the *Little House* books, the director let me stay. Four afternoons a week, while my mother attended graduate seminars, I descended a wrought-iron circular stair in invisible hoopskirts—sometimes as Sara Crewe (a quiet nobility of posture), sometimes Caddie Woodlawn (three leaps and a thump)—and sank into the worlds of Melendys and Bastables, Mowgli and Green Knowe. High up in the toast-colored walls, small square windows with wavy panes framed collegiate ankles passing by the hundreds, argyle or cable-knit, as the lake light faded to grey, then gentian-blue, the whisper of my turning pages the only sound in the tall old room.

But by fourth, fifth, sixth grade—'66 to '69—the University of Wisconsin was a front line of Vietnam protest, like Berkeley and Harvard, and to see documentary footage from those years is like watching home movies. Some professors gamely took on all comers in class ("Your arguments are illogical!" "Define illogical, man!") but lecture-room debate turned swiftly to exhausting public theater, all sides driven by the academic's terrible need to be right. Once or twice a century, people on campuses are caught up in genuine argument about serious ideas: secession, evolution, civil disobedience, foreign wars, the custody of social power. The campus rarely knows its own strength. When confrontation comes, when theory has consequences, life there becomes as exhilarating and dangerous as a summer storm.

Grade-school classmates and I tried looking up "Protest" in the big card catalogue; also "Demonstration" and "Civil Unrest," learning a lot about Mother Jones and Gandhi but nothing that would explain the grown-up voices shouting about the war far into the night in living room and kitchen, parent against parent, professor against student. We pooled milk money for illicit bus rides down to central campus, to watch the big kids riot—the brisk undergraduate *au pairs* who had once migrated in and out of our spare rooms, the formerly jovial graduate assistants from our fathers' labs. Always before, the big kids had made us marshmallow-fudge brownies, taken us swimming, shown us how to stand eggs on end at the vernal equinox. But by summer 1970, the Wisconsin campus was a combat zone. The bright Madison mornings smelled of Mace and pepper gas. Many classrooms and offices were trashed and looted; State Street, once merry with head shops and record stores, was boarded up from end to end. Urgent scrawls smeared the splintered plywood: *Death to the Pigs, Power to the People, If You Are Not with Us You Are Against Us.*

Near four on the morning of August 24, 1970, beds shook all over town, strong, even tremors, but there was no flash of light, only a monstrous roar, a wall of sound that died to ab-solute silence in the humid dark. An antiwar group called the New Year's Gang had made a giant fertilizer bomb and blown up the Army Math Research Center, housed in Wisconsin's main physics building. The explosion damaged twenty-six campus buildings, and was felt thirty miles away. The saboteurs were ambitious, but unskilled. A young postdoctoral physics student, working late (married, the father of three), was in-stantly killed, crushed beneath a heap of masonry and steel, as innocent a victim as those at Kent State three months before. At Wisconsin that September, as at Ann Arbor and Columbia, Chicago and Yale, fall term opened on schedule: an uneasy truce, freighted with unfinished business. I went back to school, too. Seventh grade. I felt very old.

The campus revolutions are history now, fit mostly for three-day symposia and other academic taxidermy. Some of my schoolyard rivals are deans or professors themselves; others are helping their own children fill out college applications, to small, quiet schools. Three of the bombers eventually served time; the fourth was never found. One operates a thriving fresh-juice stand on the university's handsome new State Street mall, just down the hill from the former Army Math center. "Hello, this is Karl the Juice God," says the jaunty greeting on his voicemail. A few summers ago, he publicly apologized for the fatal campus bombing. Student customers were polite, but baffled; many of them think Vietnam is the war fought in old "M★A★S★H" reruns.

Just after the Wisconsin bombing, I do remember watching a campus cleanup crew scrub graffiti from the large bronze tablet mounted near the crown of Bascom Hill. In 1894, a university trustee had accused a radical young economics professor, Richard Ely, of supporting, even teaching, unorthodox views—the right to strike, the right to speak. Not all college students are ready for such fare, the professor conceded. Campus regents agreed, but added that to thrive in modern times, a school must advertise. A climate of free debate, they decided, is the best campus publicity of all.

"We cannot for a moment believe that knowledge has reached its final goal, or that the present condition of society is perfect," their final report declares, "and therefore we welcome from our teachers such discussion as shall suggest the means and prepare the way by which knowledge may be extended, present evils removed and others prevented." Students and alumni commissioned a commemorative plaque to record the clash of views, a heartfelt gift to a long-sighted alma mater. The memorial was refused when first offered, then tactfully stowed in the administration building's cellar for years till all involved in that particular campus battle were aged, or dead. Yet eighty years on, under the janitors' patient hands, the old words again shone bronze in the late-summer sun. "Whatever may be the limitations which trammel inquiry elsewhere, we believe that the great state university of Wisconsin should ever encourage the continual and fearless sifting and winnowing by which alone the truth can be found."

A few years ago, at the end of August, I traveled to Manhattan on a commuter train with no air-conditioning, heading to a conference on higher-education goals for the new century with two middle-aged colleagues, one female, one male, big kids from long ago. All the way there, both wistfully recounted the campus wonders of summer 1970: the long hair, the short skirts, the defiance of curfews, the glory all around. I sat in the train's steambath heat, looking west over the Jersey swamplands, wishing for September first; for a cooling breeze; for a winnowed field.

FALL:
Dreaming in C

In college towns, postal workers dread September. For the first three weeks of fall term, campus mailrooms in fifty states fill and refill with damp bulging packages of emergency rations, mailed express to first-year students: real Tennessee barbecue sauce, homemade salsa and tortillas, a comforting gross of Philadelphia TastyKakes. In college brochures it is always summer (though the University of Minnesota includes a few artistic shots of snowflakes, for truth in advertising). But when fall term begins in southern California, students from Maine must learn about lizards on the ceiling, and the aromatic mud of black olives crushed underfoot on campus walkways. In New England, Californians huddle over their new space heaters and worry that acid rain is adding strange colors to the maples in the quad. Southern students who come north flinch at nasal accents and abrupt impersonal ways; at warm-winter schools, enormous roaches in the shower bewilder Northerners, as do public manners so perfect that you cannot tell what anyone is really thinking.

Throughout the eight waterfall weeks of September and October, first-years everywhere cling to their belief in the power of a campus to transform. Some sit back and wait to be reinvented. Others pace, complaining; to them the campus seems a way station full of arbitrary demands on the road to somewhere real. Turning civilians into collegians has always been a process that is half romance, half intimidation. Some schools dispatch a cappella singing groups to serenade newcomers as they unpack. Others dispense free merchandise: pocket Bibles, sugarless gum, tanning tip sheets, dental dams. Student handbooks cover the rest, mostly—no woks in dorm rooms, no riding on top of elevators, no cheating on exams. Two undergraduates in three will eventually cheat anyway, and a great many will learn to elevator-surf, but the formal prohibitions remain, for tradition's sake.

Though campus libraries offer jazzy orientation-week tours of the reference room, hardly anyone comes. The social training schedule is too tight. Guess the number of condoms in the jellybean jar. Come to the Orgasm, Pleasure and Pizza open house. Crime-watch pamphlets and alcohol-policy briefings abound. Mandatory multicultural awareness hours ("bring and discuss a symbol of your ethnicity") upset some first-years. "But I'm adopted." "No way am I holding up a Polish sausage in class." Mixed-race students get very quiet. In a thousand assembly halls, bonding exercises like the Name Game commence ("Share with us now a self-descriptive adjective that begins with the same letter as your first name").

> "Okay, well, basically, hi, everyone, I'm Approving Abby!"
>
> "Enthusiastic Ellen."
>
> "Jaunty Jack."
>
> "Disgusting Dan."

Mostly the new undergraduates are patient with their keepers' earnest, improving ways. Many have other worries. Quite a few throw up outside the first-day classrooms; janitors hate September. High school athletic stars wear last year's letter jackets everywhere but the shower, then quietly fold them away after the third week. Oh, yes, a professor assures a startled boy from Maui, Remedial English is required for all foreign students. A squash player from Connecticut, his father laid off four years from IBM, is asked on a registration form to name his class; hesitantly, he prints "Upper-middle???" though the registrar wants only a graduation year.

At many campuses, the first two weeks of term are known as shopping period. Undergraduates crowd into lecture halls, sling their legs over chairbacks, and wait for life-altering revelations, but professors hand out reading lists instead, then drone about lab and writing requirements. Some students roll their eyes after five minutes, mouth "*Bor*-ing!" at their new friends, and vanish. Others go buy the required texts, and the recommended ones, too. The only way instructors can connect desires and histories to the hundreds of smudged names on the course-enrollment printouts, and to the blank, cautious faces beneath tugged-down cap brims, is to study the hand-scrawled student-information sheets, fluttering onto the lectern at the close of class.

> #1) Please print clearly the following: name, intended major, hometown, Social Security number, E-mail address.
> #2) Tell me something interesting about yourself.
>   —I speak Cambodian.
>   —I am interested in alkanes, aldehydes, ketones and their residues.
>   —I can juggle keys one-handed behind my back.

—I had an actual lab rat in my bookbag today,
did you guess?
—I have a 70% hearing loss; please don't tell
anyone.

Some first-years make longer journeys to campus than others. Bernard, from South Chicago, could have attended a good
midwestern state school on a $100,000 minority fellowship;
instead, he accepted an Ivy League offer but is not yet sure he
chose well. "I knew this school was trouble when they held
the information meeting at a country club in the super-rich
northern suburbs. These people mean well, but they just don't
think. So why am I here? Face it. I went for the video. I played
it and played it, I completely fell for the line that people at this
place constantly debate issues, and meaning, and truth. Instead,
they hug. Enough with the hugging. I'm, like, get *away* from
me; you'll ruin my cutthroat competitive edge."

Many, many undergraduates never speak to a senior professor from one year to the next, or ever. Sometimes the problem
is first-term awe (encountering eminences in the supermarket
produce section, students often blurt, "My God, you *eat!*").
Veneration wears off fast. But campuses where undergrads talk
excitedly with faculty about ideas are, as Bernard suspects, un-
common. Student silence—courteous, terrorized, stupefied—
forces college instructors to picture the minds arrayed before
them mostly through the written word: essay exams, notes in
an office mailbox, late-night E-mail.

Luring students into a language of argument and evidence,
as well as a language of feeling, gets harder every fall. Mock-
ing the customers amuses some professors, as it has for centuries, but today far more faculty are genuinely worried, and a
few despairing. The annual statistical profile of the nation's
freshmen in academe's trade journal, *The Chronicle of Higher
Education,* offers some clues: Eighty-two percent are white.

Twenty-six percent born-again Christian. Twenty-eight percent interested in politics, an all-time low. Four in five want gun control and a cleaner environment. Over a fourth want married women back in the home. A confident 54.8 percent rate themselves "Well above average" or "Top 10 percent" in academic ability. But when a recent survey at a Big Ten campus requested views on the quality of undergraduate written work, faculty replies shimmered with frustration.

> I am outraged at the level of incompetence we tolerate! [Department of Germanic Languages]

> I do what I can in my upper-level courses, but there is a limit, because I also have to teach content. [Psychology]

> Students have no idea their work is so poor. [Kinesiology]

> It's difficult in many cases to determine what a student knows or understands. [Plant Pathology]

> Pre-college training seems deficient. Intelligence is not the issue. [Sociology]

Undergraduates would like to spend more time on their course work, they really would. But even the noblest intentions are often derailed by the rest of their complex hidden lives. First-years, especially, are personalities under construction. They arrive at office hours to discuss punctuation and bibliography but stay to talk with a neutral adult—neither parent nor employer nor high school teacher—about the constant early shocks of campus life. Theirs are some of the voices I remember best, encountered in undergraduate conferences or read in course journals at schools in New York, New Mexico, Oregon, Florida, Connecticut, Wisconsin, New Jersey; a collective fall-term diary entrusted to me by many hands, and a time capsule of their last weeks of adolescence.

It's 2:11 A.M. What is the Taylor series expansion of the sine function at the point x=1? And why do I care? I want to be an orthodontist.

I want an extremely "liberal" arts education, because I truelely want to be "well rounded." With this "out of mind" (ha ha) I want to get filthey rich.

Last night was pledge night at the Chinese restaurant and Jennifer our president brought out a big basket decorated with pink ribbons and threw handfuls of pink condoms to every table. We all started cheering and screaming "More, more!" The chapter advisor, a nice but clueless suburban type, looked like she was going to faint but the sisters were pretty drunk and she intelligently did not interfere with our revelry.

When my advisor went for more add/drop forms I read my student file and it said "nice Christian Asian girl." A Twinky, he means. A banana.

The vegan co-op elected me Soymaster! When answering the phone I have to say, "House of spelt and honey—vaya con Gaia."

Eating squid is like eating erasers, but at least now I have had the experience. Also, always put peanut butter on 'shrooms, they taste much better that way.

I have shaved most of my head and taken up Thai dance. When asked where I am from I cunningly change the subject. (Denver, if you must know.)

I will not will not will not be ashamed my mom is on welfare.

This school is a whirlpool, most people are left out on the edges.

This school is the anti-"Cheers," where nobody knows your name.

I did the personality test from *Cosmo* while in the bathroom and all my hall mates rushed in and read my answers afterward. It's hard being an intuitive introvert surrounded by heartless extroverts.

I signed up yesterday to tutor math in public grade school. I have zero experience but the lady said it didn't matter, that mostly they need to see a responsible man. One kid called me "sir" and like an idiot I quick looked behind me for my dad.

There are actual debutantes here, I thought they were extinct.

The first violinist has a smile like a falling star, but she doesn't know I exist.

Gay people like the movie *The Wizard of Oz* because they see Oz as an emblem of their subculture, they also admire Doris Day, I never knew this.

Once they let us out of the car trunk we knew we had made it in so Mike and I grabbed each other in a non-homo hug and then started smearing raw eggs and mustard in each others hair and the other pledges did too, I was so happy and know I will make many valuable business contacts for the future.

I had an Uzi at the beginning of the year, but sold it to a guy for $750, which will cover Christmas presents plus airfare home and back. I do not really fit in here but I get from it what I want. I always had this secret desire to be an architect, because I like buildings, even the ones my friends used to write all over. And I always liked math—I could multiply polynomials in the fifth grade. I mean, forget those little language handouts, but give me a math book and I'll blow it away and ask for another.

I miss my older brother so much. He hung himself in his dorm room last month and did not leave a note, I thought he would leave a note for me at least, we shared everything for eighteen years, except this.

Team rage last night!! I said I was dry, because of all my sports, so instead they made me chug four big cups of chocolate syrup with tabasco sauce, vinegar and milk. But I still hate the way Coach refers to us on the volleyball team as the babes, I do not think this is fair and it makes me feel helpless.

Beer Frizz, Robopound, Tequila Races, these are my beloved intramurals. I was a medical case last weekend, it was so great, I drank so many Alabama Slammers that I blacked out and fell forward, hit the edge of a table and knocked out three teeth, the guys were freaking over all the blood but they got me to the hospital and the doctor asked me if I was OK and I told him all I needed was a beer and then I booted all over him, it must have been hilarious.

Everything baffles me now, except engineering, which is definite and invulnerable. I like to think I am a constant surrounded by variables. But I fear I may be educated here in ways I never imagined.

It's only November, but my brain is full.

I went back to my high school last weekend but my old locker had been reassigned and all the freshmen looked like utter babies and my house seemed smaller somehow; my parents too. I was actually glad to get back to campus.

I'm eighteen and one day! The parents can't be responsible for my screwups anymore. I can handle that. I feel mature. Semi-mature.

Although if one more person from the outside tells me, "Remember, these are the best years of your life," I am going to scream and scream.

Adapt, thrive, and the bachelor's degree floats nearer each day. American campuses are structured very much alike, from minute colleges like New Hampshire's Thomas More (enrollment seventy-six) to conglomerates like The Ohio State University (enrollment fifty-eight thousand). A president or chancellor plus a board of trustees or regents oversees a corps of administrators; that loose coalition of deans and vice presidents turns the governing board's wishes into fact. Some watch the money, others monitor the various academic departments: molecular biology, recreational science, Spanish and Portuguese. Departments and their professors must offer enough courses to process students through the 120 credit hours commonly required for the baccalaureate. Every four-year American college awards roughly the same categories of diploma. Studying sciences and social sciences leads to a B.S., bachelor of science. Engineering programs award the B.S.E. Math-free majors yield a Bachelor of Arts diploma, the B.A. or, sometimes, A.B.

Ask what else a campus does and you get, eventually, a triple answer. The first task of a campus is the advancement of knowledge for its own sake. Scientists scout the future's edge, social scientists make sense of the present, humanists are professional rememberers, keeping roads to the past open and clear, explaining vanished lives. A second campus mission is putting knowledge to work, by offering practical courses (from pharmacy to range management) and pushing faculty to repackage pure research as product: pollution-eating microbes, smart cars, frost-resistant peas. A fourth of all college students now major in business, and most of the rest want career-training majors like health care and elementary-secondary education. Definitions of "applied" and "pragmatic" are always changing, but the practical face of campus moves the most bodies, and pays the most bills. The third great purpose of a campus, and its high-prestige loss leader, is general enlightenment. The four most popular college courses are American Studies, basic composition, remedial math, and statistics; only about a quarter of U.S. undergraduates still follow a liberal arts track, which leads to periodic agonizing that history and literature and philosophy are dinosaur pursuits, but that, too, is relative: the nation's campuses still annually produce over twenty-six thousand art majors alone, more fine arts graduates than the entire population of Renaissance Florence.

A campus may shelter a single undergraduate college, or embrace half a dozen; it may house undergraduate programs plus a smorgasbord of advanced or postgraduate degree tracks—the forestry school, the medical school, the law school. Then the enterprise is no longer a college but a university, more imposing but not always better. Colleges usually stress teaching, and universities research, but name inflation only takes one press release. Alaska and Montana both recently announced that most of their state colleges and community colleges were now universities, a free overnight upgrade. And outside most U.S. campuses now, public or private, the same investors and interest groups circle, and second-guess: business, government, the media, the local community, parents, alumni. Who's in charge is not always clear. At some schools, the athletic department rules, at others the donors do, or the legislative budget committee, or the big powerful departments like economics and medicine. The American campus may well be organized for the convenience of its administrators, but without a bright faculty any school is doomed to mediocrity, no matter how healthy its bank account, and senior professors negotiate accordingly.

But to all these fraught and weighty matters, undergraduates are oblivious. They must be. To have any hope of surviving a first campus fall, students need to learn thoroughly, then cling to, a handful of campus environments. The classroom, where public performance is suddenly serious. The dorm cubicle, dull and bare, waiting for posters and pillows bought on a first credit card. Dining halls, where walking down the aisle alone, balancing a tray, brings high school uncertainties flooding back. Computer clusters, airless under fluorescent light, packed with strangers who all seem to know far more than you do.

Although not often discussed in recruiting brochures, the campus after dark can also be a formative environment. Most college students discover this world within a world by the first week of school. Some go to bed contentedly at ten, assignments complete, prayers said, and never see their school's other face. Some feel infinitely more alive on the night campus than on the daylight one, and far more accepted.

When you get to South Dakota State Highway 18, just beyond the campus parking lot, Sinte Gleska University is a hundred miles from anywhere, no matter which way you turn. Come north to SGU through the Nebraska Sand Hills, and you may travel half a day and never see another car. Set out from Wyoming, and you must navigate first the Black Hills—in Lakota, the *Paha Sapa*—and then the breaks and drainages of the western Dakota badlands, which look from the air like vast dark ferns pressed into rabbit-grey earth. Drive south to campus from the Missouri River valley—past rosy buttes and chalk-white rivers, the radio stations in Pierre and Mitchell getting fainter every mile—and along rangeland fence lines the bending autumn grasses glow like pheasant plumage, chestnut, topaz, bitter yellow.

Sinte Gleska is the nation's first Native American university. Named for the nineteenth-century Sioux leader, Spotted Tail, awarding its first B.A. in 1984, the main SGU campus borders the tiny trading town of Mission, near the heart of the Rosebud Reservation. The Rosebud's five thousand square miles are lightly populated by eighteen thousand Sicangu Lakota plus ten thousand others—white ranchers and townspeople mostly, plus the university's lone exchange student from Nigeria. Sinte Gleska has a modest frame science building, a good small library, and a bookstore/arts studio erected by students in the construction trades program. A prefab log cabin houses Lakota Studies. The rest of the university is a straggling circle of trailer houses near a gravel pit. Beyond lies a slough loud with mallards, then open prairie. Sinte Gleska has no food service, no sports facilities, no student center. People study in their pickup trucks or sit reading on trailer steps. The cool bright fall air smells of wood smoke. Beside the satellite dish, striped frogs bound in the long grass.

Duane Hollow Horn Bear, a stocky man in jeans wearing a red and green blanket vest, silver necklace, and worn brown boots, his gray hair bound in one thick braid, paces a basement classroom as his students find seats around a long wooden table. SGU's catalogue lists courses in literary criticism and calculus, ethnoastronomy and traditional featherwork, plumbing and commercial graphics. One requirement is absolute. All students must pass two terms of Lakota culture-and-language instruction. In the 9:00 A.M. section of Lakota I, one woman is Anglo, two more are German nationals, the other eight Sioux. Jackets stay zipped to the chin, hands curl around plastic coffee mugs. A lemon sun and shell-white moon both hang in the faultless October sky over SGU, but frost etches windows and windshields. Off the reservation, it is Columbus Day, but here that holiday is not observed, except by those who call it Indian Day. Thanksgiving is not popular either.

"White society follows what, the Georgian, the Julian calendar? I forget," muses Duane Hollow Horn Bear, arranging his notes. "But theirs is not accurate either, just like Christmas in their Bible is really spring. We go by winters, and our language is phonetic and descriptive. Terry, how do you say, 'How old are you?' or literally, 'How many winters are you?'"

Terry winces. *"Wahiyeto?"*

"You need to put it in second person. Try again."

Terry mumbles, looking desperate.

"No, you need the prefix. It's not an active verb. Lisa?"

"Ni. Second person."

"Ma goes with *ni, wa* goes with *ya.* Now form the sentence, Terry."

"Waniyetu nitonahe."

"Good. Repeat, everyone. Watch that enunciation. Nice

and clear. And if you asked me my age, I would say—" He leans to murmur in a student's ear. She falls face forward onto her notebook, giggling. "Forty-five! You're forty-five! I understood that!"

Duane nods, turning to a girl with clear tan skin, a shag haircut, and a Coed Naked Beer Games T-shirt. "Tessa, give us thirty-three. Say it as ten threes, remember, and imply the winter."

The lesson moves to winter counts, traditional pictographs painted on elkhide, each icon recording one year's distinctive event. The winter a trader built a store. The winter many died of smallpox. Some winter counts are in museums now, some in collectors' hands; a few are reservation heirlooms still. Anthropologists have tried to locate the very greatest examples but—Professor Hollow Horn Bear smiles faintly—all seem to have disappeared. He takes the class through the Lakota lunar calendar of thirteen months, and the meaning of each name.

January is the midwinter moon of hard times. "Your food and wood rations are halfway gone, you can't get out to hunt fresh meat, your car's froze up—an excuse I only accept in Lakota, by the way, come exam week." February, Wi-na-po-pa-wi, moon of popping trees, suggests the effect of winter sun on ice-glazed leaves. March, Is-ta-wi-cay-zan-wi, moon when your eyes hurt. "In other words, snowblindness. Get out your Ray-Bans." April, the moon when ground begins to thaw, Wis-tu-ta-wi.

"I hate mud," says a Sioux student. The professor looks stern. "For your first sun dance, the spirits may test you, with heat, rain, wind, dust, mud. In the sweat lodge, you may have to undress in thirty-two below. Accept the weather. All days are good. Don't try to control, just concentrate on being alive in the elements."

"I would *never* do a sun dance," mutters a Sioux girl. "Stab yourself with steel hooks through the chest? Gross!" Duane sighs; student pride in an ancient heritage is clearly slipping. Too much television. A middle-aged man in a Sinte Gleska Warriors cap slips into class late, squinting at the board. "Say, you left out a syllable in February. Need an extra *chan* in there." "I'm totally spaced today," says the professor, erasing madly. The German women fidget. One raises a hand.

"Sir," she says resolutely, "I still do not understand what means yesterday's lesson. How can the word for blue be the same as the word for green? Logically, a thing is either green or it is blue." "Explaining would take a whole extra paragraph of description," says Duane firmly. "We shorten it down. Sometimes. Or maybe not. Depends on how we feel." The Germans shudder. After class they describe the double shock of American higher education plus the Sioux nation.

"I lived with an Indian family for eight weeks," explains one. "But I had to move out. You cannot imagine the drinking, the violence. The *dirt*. My parents think I am mad." She meant to attend a Navajo college, but fate and omens sent her here instead, she explains, twirling the black-velvet bow in her long blond braid. "Yet beyond the externals is a most marvelous philosophy of wholeness. That is why I stay. Besides, my Lakota accent is best in the class."

Duane Hollow Horn Bear agrees. Thanks to their nasals and gutturals, Germans make splendid Lakota speakers. Half the Native Americans he teaches hear no Lakota at home. They are learning it in college as a foreign language, like French. The course final will be a portfolio of translations, a self-assessment, and an extended conversation with a tribal elder. After high school Duane himself studied with an elder for ten years, joining a century-old underground of advanced instruction.

"Until Jimmy Carter passed the Freedom of Religion Act, no Native American could legally teach our own religions, or study the ancient ways. Amazing." He rolls a sardonic eye, taps the Lakota I vocabulary quizzes into a crisp stack, and heads for his eleven o'clock class. Across the small crowded lounge, a student assistant double-checks fall enrollment names: Lester Kill the Enemy, John Leading Cloud, Regina Thunder Hawk. A trio of undergraduate women stops by to chat. "I had a dream last night," announces one. "Oooh!" say her friends; all huddle to hear details. Sinte Gleska's language courses seem to be working; except for one squeal of "That's *soooo* cool!," narration and comment are all in firm, fluent, singing Lakota.

Of all America's campuses, the Carnegie Foundation has declared, tribal colleges best know who they are and where they want to go. Twenty-nine exist now, twenty-seven of them west of the Mississippi, from Salish Kootenai, deep in a Montana pine grove, to northern New Mexico's Crownpoint Institute of Technology. All are very young, born of Sixties civil rights and higher education acts, strengthened by Indian self-determination laws passed under Nixon. Sinte Gleska students range from seventeen to sixty-four, but the average undergraduate is thirty years old, a single woman with children. Enrollment averages six hundred and fifty students in the fall but swells to seven hundred by spring as young Sioux return, discouraged, from off-reservation tries at higher education. Can't take the pace, they say. It's madness out there. In here, instructors work very hard, knowing they have about sixty days before the empty seats reappear. SGU has tried learning centers, correspondence courses, community outreach, individual tutoring, but midsemester slump remains a major problem. At many U.S. schools, undergraduates at midterm will stop taking notes or start skipping lectures. Here they vanish, walking off suddenly and, too often, never returning.

"We're a junior college in disguise," says a science professor. "Over half our students need extensive remedial help. About one in four has real trouble with English. But we get rez kids used to being around whites. And every year some transfer to bigger campuses, especially in health sciences, and do well." Don't think of SGU undergrads as disadvantaged college students, one staffer warns me. Around here, that's a contradiction in terms. Those we see are the survivors.

Campus vans provide free daily door-to-door service for every SGU student. Eighty-mile round trips are common. Never leaving the reservation, the van fleet travels a quarter-million miles a year. But SGU students still take a long time to journey through degree programs. Some years 100 percent of those enrolled are on financial aid. More on-campus classes in parenting would help, SGU staffers say, more day care, more early childhood education, more counseling, more anti-alcohol programs, more jobs. But federal funding, in the way of all treaties, is constantly granted, cut, granted, cut. Outreach by other campuses is welcome but fitful: faculty from South Dakota State University in Brookings, three hundred miles east, used to visit weekly to teach nursing courses, but the program was recently discontinued; flying in small planes to the Rosebud in winter wore everyone down.

Sinte Gleska has a tiny endowment, and hopes to start a foundation, but any suburban grade school is better equipped. At SGU anything will make a lesson, from NASA surplus to old novelty toys from decades past; the physics classes learn Newton's laws from the clacking steel balls of a Seventies-era perpetual-motion novelty toy. The entire SGU budget was $4.5 million in 1994–95, a year Congress approved $651 million in purest academic pork: $25 million went to the University of Alaska, to develop a supercomputer to help harness the energy of the aurora borealis; $8.7 million to buy a planetarium for a Michigan community college with no astronomy department; $25.5 million in NASA funds were secured by Senator Robert Byrd to build high-tech classrooms at Wheeling Jesuit College (enrollment 1,511). Meanwhile, Sinte

Gleska faculty comb the local yard sales, looking for used books and shelves to put them on.

"The Rosebud is the Third World," says one computing professor, matter-of-factly. "It speaks the same language, sometimes; drives the same cars, watches the same TV shows. But the bedrock culture is perpendicular to everything else." He did graduate work at Clemson, spent years in the California computer industry. While teaching at the University of the South Pacific in Fiji, he discovered SGU's home page on the Internet and applied for a job. Some of his faculty colleagues are white educators from the area who received their own master's degrees from SGU, some are Sioux old enough to recall when Indians were only allowed to swim in public pools on Tuesday afternoons, just before the weekly cleaning.

"We don't want to discourage," says Mike Beach, a tribal member, head of student services. "And we're trying to assemble reliable norms, to see if Native Americans have some distinctive learning pattern. But people around here assume that the campus automatically transforms lives, when it's really up to them." Perhaps half of SGU's undergrads sign on, professors say, because they can get government grants, and courses pass the time. The other half are good students, by any standard. With another tribal school, Oglala-Lakota Community College, SGU is applying for a $10 million grant from the National Science Foundation to start a four-year computer sciences program, hoping to demonstrate minority success at the B.A. level.

"Without decent equipment, the whole exercise is pointless," the bearded computing professor says, rocking in his chair. "But the talent *is* there." In a dry scuffed yard nearby, three male undergrads toss a football, going out for a long one, faking left, faking right. "Hoka-*heye!*" the undergraduates shout, at Sinte Gleska sports events. "Hoka-*heye!*" The cry that

Custer heard so long ago can still unnerve opposing teams from white colleges, on field or court. *It is a good day to die.*

Sinte Gleska personifies the oldest anxiety on American campuses: Who shall come to college? And on whose terms? Educating masses and minorities has made campuses nervous for centuries, though the outsider faces constantly change: Indians, women, the poor, Jews, Catholics, artists, blacks. But customers who define themselves by difference are an expanding market; special-interest or special-audience institutions now enroll more than one U.S. undergraduate in five.

Some American identities remain linked to landscape. The tribal campuses understand this; so does Kentucky's Berea College, tuition-free to Appalachian undergrads, as the work-study University of the Ozarks is free to many of its mountain students. Religious battles, too, have spawned American campuses for centuries. Yale was a conservative retort to Harvard's laissez-faire theology. By 1766, the Dutch Reformed sect had founded Queen's College, later Rutgers. Dartmouth began as a Congregational wilderness mission to the Indians. But the rigid collegiate quotas of genteel Protestantism take three hundred years to fall. Meanwhile, other faiths erect their own compounds: Notre Dame, Brandeis, Brigham Young.

Ethnic massing ebbs and swells at U.S. colleges, often in response to ethnic money; education by heritage is another old dream, and a strong one. In 1940, the Boston Irish coolly underwrote an entire department of Celtic Studies at Harvard, stipulating special attention to the Irish immigrant experience; Harvard harrumphed mightily, but cashed the check. More than 20 percent of African-American undergraduates now attend historically black campuses like Morehouse and Fisk, Tuskegee and Spelman, all founded after Reconstruction in what W. E. B. Du Bois called a frenzy for education, among a people consumed with the desire for schools. At Florida International University in Miami, at New Mexico Highlands University in Las Vegas, you hear more Spanish than English in the halls, and sometimes in the classrooms, too.

Special-mission schools are social weather vanes. When the District of Columbia's Gallaudet opened in 1857, deafness was a curse; now it's a culture. Educating makers—painters, dancers, musicians, engineers, architects—has always puzzled academic campuses; arts schools like the Rhode Island School of Design, technical institutes like Rose-Hulman in Indiana, emerged as partial answers. Women's colleges took root before the Civil War and withered with the spread of coeducation in the Vietnam years. Well over two hundred all-female campuses still operated in 1960. Today about eighty remain. But applications to the survivors—Mills College in Oakland, California, the College of Saint Catherine in St. Paul, Minnesota—are rising strongly. Some female-only colleges, like Ohio's Ursuline, design whole degree programs around what they term women's ways of knowing. Others merely observe that one-third of the highest-paid female executives in *Fortune* 500 companies attended single-sex colleges, as did one Congresswoman in four.

Separate but equal, separate and better, are powerful lures in the college market, what advertisers call a product point of difference. Less openly discussed is the pull of the group, the comforts of enclosure, the whisper in the brain that can sap or goad: *Don't go beyond us, you will lose yourself, forget where you are rooted, who you are. Stay. Those outsiders will betray you.* The vast majority of citizens who go to college remain close to their various roots, both in their choice of campus and after graduation. Most Sinte Gleska graduates stay in the community, too. The Lakota need all the professionals they can train: programmers, public health nurses, agribusiness planners, teachers in the public schools. I asked the school's grantmeister, a tribal member, if he had ever considered a career at a larger campus, an Iowa State, a Stanford. He glanced out the window at the dark-haired students walking quietly to tutoring appointments through a golden shower of cottonwood leaves. He said, "Why should I? This is my home."

In times of plenty, campuses and fields of study expand. In financial droughts, they contract. Let the market work, say education economists and managers of campus portfolios. By that measure, the tribal colleges are a wild success, even more than the women's schools and the historically black campuses. In 1982, twenty-one hundred students attended tribal campuses. Today sixteen thousand do. Enrollments for reservation campuses are up 60 percent in the last nine years.

It is a mixed blessing. Sinte Gleska's crowded trailers and fragile resources also illustrate American higher education's deepest fear: that the next century will be winner-take-all. A two-tier universe is already forming, fifty or so extremely rich schools and below them, in varying degrees of distress, everyone else; campuses of permanent abundance, campuses of grinding scarcity, with less and less middle ground.

On an October midweek morning in upper Manhattan, overcast and chill, I explored the dim narrow corridors of a Columbia University dormitory. To get there, I surrendered my campus ID at the lobby security desk and left a credit card as extra hostage before ever reaching the residence-floor elevators. Columbia's Beaux Arts campus is formal and grey, walled and fenced, each gate double- and triple-guarded. If you stand on tiptoe by its Broadway security checkpoint, and look west beyond six lanes of traffic, beyond the polyglot crowds swarming bookstores and health-food emporia, beyond the elegant apartment buildings on Riverside Drive, the basalt palisades along the Hudson River can just be glimpsed. In the university's central quadrangle, minute squares of lawn are chained off like museum treasures; Columbia's great quad is gorgeous with domes and pediments, marble and granite, a paved garden of stone, timeless, nearly treeless.

But the hallways of the high-rise undergraduate residence hall near Butler Library smell ripely of industrial disinfectant, cold french-fry grease, rotting citrus peel, urine, used tampons, bathroom steam, and advanced athlete's foot, a chaotic, mock-erotic slum. Double-locked room doors display slogans ("Jessica, Trained Extrovert") or shiny pages torn from magazines: a close-up of a pistol barrel, a basket of kittens, women in chain-mail bikinis, men in chain-mail bikinis. At eleven in the morning, dorm hallways remain very dark; many inhabitants are sleeping still. Bleary undergrads wander by in towels and T-shirts, peering at flyers for TB testing and procrastination support groups, complaining gently about impossible workloads for their courses in Jewish mysticism and South African politics. Two students, male and female, suddenly dash past, screaming.

"I *told* him there was a pizza under the sofa!"

As at nearly all campuses, the Columbia dorm rooms are in size and style Early Federal Penitentiary, but house an astounding number of accessories. In 1950, your basic undergraduate needed reading lamp and record player to feel *au courant*. By 1970 dorm-room essentials translated to clock-radio, stereo system, popcorn popper, hair dryer, electric blanket, maybe a rabbit-ear black-and-white TV. The children of the children of the consumer-media culture are more exacting. Dorm rooms everywhere now house cell phones and headphones, computers and laser printers, surge suppressors and sound systems. Powerbooks. Calculators. Beepers. Large-screen color

TVs plus VCRs. Custom-built lofts with excellent sound systems. Walkmen, Discmen, Gameboys, camcorders, CD players. Microwaves, coffeemakers, toaster ovens, blenders. Hotshots, mini-grills. Electric toothbrushes, blow-dryers, contact lens sterilizers, small whirlpools for sports injuries. Fire inspectors hate Information Age dormitories. Some U.S. schools have wiring from the 1940s, some from the 1970s. Neither decade imagined the power hunger of the Nineties undergraduate.

But just as the fat college textbook is a dying campus life form, replaced increasingly by photocopied coursepacks or assignments downloaded from the World Wide Web, so the college dorm is vanishing from the common reservoir of campus experience, and with it the dear old college roommate. Florida State recently found that four in five of its freshmen have never shared a bedroom, and don't plan to start now. Eighty-five percent of U.S. undergraduates no longer live on campus after the first year, preferring apartment rentals, house shares, a relative's couch, or (for older undergrads) their own homes. Some campuses have boarded up much student housing; a few, like the University of Cincinnati, have dynamited million-dollar high-rises, to alumni cheers. Some rent the old cramped cinder-block rooms at bargain rates, or create special floors for community activists or musicians. Others renovate the behemoth towers of the Cold War campus to suit the cocooning Nineties, replacing pool tables with Stairmasters, installing sybaritic bathrooms and premium cable—and creating new problems for resident advisors, as students hibernate for days on end, skipping class after class to sit in the dark, eating red licorice and channel-surfing.

Yet even the cushiest updatings still mean supervised communal living, a free-floating chaos that some inmates adore and others detest: the ritual midnight howls, the crowds in the laundry room at 2:00 A.M., the unsought intimacy of rooms with walls so thin you can hear a neighbor take the cap off an aspirin bottle. Valerie, an engineering student from New York State, arrived at my office one morning, her delicate Afro completely flattened on one side, eyes weary and red. She handed me her campus journal. I read the first paragraph, then looked up to ask a question. She was already asleep on the couch.

> It's 2 A.M. The politics major across the hall has flown in his girlfriend again (five weeks into term, and they can't be apart?) and now through the tissue-paper walls I hear her say, "What's a thousand miles when negative six inches is so much more rewarding?" I just peeked around the door. He's trying to make it to the bathroom with his hand between his legs to hold the condom in place. I am sick of weathering all these sexual storms. I want a cigarette, and I don't even smoke. This is the second night I have had no quiet, no time to myself or to do my work. Tuesday I sat up with a first-year woman who got smashed on White Russians and had unprotected sex with a grad student she met at an orientation-week party. Never got his name, of course. I try to help, I really do, but sometimes I feel like the catcher in the rye.

College has always stirred new tastes, and unexpected appetites. But until recently, campus sophistication stopped well short of the dining hall. Though early American campus tuitions could be paid in loaf sugar or bacon, Harvard students in the years around 1800 endured weevily bread the texture of wet wool, rancid meat, and sour college cider fortified with raw whiskey. When moldy butter joined the menu, they rioted for days, ignoring the elderly alumni (John Adams included) who wanted them flogged. At 1840s Princeton, hungry boys speared suppertime chops to the underside of the dinner table for breakfast retrieval.

Gradually, American schools generated more attractive food traditions. A chafing-dish cuisine of rarebits and fudges, invented by Vassar and Wellesley girls as an excuse to stay up late, became a national food fad in the years before World War I. The great Oxford colleges like Christ Church might produce crème brûlée or meringues for high-table dinners; Mount Holyoke boasted Deacon Porter's Hat, a steamed molasses pudding named for an early supporter of female education.

Alumni of the 1940s and 1950s nationwide remember breaded veal, shepherd's pie, or tuna-noodle casserole slopped onto thick china plates, the only garnish cold canned peas and white bread lumpy with margarine, the only beverages milk and water. Depression-era students from rural campuses recall that a hot college date frequently meant banana-cream pie and Grain Belt beer for two at the local café. By the time you walked the mile back to campus in sub-zero weather, survivors say, you were always perfectly sober. Always, everywhere, students from small towns and immigrant families learned old-money manners at college, sometimes the hard way; one thinks of Sylvia Plath's *Bell Jar* heroine at a scholarship dinner, drinking the finger bowl, cherry blossoms and all, believing it a strange Japanese soup.

Many American campuses produced and processed much of their own food until well after World War II. Cowyards and kitchen gardens kept costs down and menus plain. As late as the 1980s, some land-grant schools still maintained in the poultry science building lobby a cooler of fresh eggs at fifty cents a dozen: blue-green offerings from the South American Araucanas, filbert-brown ovals from the Buff Orpingtons, all still faintly warm, and stippled with bits of feather or dung. Theft and fears of salmonella ended the academic egg business, as budget cuts have made most of the traditional college cheeses extinct, though Clemson Blue and Washington State's Cougar Gold cheddar still thrive.

Contemporary undergraduates, raised on takeout and food courts, crave meals that look and taste commercial. Campus food is now a $7.1 billion business. Over fifteen hundred schools outsource their dining contracts, mostly to international purveyors like Aramark and Marriott. At Trinity College, a private school in Hartford, Connecticut, the dining hall is bright and inviting, the menus copious and healthy. The food director still receives a daily bombardment of anguished notes on paper napkins.

> Dear Dave. What is up with never having sprinkles out for the frozen yougourt. I continually have to ask for them. Also, your workers lied and said they were all out, but they weren't.

> Hey Davester—the vegeterian chili is superbe, best thing i've eaten here in 3 years. Spicyness is great.

> Hey Dave, when you have a buffet of fried vegetables, why do you not have okra??!! you are letting down your southern customers. signed, the good ole boy.

> Dear Dave. 1) the grapefruit stinks. At least you could thaw the sections and con us into thinking they're fresh. 2) While enjoying my turkey noodly soup, I found a big bone in my bowl, I could have choked. 3) ID-takers at the door are rude and grumpy. I think the hell my parents go through to send me here merits a better cafeteria. Thanks.

Plenty of college students take fourth helpings, of course, while others spend instructive minutes exploding grapes in the dining-hall microwave. Eating in class is very common, more common than taking good notes: professors in mid-lecture may notice their audience unwrapping burgers and passing tortilla-chip bags; a two-hour seminar can mean a table awash in lettuce shreds, half-scraped dressing containers, and natural-juice bottles. Undergrads in states with sparse economies sometimes turn to food stamps; everywhere, students on budgets learn the traditional hotplate cuisine of macaroni-and-cheese, or ketchup soup. But for about one undergrad in four—especially those from California, the Northeast, or the South—college eating means not appetite but anxiety. More student voices, male and female, from campuses around the country.

> We keep scales in our rooms for weighing food, and have these long debates—does digesting a Diet Coke wear off the 1.5 calories involved? What about half a Cheerio?

> People smoke constantly for weight loss. Catalogues and magazines are very influential. *Vogue, Elle,* J. Crew are what really gets read.

> A girl from the University of Zurich came to dinner and *drank whole milk.* It was the topic of intense conversation for days.

> I am frankly baffled by white eating obsessions. To me a husky figure means power. Strength.

> It's a faux ideal, that you can have a mind and a glamour life. "This place isn't fully coed," the guys say, "there are no bigbreasted women." But they

work out insanely, then announce, "The girls here don't look so good, but the guys are great."

Here's what we really consume, especially before exams. Ramen noodles and powdered iced tea, dumped straight from pack to mouth. Jumbo jars of marshmallow fluff. Nutella. Baby food. Trail mix. Vivarin and multivitamins. Mountain Dew, for the extra caffeine. Numerous tubes of raw chocolate-chip cookie dough.

Food is the real peer pressure, not sex. Body put-downs, self-defense classes, powerbooting after a party night, it's all a continuum.

———————◆———————

As the fall days shorten, as course assignments grow, students develop circadian rhythms. We have no time to study, they explain. Lecture, lunch, and then the soaps—can't miss the soaps—segue so quickly into afternoon sports practice and activity meetings that serious work, at least during the day, is out of the question. Not everyone on campus has the luxury of an upside-down life. Office staffers are rinsing out the coffeemaker by four-thirty and locking up by five as the administrative urgencies of the day campus fade with the light. Faculty endure a last round of budget and hiring meetings, then gratefully vanish by six P.M.; some commute between towns, or across state lines; others must hurry to other campuses to run evening classes. Computer-center sysops are really the first to see the night campus rouse. Just when afternoon fades to dusk, food-services home pages receive a flurry of hits as students go on-line to criticize the dinner offerings, a nocturnal species beginning to forage.

"I hear that after dark this school is real *Lord of the Flies* territory," say employees at school after school as they head for parking lot and bus stop, but few payroll managers, lab assistants, religion professors, or vice presidents for development ever stick around to see. Once sundown comes, security patrols and health-services workers are among the very few adults left on any U.S. campus. Of course, the undergraduates are also adult, as college and university attorneys firmly emphasize in campus mission statements. Our students are of age. We encourage them to make their own decisions. And so they do.

Nine P.M. Adult-ed classes and extended-day courses are dispersing, an educational swing shift shutting down. In their varied residences, students have begun to cast about for fun. Undergraduates say they live on vampire time, sleeping in class, active after dark. The post-dinner hours are a curve of rising energy. Scientists experiment ("Fifteen hundred pounds of freshmen on a single bunk bed, and only two springs broke!") or else make a water balloon fly really, really far using two lengths of surgical tubing and a funnel. Gymnasts practice dismounts from sofas. Swimmers brace themselves above hallway doors, hands against one wall, feet braced on the other, ready to pounce screaming upon luckless passersby.

Eleven P.M. On a Saturday night before fall midterm exams at Georgetown University, students put away notes and shut down laptops in the library reading rooms, then line up to display their bookbags to a security guard before ducking through the electronic theft-detection archway and out into Washington's chilly autumn air. Some start down the red-brick sidewalks of residential Georgetown, heading for the M Street clubs. Others turn toward the nearby computer labs.

Everything is nearby at Georgetown; it is a small campus, but as ingeniously layered as an Italian hill town. A massive teaching hospital and conference center lie only yards from dorms and classrooms, and these in turn hem the brownstone towers and stained glass of administrative Healy Hall, built to impress the Washington of Henry Adams. The old walled upper campus links to exercise fields below and beyond via a cascade of enormous new buildings, cliffs and canyons of limestone and terracotta. Five undergrads, three men, two women, all dressed as soberly as tax lawyers, pause to survey these darkened plazas and towers.

"So how do you get from that second ledge to the turret, huh, huh? You'll be lunchmeat."

"Not at all," says a small sturdy girl, hugging an attaché case. "Consider the window bracing to the left."

They rise on tiptoe, peer thirty feet up, then subside, nodding; college debaters always respond best to evidence.

"Step sideways and push, step sideways and push," says the tallest boy sagely. "Push *real hard*. Thank you, Shanti. Applied architectural appreciation at its finest."

The night campus means action above the ground, and below it, too. Roof trekkers and academic spelunkers have plagued administrations for at least a century. A young Amelia Earhart is said to have explored Columbia's underground storm drains; today's devotees confer on good routes via Internet, and make special trips to view Boston's night skyline from the roofs of MIT, where the fine is fifty dollars if caught, five hundred dollars if caught atop the Great Dome of the Barker Engineering Library. Even the most proudly lawless do observe some rules. Keep your hands out of strange machinery. Try not to get parboiled in steam tunnels. Avoid sewers near nuclear labs.

In the Georgetown humanities buildings, no lights are on. Only a few psychology and econ office windows glow. But the science areas are beacons in the windy darkness. At the math department's ground-floor computer cluster, all forty workstations are claimed as students call up network links to course materials for Russian Art, Neuroanatomy, Introduction to Greek Archaeology, Biology 124. Latecomers line the walls, staring at the C and C++ programming languages scrawled on the blackboard, willing classmates to finish up. The wails around the long room suggest a long wait.

"How do you get it to do margins?"

"How do you make a binomial tree again?"

"Did I drop peanut butter on this disk?"

"I've been debugging for *four hours,* can you believe it?"

"I'm ruined! Where's my H file? *Where's my H file?*"

In computer clusters like this across the continent, college memories for a new century are being made, most of them traumatic: fistfights over printers, terminals that freeze on the last paragraph of a twenty-page politics paper, torrid E-mail love affairs that end in Dorito abuse. By the end of exam period, in order to get work sent over the network to waiting instructors, some people will be lugging in futons and cell phones, the public computing cluster as life raft.

In cyberspace no one knows if you are old, young, brown, red, female, male, rural, urban; if you are typing from a wheelchair, or from a kitchen late at night. At thoroughly wired campuses like Dartmouth or the University of California–Santa Cruz, seventy to one hundred thousand messages pass daily through the local system, a true fiber-optic village. Students can E-mail professors 24–7, or around the faculty, with a keystroke, alert four hundred members of a lecture course to changes in a field trip or lab schedule. Any course or seminar, anywhere, may form its own newsgroup or home page on the Web. The only drawback, students say, is that now mothers also have modems. They follow along from Michigan, or Osaka, then phone to ask if the homework is done.

To some undergrads, computers are smart typewriters. Anything more complex brings angry resistance, or quiet dread. Others delay work for days with game orgies of Minesweeper and Bloodsucker. Drunken and weird E-mail forwarded by friends and enemies is one great undergraduate time waster; another is choosing avatars. At some Web sites now, you engage in live on-line chat with fantastic beings— smiling chess pieces, blowfish, lionmen, or female warriors in strapless tunics, the secret selves of many an undergraduate. Another site (named "School Sucks") offers free college research papers, to be downloaded at will. Many faculty call it an electronic term-paper mill; the creator, a student at Florida International University, calls it a public service.

Tinkering with a home page also counts as educational. Some pages are collective, as in Carnegie Mellon's "Girl Geeks: Girls Who Would Rather Have Modems Than Ponies." Others are scholarly, as in a lovingly tended page at Rice University on proofs for Twinkies as supreme life form. The software is so easy now that even creative-writing majors, least technical of campus dwellers, can post opinions on the Miami Dolphins or Swinburne, or display doctored home-page photos (pets wearing hats, ex-lovers wearing nothing at all), the academic rite of cartoons, and silly quotes taped to room and carrel doors gone global. From the Angst home page to the Surrealist Compliment Generator to Jen the Procrastinatrix, everyone browses everyone else, cruising the electronic causeways between campus islands. When a Cal Tech or Amherst person discovers some Georgia State sophomore is faster and funnier than she, the shock can be severe.

Many students customize their screensavers. Opus the Penguin, shooting down flying toasters. *101 Dalmatians*. Women of *Playboy*. Mime Hunt. Discard an item, and Oscar the Grouch may pop up to sing "I Love Trash." Others like to monitor the graduate student at MIT who has lived for years with a camera on his head. Steve Mann's goggles contain a screen and lens; his belt has a keyboard and wireless Internet connection. He can receive E-mail while waiting in line at the bank, or stare at items in a store and wait for his wife to log on: *"Buy." "Don't buy."* Anyone on the Web can watch Mann's life proceed. Highly unnerving to have in class, his professors say. But undergrads around the planet yearn for such wired stardom, cyborg wannabes.

Faculty formed by the lost empire of print are sometimes baffled by students who move, work, and mate in an electronic fog. Undergraduate perceptions are increasingly image-driven and cybercouched. It affects apologies ("Sorry I downloaded on you like that, my life just bombed"), critiques of the long-winded ("He's always playing that tape, can't the guy fast-forward?"), and learning patterns, too. In an art history discussion section, a professor waits as twenty students stare at a Rubens slide.

"What's the story line on this thing?"

"It doesn't have one. It's a seventeenth-century portrait."

"It doesn't move at all?"

"Unfortunately, no."

"But I can't see things if they don't move."

Midnight in a northeastern computer lab. Forty students are coding furiously for an interactive computer graphics course. A dozen more power-nap, or slam toilet paper rolls at the walls to relieve stress. Dr Pepper cans and empty Skittles bags dot the long tables; this is a sugar, not a caffeine, crowd. The male-female ratio is ten to one. Many undergraduate women who would like to major in computing or hard sciences soon change their minds on purely practical grounds; serious work in these fields demands late hours in the lab, and many fear for their safety on the night campus. The students working now

are insanely fast typists ("My hands literally won't write anymore, it's too slow") and faster talkers.

"Void pointer? Compile for assembly code, you jerk!"

"That has the possibility of too much fun," says a boy lying
between two Sun Microsystems monitors, eating stray Chee-
tos off a grimy floor. A tall redheaded senior woman behind
him calmly coaches two floundering male colleagues.

"You're implementing library functions, see—" A soda can
beside the keyboard rattles as her fingers dance from command
to command.

"So I make a stack, and then a stack pointer from assembly
code?"

"Exactly. Pop, pop, pop, pop till your information gets out
of scope." Silence, then a storm of curses from the tutees.

"Abort the function, or you'll blow the stack!"

"Throw an exception."

"If I said, 'Throw zero,' then what?"

"Restore and do cleanup."

"I feel compelled to inquire: how the hell do you know
this?"

"A first-order approximation. Do it."

It is like overhearing young pilots at an RAF briefing in
1940, new language for a new world. A slight, soft-voiced student across the room is pointed out, reverently; he has already
received royalties on his work. In program design and computer music, undergraduates often make the best software
writers, flowering early, with an instinct for the edge. Always,
younger, faster minds are close behind. At eighteen and nineteen they are all ardent focus and devotion, happy to code
forty hours a week. But a junior may digress for eight weeks
into juggling or Russian, and never recover.

Computer science majors (and engineers, too) have different worries than other undergrads. They brood about how to
remain ethical in industries where they will soon be making a

great deal of money. And they think a lot about personal style. Some people code with instinctive elegance, using few lines, their output sleek and succinct; others can produce only ugly, rough code, lots of empty space, but powerful and direct. Coding style is like a fingerprint. A good professor knows when you do the work and when someone else does it for you. One misplaced curly bracket, one badly chosen algorithm, gives you away.

It is past midnight, but the lab's bright lights and constant murmuring make it hard to tell. Design assignments at nearby terminals range from automated highways to bicycle-riding robots to neural-network helmets. Some students are clearly on dawn patrol (they're still going to be there at daybreak), a few are going postal (showing severe stress), and others are thrashing (trying to trigger obscure interactive features). Outside, in the dark, in meatspace, the technopeasants roam. Occasionally local gods pass through—graduate-student teaching assistants, the stack rats, the theory heads, going for Ph.D.s in computational science. They are envied a bit, because they will spend their lives eating cold pizza in rooms very like this; pitied more, because they are already so old.

Advanced computing is like being in one of the science-fiction novels these students love. Your mind becomes the supreme creator, bodiless and beautiful and supernally alert. Nearly all their courses are not only paperless but collaborative. Computing is a surprisingly social activity, best done in teams and groups. Sometimes, such students seem to learn as one mind. "The sanity coefficient is not very high here," most acknowledge, but working alone is too slow, and too dangerous. You stare at the screen, and it becomes transparent, you fall through and are transformed, losing sleep, losing touch, losing any grip on place and time.

"I just want to code, I can't relate if I'm not coding, it's such a high when it works," says the redheaded senior ruefully.

Since freshman year she has kept a notepad beside her bed, for programming breakthroughs at 3:00 A.M., when she wakes with a solution waiting in her brain, whole and clear and necessary and right.

"You know it's working," she says, "and you know you are changing, the night you start dreaming in C."

One A.M. Two thousand miles west, the evening has peaked at Arizona State University, the nation's sixth-largest campus. Some twenty bars lie within walking distance of ASU; from Wednesday noon to Sunday night, business is excellent. When asked at one in the morning, "Why do you drink?" students are succinct.

"Stress!" says a blond business major in pink polo shirt and tennis shorts, wandering the courtyard of a café-bar on Mill Avenue, the mile-long shopping strip that forms the western campus border. "Yessss," he says, thoughtfully. "Very great stress." Watched by a bored bouncer, he vomits loudly ("Manymany Heinekens") into a crimson bougainvillea.

"Stress, I guess," whispers a plump elementary-education major in a purple spandex bodysuit and gold ear cuffs, on hands and knees beside an off-campus patio where the carpets squish with beer and some sixty guests dance with cans in hand, downing whole Coorses in one long practiced gurgle. A pair of bull-necked boys (their T-shirts read "Take Me Drunk, I'm Home" and "From Zero to Horny in 2.5 Beers") hoist the education major by the ankles over a nearby keg. Giggling, she seizes its plastic hose, inserts it into her mouth after three tries and, hanging upside down, begins to gulp.

"Personally, I drink to maximize fun," says a leisure-studies major, aiming her too-drunk-to-walk roommate at the front seat of a silver BMW. The roommate promptly hangs out the car window, hiccuping and retching. Two friends in the back seat haul her in, whip moist towelettes from their purses, and, crooning gently, wipe her contorted face. A pleading, rumpled boy circles the car, pounding the hood, the roof, the trunk.

"Let's party, you said we could party, I'm very caring, I promise you safe passage, let's go find some fun." "Fuck off, moron," says the recreation major. A girl in the back pokes out her head. "Wait—don't you have any good-looking friends?" He gestures vaguely at the crowd struggling down the fire escape of the nearest club, screaming, lurching over railings, being hauled back by companions equally drunk. The roommate howls louder, attracting a dozen extremely large young men in fraternity caps. They advance on the car, hooting and whooping and grunting, but the girls roar away into the desert night, shrilling in excitement, crossing four lanes of traffic in a $36,000 blur.

Like all big public universities, ASU is a school where you can get a very good education, if you want one. Plenty of students there earn straight A's or join the chess club, give up weekends to work in barrio clinics or build housing for the homeless. Professors photograph far galaxies through the Hubble telescope, take their geology classes to the Grand Canyon, study the role of fire in world history. Half an hour from downtown Phoenix, three hours from good skiing, four hours from Mexico, ASU's suburban Tempe campus is groomed like an expensive tennis resort. Royal palms shade tiled fountains and hibiscus hedges. Classroom windows frame the jagged Superstition Mountains, violet and umber in the midday sun. Prone undergraduates decorate perfect lawns. Some drape econ textbooks across their faces or tuck foil reflectors under chins; others talk languidly of silk-wrap manicures and Baja getaways. Students in wheelchairs zip about like dragonflies. Good ramps plus near-perfect weather make ASU a magnet for wheelchair users.

At noon on an autumn weekday, the central campus mall is crowded with fund-raising tables—a black sorority's bake sale, *De Sangre y Corazon* T-shirts from the Puerto Rican Student Association, campus Muslims selling Great Mosques of the World posters—but the main library is cool, quiet, and underpopulated. Closed Saturdays at 5:00 P.M., says the sign on the door. Upstairs in the student union, a hundred undergrads practice line dancing, sliding and twirling to a live band. Downstairs is a brown-bag session on sexual assault, with men doing most of the talking. ("So, legally, how plowed does a woman have to be, before it counts as rape?") At the nearby Newman Club, a dozen students file quietly into a large dark room, sitting far apart and looking at the floor, waiting for the daily Alcoholics Anonymous meeting to begin.

At the head of the mall, beside a grove of orange trees, glitters a pyramid of empty beer cans. Five ASU students are starring in an alcohol field test. Tempe police officers supervise, practicing careful crowd surveillance. ("Outrageous babes!" "Keep your voice down, man.") Enthralled undergrads crowd to watch as the volunteers chug beer after beer, then attempt to walk sidewalk cracks or touch fingers to noses. After two hours, all test subjects have gotten exceedingly smashed in the cause of science, or nearly all.

"I don't understand it, he should be drunk as a skunk by now," an officer mutters as a smiling Asian boy, hands steady, reactions precise, sails through every test and bows to his fans, who howl approval. "Antabuse! Antabuse!" shout passing tennis players, rackets held high in salute.

ASU has thirty-two thousand undergraduates. Their graduation rate hovers near 42 percent, slightly under the national average. Only about three thousand live in campus dorms. Far more commute from the Phoenix metro sprawl, or roost in an amorphous off-campus zone of condos and apartments. Despite administration efforts, midweek bingeing has been rising.

The alcohol-awareness week held at ASU each fall features a simulated DUI wall crash, a wellness day, field sobriety testing, talks by peer educators, a car wrecked in a drunk-driving accident, a comedy club, a sober dance. The bars at the edge of campus stay as busy as ever, starting at 11:00 A.M., monster beers only ninety-nine cents; a sixteen-ounce Southern Comfort and Cuervo, or a giant melon margarita, $1.95. Students go Greek to make friends, or hang out in bars for the one-cent drinks and the wet T-shirt contests and the Deke Fight Nights. College life turns shallow and disconnected, like a stone skipping across a pond; as at many party-minded campuses, counselors and health-services personnel report frequent crash-and-burn semesters. On a campus this size it is easy to feel alienated. Over the 1995 winter break a wheelchair student from Alaska died in his dorm room. No one remembered he was there.

Arizona State is in the U.S. region where college students drink *least,* the West and Southwest. Bingeing (defined as four drinks in a row one or more times in a two-week period for women, five drinks for men) is far heavier in the Northeast and Midwest. Anglo men drink most. Anglo women are right behind, then African-American men, Hispanic men, and Hispanic women. Black female students drink least; Jewish students also tend not to drink to excess. One Asian student in five binges, as opposed to half of white undergrads. ("We can have more fun on one drink than any self-loathing WASP can on six," some minority undergrads like to say.) International students find it all very odd. When the drinks run out, they inquire, why does everyone flee the party? Undergraduates everywhere drink in bars, at room parties, on road trips, legally or illegally; fake IDs cost no more than fifty dollars in most states.

After dark, American campuses split into two cultures, the reasonably civilized and the deliberately out-of-control. According to a 1995 Harvard School of Public Health study of 17,500 students at 140 representative campuses, about half the undergraduate population is drinking less, and the rest much more. The divide is not consistent; at some schools, 1 percent binge, at others, 70 percent. But nearly half of all American college students now qualify as binge drinkers. First-years are often the most adventurous, those recently liberated from protective homes often the wildest of all, their evening schedule often described as "drink, dance, scream, puke, pass out." Binge drinkers are seven times as likely to have unprotected sex, ten times as likely to drive after drinking, eleven times as likely to fall behind in course work. They are also most likely to have trouble with police or campus security, to wreck property, to hurt or be hurt. At colleges with high binge rates, students are twice as prone to get pushed, hit, or assaulted. The Harvard survey found that most students in four-year schools had study or sleep interrupted by drunken peers. Over half were forced to care for drunken students. One in three reported drunken insults or humiliations. One in four had repelled drunken sexual advances. In a generation light on heroes and heroines, the college-age turn to each other, and sometimes turn on each other. Those trying for balanced lives still must watch friends struggle, and sometimes lose. The conspiracy of student silence means one does not rat on one's peers to the grown-ups, even if you technically are the grown-ups, even if property damage and insurance costs mean tuition increases for all, and hospital bills for some.

One of the last places where public drunkenness is tolerated, even expected, is the American campus. At Pennsylvania's East Stroudsburg University, off-campus keg parties grew so uncontrollable that the local mayor threatened to declare a state of emergency. In Austin or Berkeley, Corvallis or Ames or

East Lansing, social pleasures abound: poetry slams, concerto premieres, ballroom-dance classes, hiking trips, bluegrass cafés. Students still binge. Administrations everywhere have tried distracting the customers with midnight basketball, classic-film marathons, natural-high nights, or novelty events like human bowling. Drinking prevails. At some schools the weekend starts Wednesday night; at others, Thursday. Fall after fall, before students finish buying their books, the drinking games begin.

> We have a drinking game called The Professor, because you gain so much knowledge. A 15-foot hose runs from the top of a staircase to the bottom. On one end is a guy with his finger over the end of a funnel, and on the other end more guys are pouring 12 beers—half a case—into the hose. A lot of pressure gets built up. You put the funnel in your mouth, and the guy takes his finger away. Your cheeks fill up like balloons, there's three seconds of total joy, then you throw up. The beer is like a ricochet, down and up. It messes your teeth, all that acid in the vomit. So it's best to only do this game once a night.
>
> (Male senior, residential East Coast campus)

Two A.M. to dawn are the violent hours. Amid the stolen bikes and lost lab keys, other entries surface on campus security blotters, night and day. Some are procedural, like the urgent note to officers at the University of Montana: "What looks like an abandoned Cadillac by the art annex is in fact a student sculpture project. Do not tow!" Others are less winsome. At the University of Iowa, a student loses a research prize, then shoots to death three professors, one staffer, one vice president. At Berkeley, the chancellor is stalked in his own home by a local woman wielding an ax. At Yale, a sophomore dies only yards from the university president's house, shot in a street holdup. At USC, stray bullets from local shootouts wound a football player on the practice field. At Virginia's Norfolk State, a student is killed in cross fire as campus gang members fight over turf. Going off to college now is full of worries—lingering acne, quarters for laundry, choosing a major, whether your new friends will like you, whether they will rob you. Thirty years ago, sneaking in past curfew was a big deal. Today it's avoiding date rape.

Sexual offenses are a frequent by-product of the night campus. Sociologists disagree about the percentage of college women—25 percent? 92 percent?—who meet some form of sexual assault, because definitions of assault range so. All-night rape by the football squad. Whistles from cars. Aggressive side-walking (groups of men occupying the width of a campus walkway, forcing woman after woman to step aside onto lawn or street.) Alcohol is nearly always involved in campus sex offenses. Usually both parties have been drinking late at night. They go to a room or apartment, the woman says maybe, then no, the man is incensed and forces sex. Campus counselors say that fall term of the first year is especially perilous; some 60 percent of the women who are sexually assaulted or raped while in college are attacked as first-years. In the 1970s, there were three major sexually transmitted diseases. Today, there are twenty, eight kinds of herpes alone, and college students contract them at astounding rates, especially NGU (nongonococcal urethritis), PID (pelvic inflammatory disease), chlamydia, and HPV (human papilloma virus, which produces genital warts). About one college student in five hundred is thought to be HIV-positive. Each year more and more, straight and gay, enter full-blown AIDS.

Campuses everywhere struggle to keep their calm, prosperous public images unflawed, their scandals in-house. A parallel justice system of school hearing boards, composed of students, faculty, and administrators, may deal with plagiarism and embezzlement one week, sodomy rape the next. For decades, pressing a sexual-assault case against another student (or a faculty member) meant traversing this private disciplinary maze. Although suits brought under the 1994 Violence Against Women Act have begun to challenge the secrecy and privilege, procedures are usually secret and pressure politics formidable, especially if the man involved is an athlete, a fraternity member, or the son of major donors.

Six A.M. On campuses everywhere, the last partiers are wandering home. They pass ROTC units out for a cadenced run before breakfast, groups of astronomers coming off shift, and here and there a sleepy biologist, locked into experiments that must be monitored every four hours for weeks on end. Architecture students go looking for dawn coffee, grungy and fretful after a day and a night *en charrette*. (In the design schools of nineteenth-century Paris, a great wheeled cart, or *charrette*, trundled from desk to desk at deadline to pick up student projects. Cart has yielded to modem, but the term lives on.) At schools on lakes, like Wisconsin and Cornell, crew teams are already hoisting the varnished eight-oar shells for portage to the shore. Winter ice is coming, and with it the long terrible hours of conditioning in the indoor rowing tanks. But for now, the boats slide into live water.

Seven A.M. The first professors arrive on campus, seeking two quiet hours before lectures to answer mail, grade papers, tinker with a difficult translation. Janitors are moving about as well, stoically purging bathroom after bathroom. Go to any party-minded campus early on a Friday to a Monday, and the student-residence bathrooms—male, female, coed—are likely to be vile. Fresh feces lie atop trash cans, or coagulate on the ground outside, where students have defecated from windows. After the first week of school, many undergrads learn to wear rubber thongs to a morning shower. Human waste may clog the drains, and floors can be sticky with dried urine: the spoor of the night campus. Soda cans, oranges, apples, and shirts block some toilets. Fresh vomit smears others. Nearly all campus buildings suffer "facilities abuse," the standard administrative euphemism for body-slammed Coke machines, exit signs shot with BB's, electronic pass-card panels kicked in weekend after weekend, fire extinguishers exhausted in water fights, head-butted street lamps, paneling turned to kindling, doors wrenched off hinges, windows smashed, toilet partitions and bathroom sinks ripped out.

At the nation's campus infirmaries, overnight injuries are triaged. Science students arrive with chemical burns, or feet swollen from standing over a microscope for sixteen hours straight. Party casualties are frequent: students hit in the eye by bottles flung from a sorority house, first-year males nauseated after eating too many raw hot dogs dredged in tobacco, a fraternity pledge ordeal nearly as popular as rubbing Ben-Gay on testicles. Many walking wounded are stoned; big schools near interstates (like UNC–Chapel Hill, or Berkeley) are the ideal drug runner's detour, and not all campus dealers practice quality control. Students may convulse, hallucinate, or bite security officers and infirmary staffers. The drinking age in all states is twenty-one; many health-services and student-life counselors say that so much campus drinking has been driven underground or onto the roads that drugs can be the more social pastime, and often the easier high. LSD, Ecstasy, crystal meth, heroin, tar heroin: they do it all.

Undergraduate women often come to campus clinics to request the morning-after pill. ("Social choices on any campus are very confined," a female University of Chicago student explained to me, wearily. "Either you're married, which is beyond going steady, or you opt for hookups—fast emotionless sex while extremely drunk—or you join a sex chain, going

out with a person who used to go out with your friends.")
Nearly all infirmaries stock heavy-duty birth-control pills,
prescribed after regretted or forced encounters. Eighty-five
percent of college women are sexually active, but more than
half use no protection, oral or vaginal. Much campus violence
is really domestic violence. Bruises, broken noses, and cigarette
burns no longer surprise campus medical teams. One college
woman in three may encounter physical abuse in a dating rela-
tionship, straight or lesbian. Michigan State recently opened an
on-campus shelter for battered women, a useful refuge when
fall romances implode.

Eight A.M. The University of Oregon has just had a 27 percent budget cut, but still works hard at hospitality; signs and
doors and elevators all over campus are thoroughly Brailled,
and recycling bins stand everywhere, though some student organizations cross out the White Paper label and neatly write in
Gringo Paper instead. The whole Oregon campus, like its city,
Eugene, is wonderfully neat, uncrowded, and agreeable, full
of bookstores and serene elderhippies and good cheap cafés
where undergraduates sit at battered wooden tables underlin-
ing key passages in *White Noise* and *The River Why,* ordering
sprout omelettes and blackberry tea, or platters of potato pancakes lavished with real butter and sour cream. Ducks paddle
in rain puddles on the brilliantly green lawns, or sit quacking
on campus sidewalks, forcing students on unicycles to yelp and
swerve. Drifts of low cloud touch the redwood grove behind
the computing center, like a landscape on a T'ang scroll. The
whole campus smells of fresh pine and fresh bread. Undergrads
with fine new hair colors—flamingo, jonquil, lagoon blue,
apple green—amble to class with fishing rod cases over their
shoulders, sipping from jumbo coffee mugs, their sweaters and
eyelashes beaded by the soft perpetual mist. People constantly
agree with each other. Any observation elicits a chorus of
"You bet!"

"I have this thing about doing the dinner thing."

"You bet."

"Angels helped us down that mountain, we were soooo drunk."

"You bet. Want a taco?"

"Joe's getting married, isn't that awesome, guys?"

"Totally is, you bet, you bet."

"Face it, I have seen women at UO who could easily rape *me*," says one tackle-sized undergraduate male to another, coming out of a sociology lecture hall.

"You bet. But would have no interest whatsoever in doing so," replies a hefty, self-possessed woman in overalls, stalking out into the rain.

At this campus the inclusion industry is very strong. To a Columbia or a Sinte Gleska undergraduate, life at Oregon might seem a touch sanitized, even pre-digested. Though customer-satisfaction surveys throng campus countertops, undergrads press for vote after vote on the need to ensure a more user-friendly U. Even a country of consideration has its casualties. At the student health-services building, two undergraduate women sit huddled in rain slickers on the clinic steps. One is fair and set-faced, the other twists her short dark hair into elf locks, brown eyes tight with worry. The pearly Willamette Valley morning light moves over their drawn young faces; both look exhausted, cried-out. The blond woman ducks head between knees for a long moment, and her friend's hand goes out to stroke her back but instead hovers, uncertain. The other girl is quivering all over, a tiny continual shaking, like a drenched cat. At 8:01, they walk stiffly to the glassed-in reception desk.

"I need—I want to see the, the. Personal things. The personal stuff person, the person who does, who gives, who tells—" She runs out of words.

"The OB-GYN nurse," says the dark girl firmly. "My friend needs to see her right away. Please, I mean. Needs to see her right away please."

A gynecology staffer appears from the back regions with commendable speed, and leads the fair girl away.

"I'll be right here," the roommate says to her retreating back.

"No—no, you have that exam today."

"I want to wait."

"I don't want you to. Just go to class. I'll see you back at the room. Just go, okay?"

Her friend stares blindly at the reception area's notebook of Student Travel Tips—carry soy nuts for protein, suck lemons to rehydrate on long bus rides, turn your socks inside out, do not give in to impotent rage. Then she snatches up her book-bag and dashes out across the wet green lawn, along the mall, toward the math building. The ducks fly up around her as she runs.

"Why is the night campus so chaotic?" I asked Dorothy Siegel, who directs the National Center for the Study of Campus Violence at Maryland's Towson State University, in suburban Baltimore. In a city where private enclaves like Johns Hopkins, Goucher, and Loyola dominate, Towson is the fallback public school, big and bland and low on frills; get the degree, get out, get a life. Many of its enrollees are working-class strivers who must regularly choose between three more credits and a new set of tires. Others are not so motivated.

"Our big campus crime use to be plagiarism. But odd stuff started appearing in the Eighties, from armed robberies to the kid who used his prosthetic arm to beat up his roommate. I decided to look into it," Siegel explains. Direct and organized, she kicks off her pink pumps, tosses me a bagel, and reaches across her desk for a thick computer printout, the first national survey of campus crime. Once she was a juvenile court psychologist. Now she is a vice president for student life. Little surprises her. But the tales from the campus front come close.

"Eighty percent of campus crime turns out to be student-on-student. Ninety percent involves drugs or drinking. By guarding against strangers, we found we were locking in the aggressors already among us. The intensity of violence is rising most. Harassment becomes assault; instead of pilfering, you get grand auto theft. Most students who commit campus crimes were not juvenile offenders. Most go on to be respectable adults. But the myth of college as a time-out, a period of total freedom, is extremely strong. Too many just want career-credentialing, not true learning. The result is a four-year madness, morality suspended."

The ripple effects of the night campus are hardest on those who expected college to be challenging and serious. About 70 percent of students do just fine in higher education; the other 30 percent are a major pain. It is hard to tell, on college applications, who will fall in which category. Many students, of course, drink socially, or choose not to drink at all, or have neither the time nor the money to pursue the party scene: instead, they run investment funds, design solar-powered cars, play soccer, start bands, plunge into union organizing. According to the Harvard study, undergraduates involved in community service or the arts or studying are less likely to be bingers.

The culture of academe—self-centered, trusting, impractical—often assumes a finer, safer, freer world. "I get to do whatever I want, but you have to protect me." Most campus crime is impulsive. Assaults, holdups, and stabbings all tend to occur after concerts or dances or big parties. Like undergraduate drinking, undergraduate violence has an extensive pedigree.

From Oxbridge hearties pummeling aesthetes to secret-society hazing, the Anglo-American educational strain has long looked the other way after dark. Young subalterns *will* wreck the mess, all very traditional.

Not all campus crime is drunken impulse. White-supremacist incidents, cool and deliberate, are rising, too. Sometimes student-age townies are responsible, sometimes enrolled students, but the aggressors are nearly always white and male. A Siegel colleague cites a recent Berkeley study suggesting that hate crimes shoot up wherever right-wing foundation money subsidizes conservative student groups and publications. Gay or minority students are favorite targets—flyers shoved under a door, yells in the night, spray paint on a car, beatings behind the gym. Weapons offenses on campus are rising, too. A 1995 survey of seventy-three institutions revealed that 7.5 percent of college students had carried guns, knives, or other weapons to school in the last thirty days. Some armed undergraduates are gang members (an increasing worry for campus security staff) and some students who do not wish to become a statistic while walking to the college library parking lot after dark.

College has always been a place of enthusiasm and excess, of identities tried on and discarded: the Pagan Student Union, the Young Republicans, the Alternative Sexualities Task Force, the Ultimate Frisbee team, the drinking crowd. When trouble hits the night campus, the most likely suspect is the white male, freshman or sophomore, who is both athlete and fraternity member. Only 3.3 percent of the college population, athletes commit 19 percent of campus assaults on women. The strongest predictor for binge drinking is membership in a fraternity or sorority: a startling 80 percent of sorority-house dwellers and 86 percent of those who live in frat houses are bingers. Like the tobacco industry, liquor and brewing companies talk responsible use but advertise hard for the student dollar. (Typical ads from ASU campus publications: "Miller

Genuine Draft Ski Utah! Round trip video bus . . . of course all the beer you can drink all weekend long!" "Lake Tahoe All-Greek Blowout . . . Booze Cruise!") Greek life is healthier than ever at U.S. colleges and universities. Of the 3 million full-time male undergraduates, 400,000 are frat members. Though their violences often spill onto the larger campus, such societies are private entities. Not all are animal houses; the gay Greeks are often better-behaved. Delta Lambda Phi now has thirty chapters nationwide, and an official toasting song: "There once was a mighty Lambda man/ Who lived by the sword/Crushed the rogue horde/With a whirl of steel he took the fight/And won the prince's heart that night."

At conference after conference, deans and student-life staffers offer theories and anecdotes on the night campus, shards of a social puzzle. For many the problem is not abstract; they badly want to know why sons and daughters, nephews or nieces were beaten or raped during undergraduate years. Some believe America's problems have come to campus because admissions are no longer selective. Others say campus residents should stop treating their schools like small towns, circa 1935, where no one ever locks a door. Security officers see the results of that attitude daily: full professors who leave keys in ignitions; students who keep homeless people in their dorm rooms like pets, feeding them smuggled peanut-butter sandwiches; alumni who steal computers or office equipment because, years later, their building keys still work.

A great many administrators (and faculty) argue that today's college students are damaged goods. They arrive dragging complicated lives. They did kidnap drill in kindergarten, learned to drink in middle school, thwarted their parents' home drug tests by eating poppyseed bagels or drinking goldenroot tea. Some arrive at college with a "been there, done that" view of campus excess, having seen too much in grade school and high school, or else at home; others plunge right in. Many Nineties students have bad academic skills, and worse social ones; even at expensive private schools like Bryn Mawr, professors find themselves explaining how to perform an introduction, or write a check. Many four-year campuses have seen a clear rise in uncontrollable students, afraid of no one, confident that there is no such thing as a permanent record or a last chance.

Other campus adults blame popular culture. This first generation of day-care kids to reach college has watched 100,000 televised murders, they say; what do you expect, if they grow up playing computer games like Night Trap, in which a troupe of ghouls captures a scantily dressed sorority girl and drains her blood with a neck drill? Administrators fear full reporting of campus crimes will make their schools look bad; many security officers and parents push for enforcement; some faculty worry that outsiders who want to oversee campus life beyond the lecture hall will also soon want to dictate class content. We are not high school, professors snap. We are a republic within the Republic, with many freedoms.

Like its European ancestor, the American college experience was designed for young adolescents. In 1600 and 1700, college students were often fifteen to seventeen. Reforming American high schools pushed ahead the college years; enter at seventeen or eighteen, leave at twenty-one or twenty-two. Many undergraduates today are adult in every sense. They have jobs, families, responsibilities; they pay tuitions, do the work, collect diplomas. Everyone wins. But others treat college as an extended vacation or private club. The most violent partiers often prove to be alumni, or students from other schools, or people in their mid-to-late twenties who are still technically undergrads. (Arizona State's *Greek Review,* a tabloid for fraternities and sororities, prints frequent valedictions to aged colleagues: "Hammer down! . . . we must bid farewell to a couple of finally graduating seniors . . . pledged in '86 for

Christs sake . . . good luck out there in the real world, I hear it licks balls!")

Academic liability law struggles to decide how much—and how little—faculty, staff, and students must be protected from one another. On a college-sponsored field trip, a drunken student falls off a cliff. Is the university liable for his broken neck? No; he is legally adult, and the accident was not foreseeable. A drunken student falls off a campus trampoline. Again, no liability; bouncing under the influence was a personal safety choice, by one who is of age. Students robbed on a public sidewalk? The college has no duty to protect. Students assaulted in a campus parking garage surrounded by untrimmed foliage where previous attacks occurred? A-*ha:* the school has failed in reasonable care.

Older campus officials observe that a disordered undergraduate life is nothing new. Since the 1960s, the Association of College and University Housing Officers has been known as the Zookeepers. If you want to see student wildness, members observe, try a high-rise dorm in the mid-1970s, when the parents of today's undergraduates were tossing burning couches out the windows and grand pianos from the roof. On campus all trends recycle, its historians say. Contemporary students drink more like their grandparents than their parents. College life has always been violent; crisis is the university's natural state. The decades between World War I and Vietnam were really an extended lull. The passionate religious revivals at Jacksonian-era colleges live on at conservative campuses like Tulsa's Oral Roberts University or suburban Chicago's Wheaton, where students by the hundreds line up to make public confession of racism and drug use. Division I Football looks sedate beside the mass mayhem of "rushing" a century ago, when hundreds of students blindly pushed at classmates on stairs or walkways, or pitched one another into rivers and lakes. (Organized sports were promoted as a character-building alternative, but in 1905 alone, eighteen college boys died on football fields. To clean up a brutal game, Theodore Roosevelt finally had to intervene.)

To the sociologist Neil Smelser, formerly of Berkeley, a taxonomy of undergraduate cultures cuts across the decades, even the centuries. One clear group is the highly competitive—pre-laws, pre-meds, bright people who are not very interested in ideas. Work and thought, for them, are two distinct activities. Next is a culture of free spirits, who identify with the faculty, value the life of the mind, and come to college hoping for peers who like to read and speculate. Other students join the politically active campus culture, once mostly liberal or radical, now also libertarian or conservative, but in all cases fond of action, and forcing issues. A culture of expressive protest (centered on personal appearance, drug use, sexual liberty, and calculated intellectual outrage) has flourished on campuses for centuries. When Shelley was sent down from Oxford for advocating atheism, he was being correctly countercultural. Niche worlds also bloom and fade, from drama and music to literary groups and ethnic organizations, though yearbooks in time yield to on-line 'zines, and missionary societies to recycling clubs.

The big man on campus is now a ghost. But the party-hearty collegiate subculture that often spawned him remains, still extroverted, confident, hostile to ideas and causes, anti-intellectualism personified. At its core are fraternities, sororities, athletes, and rich alumni. Many of these people binge. Later, they also give. Antagonize them now, lose a track-and-field complex in 2030.

We are a family, we handle our own, institutions say. Remember goldfish-swallowing, and kids cramming into phone booths? We will survive this, too. But that mind-set—minimize, deny, deny some more—frequently means trouble in an age of live hand grenades in the cafeteria, in a time when dormitory suicides can require an AIDS-alert team in full decontamination gear to sterilize the bookshelves and bedding, and hose away the blood.

In a crowded basement at the edge of Brown University, the school's chief of police steps forward one perfect military pace. "I wish I could say you will all be safe here," says Dennis Boucher, in a strong New England twang. "But even I've been attacked on the street, in full uniform"—he gestures at his crisp khaki shirt, his mirror-bright shoes—"so you must stay alert. Aware." The international students around him, some just hours off a plane from Vienna or Rangoon, murmur in dismay. Seventy-nine nations are represented in the Brown student body, and Boucher knows some come from countries where a reasonable citizen fears uniforms. "America is full of wooden floors," says a woman from India, clutching a camera, "and rats with furry tails!" Everything about a U.S. campus fall is so strange to them, squirrels included, that senior policemen giving special lectures on how to walk in public seems one more inexplicable.

"Head up, confident stride," Boucher continues. "Use the shuttle or escort service rather than walk alone after dark. If you leave a car or a bicycle unguarded here, I guarantee it will go away. Lock your rooms when you go down the hall to shower. If you feel at risk, anywhere, any time, call me." A hand shoots up in the back row. "Do you recommend that we equip ourselves with Mace or stun guns?" "Arm yourselves with information," Boucher says. "Memorize the university emergency number: 3322." A hundred pens hurry across notepads, double- and triple-underlining.

Half a mile from downtown Providence, Rhode Island, Brown is a hilltop inner-city campus of 235 buildings. The neighborhoods around it range from working-class grit to a gleaming colonial district with streets named Benefit and Jenckes and vast clapboard houses freshly painted mustard, slate, and pumpkin. Like many campuses—USC, the University of Chicago, Yale, Columbia, Clark, Trinity, Marquette, Yeshiva, Fordham, Oakland's Mills College—Brown must live with the consequences of long-ago real-estate decisions; neighborhoods may alter, often for the worse, but campuses are fixed. The Brown campus is unwalled. Campus police, Chief Boucher says, may receive some two thousand suspicious-person calls each year. Police work here is mostly service—lockouts, free whistle distributions, bike registration, a rumor-control hotline, discreet room checks on behalf of parents who haven't heard from a child in weeks. Brown is the easygoing Berkeley of the Ivies, no course requirements, all grades below C purged from student transcripts, lots of choreographed liberty. "Are you feeling okay?" one Frisbee player asks another as they stroll the college green. "You're actually wearing a Brown sweatshirt." "I know, I'm so sorry. Don't disown me." This is *Brown,* students say every year, with great hauteur; do we really need security people at all? On this campus, everyone jaywalks, even the cops.

In the Brown student union, a dozen women, most young, one silver-haired, one heavily pregnant, lie on a carpeted floor looking up at a young Asian-American special-services staffer. "Let's review an oral-sex scenario," she says, her voice level and professional. The sole man present, a visiting student from California, nods politely. "It's called Bite and Volley. If you wake up in your apartment or dorm room and find a 240-pound assailant on your chest, or if what began as consensual activity turns to date rape, chomp down on the offending anatomy ["Sure hope it's someone I know," says a nearby woman], brace your feet against the mattress, bring your locked hands up like a volleyball serve, scraping the scrotum as hard as possible, then heave him off with a strong fast hip thrust and come around with your leg cocked, ready to kick. Try it. Make your intentions clear."

Flailing feet fill the air as the women grunt and lunge. They practice instep stomps, screaming *No! No! No!* They master shin kicks and breast-bone jabs and nostril slams and knees to the gonads. The California student is pressed back against the sofa cushions now, eyes averted, face pale. "Rats, I have physics lab," says a petite senior, sending her last invisible rapist reeling. The instructor bounds to her feet, looking proudly at the panting class. Some are somber, some grinning. "Next week," she tells them, "knockout blows." Brown first-years all discuss sexual assault with peer educators; each group must agree on a definition of consent. After class, I ask the self-defense instructor if classes like hers should be required for every student. As a recent graduate, she finds the idea of requirements disconcerting, distasteful. "This is Brown. We don't do mandatory."

Generational amnesia strongly affects the ebb and flow of campus rules. For thirty years, *in loco parentis* seemed a campus artifact, dead as the bonfires that once hailed debate-team victories. But the concept is again alive. The assumption that a college or university represents a student's parents, safeguarding life and morals, flourished between 1914 and 1945, weakened with the arrival of GI Bill students, vanished following Sixties demands to treat students as adults. Like the Berlin Wall, *in loco parentis* fell bloodlessly. Students sought freedoms and colleges retreated, shrugging; most were glad to escape an administrative Vietnam, despite apoplectic letters from alumni. By the mid-1970s, the lowering of voting and drinking ages to eighteen had cemented the shift from student ward to student citizen.

Yet many contemporary undergrads, trained as consumers from the cradle, prefer service to empowerment. Few schools lack a Food Preoccupation Group, an In-the-Closet Support Group, a Bereavement Group, a Self-Hypnosis for Better Grades Group, a Students with Mentally Ill Family Members Group. Twenty-four-hour campus hot lines flower. Brown alone has offered Dean on Call, Women on Call, Chaplains on Call, Psychologist on Call. Sometimes student protection means tighter rules about who may be in campus housing when. Sometimes it means party monitors, once known as chaperones (today, usually moonlighting police officers). Sometimes the demands for perfect protection and perfect freedom leave student employees caught between their peers and their paycheck. "Should I go to the library now?" inquire resident advisors, when the first kegs roll down the hall.

What, if anything, should administrations do about the night campus? Planning response in advance of violent crime is an excellent policy, and so is a clear behavior code. Researchers Andrea Parrot of Cornell University and Carol Bohmer of the University of Pittsburgh have catalogued the classic administrative reactions to sexual assault cases. Some schools favor the much-parodied Antioch model of step-by-step request and consent—May I kiss you now? May I place one hand on your breast? Ethical campuses (Parrot cites New Jersey's Stockton State, or small Catholic colleges like St. Norbert's in De Pere, Wisconsin) are realistic but firm. They will suspend students for sexual assault. If asked why, ethical campuses reply that they really don't want people like that around.

But most campuses fall into other Parrot-Bohmer categories, just as clear. At There-but-for-the-grace-of-God institutions, the first reaction is selfish gratitude. Spared big-money lawsuits, they count their public-relations blessings. Protecting students—oh, right, them—is a distant second. For barn-door closers, only extreme discomfort (like a big-money lawsuit) produces policy changes. Ostrich schools stonewall. We've never had an assault reported, they will say. All our students are decent and kind. Victim-blamer campuses are as self-protective as barracuda. A female student files a sexual assault charge. Where? school lawyers demand. A fraternity? How many drinks did you have? What were you wearing? Did you lead him on? Be glad that's all that happened. Soon thereafter, the student finds two administrative letters in her mailbox: a complaint against her for filing false complaint, and an alcohol-violation summons.

Tired of stabbings and shootings when outsiders crash large campus parties, MIT now uses metal detectors to deter non-students packing guns and knives. East Texas Baptist University enforces curfew with electronic locks that confirm the time of late arrival, then transmit data via fiber-optic cable to administration computers. The University of Southern California, in southeast Los Angeles, invested in a $2 million access and surveillance network of TV cameras, alarms, and card-key readers used by seven thousand students over twenty-five thousand times a day. Computer-controlled cameras can zoom in on the license numbers of suspicious cars. Two-way speakers warn intruders to leave USC property. In stairwells and parking garages, voices come out of the air. "Hold up your ID to the camera. Thank you. Move along."

Other institutions take refuge in paralysis by analysis. Campus lawyers point out that undergraduate rapists have rights like anyone else; professors warn against paternalism, defending partying as student cultural expression; administrators wince at student arrests for drugs or drinking because all campuses must (in theory) certify that they are drug-free workplaces to receive public funding. Others try prevention. Howard University, in Washington, D.C., is moving all freshmen back on campus. The University of Minnesota holds mandatory briefings for its five thousand first-years on campus safety, sexual assault, and self-defense. The University of South Carolina offers a for-credit course on being a freshman, and claims that students who take it get better grades and are more confident about their undergrad careers. The University of Rhode Island, long a champion party school, banned alcohol on campus in 1995. Cornell has required athletes to attend awareness sessions on sex, crime, and violence. Try the *cum parentibus* model, suggests Connecticut College; ask not only your students but their parents to read three specified books each summer; have faculty run discussion on the reading at parents'-weekend panels; get parents, students, and faculty to help draft campus drinking policies.

Another possible response to night-campus syndrome is assigning more homework. Many American undergraduates have a lot of time on their hands. The average national college workload hovers near a twenty-nine-hour week, an all-time low, as opposed to about sixty hours of schoolwork in the early 1960s—though whether quantity is quality, then or now, sends faculty instantly into bitter defensive debate. So does the question "What should an educated person know?" Competing answers tumble forth: the information explosion has killed survey courses on common knowledge, and high time. Handing students born in 1980 the mental furniture of an eighteenth-century gentleman is no kindness. Ensuring they have something to think about while doing telemarketing or changing diapers, however, is. Why require Western Civ courses in a transcultural America? some faculty demand. Students don't know what they don't know, other professors retort: 80 percent of undergraduates now study anything they want, too much of it warmed-over high school. Meanwhile, only 35 percent of first-years do six or more hours of weekly homework, as opposed to 44 percent as recently as 1987.

The night campus has long been a matter for undergraduates and administrators—but to create a more responsible and engaged campus life, involving faculty is essential. What works? Informed academic advising, as hard to find on expensive campuses as at factory schools. Small, targeted commonsense innovations: the New York nonprofit that helps buy PCs for poor first-year black and Hispanic students interested in engineering and science, since low-income undergrads are 50 percent more likely to arrive on campus without their own computers. The Berkeley professor who formed calculus study groups for black students after noticing that while whites and Asians readily worked together on hard problems, black kids tended to suffer proudly in silence, convinced that asking for help would make them look dumb. The studies noting that many undergrads are growing adolescents still; sleeping late, for them, is not always sloth, and many learn most efficiently from early afternoon on—suggesting that scheduling fifty-minute lectures at 8:00, 9:00, 10:00, and 11:00 may be the worst of all campus learning formats. Seminars of ten or twelve students remain a very effective way to learn in college; taking even one small-group class, especially in the first year, does wonders for undergraduate morale and grade point averages both.

Intensive courses wear out professors but stimulate undergrads, from the language schools at Middlebury College that immerse students in Russian or Arabic 24–7 to Yale's legendary Daily Themes course, its requirements simple and brutal: an essay a day. Honors colleges, especially at enormous state universities like Wisconsin, Michigan, and Michigan State, help smart, serious students find one another in the crowds. Faculty everywhere are famously bad at calm negotiation, or bargaining for change (at many schools, some courses have not been seriously updated for forty and fifty years, because all know the fights with colleagues will be so exhausting), but when professors do take charge they tend to get results: after Louisiana State's faculty senate persuaded the public schools to require a year each of chemistry, biology, and physics as a requirement for LSU admission, enrollments in Louisiana high school physics classes quickly doubled. And when rich campuses help poor ones, both learn: Sinte Gleska did get its $10 million federal grant for computer instruction, and Stanford faculty have promised both syllabi exchanges and access to Silicon Valley's powerful internship and job-placement network. Some of the National Science Foundation money will also wire the tribe, buying a Powerbook with modem for every Sicangu Lakota who wants one, allowing a good portion of the Sioux nation to surf the Net, and dream in C.

The quality of student resident advisors, or RA's, will either ease or hinder first-year adjustments. Some RA's can recommend a good literature professor, explain the fine points of course-change cards, and locate both the math help room and the best local pizza; some are coolly absentee; some deal drugs in the dorms. At Haverford, a small Quaker school in suburban Philadelphia, entering students are assigned to "customs groups" of twelve to fifteen students, a ready-made tribe for study breaks, hikes, concert trips, birthdays, and moans about exam stress; older students serve as advisors. At Haverford an honor system covers exams and private life. Behavior that bothers others gets discussed to death, the price of collective civility.

Another way to defuse the night campus—to help students belong—is for all undergrads to help tend the campus infrastructure, spending several days each month in painting, cleaning, grounds work, or helping in food service or library, as happens at Blackburn College in southern Illinois. Expenses fall, emotional investment in the campus climbs. And Duke is trying to break up its entrenched undergraduate partying patterns through social engineering—by recruiting students who study for fun, by persuading faculty to live in freshman dorms, by reworking housing assignments to keep younger students away from upperclassmen, many of whom resent the administration's attempt to introduce intellectual activity onto campus. "You can lead me to college," declare their protest T-shirts, "but you can't make me think."

Behind the clash of cultures—an entrenched student tradition of Dionysian excess, a new protective puritanism—two very old models of what a campus should be are also at war: the college way versus the university way, tradition or sentiment against size and money, the finishing school and the trade school. Design students' time, or let them do it. Provide more structure, prune the choices, or keep the system neutral. A hundred years on, campuses are still debating John Dewey's query: are undergraduates wayward, ignorant, and in need of firm guidance, or is experimenting the best way to become self-confident, self-reliant, self-propelled?

Brown University's president, Vartan Gregorian, suggests that campuses have already discovered a third way out: the frankly commercialized operation. "Campuses today are Athenian city-states," he told me, gazing with urbane weariness at the ceiling of his eighteenth-century office. "Laundry, concerts, parking, catering vegetarian, catering kosher, too much government regulation and not enough government funding—some days I feel like Job: 'Hit me again!' But as Neil Rudenstine up at Harvard said to me recently, 'Where else in America can you get hotel, health club, career advice, and eighteen hundred courses for ninety dollars a day?'" As at any exclusive resort, what you do of an evening becomes your own business.

To say "We are responsible" admits liability, and most campuses will do almost anything to avoid a lawsuit. Professors sue their schools far more than workers in any other industry, but students are right behind: a University of Idaho student mooned friends from a third-floor window, fell out, and sued the school for not explicitly warning him of the dangers associated with upper-story windows. Malpractice insurance for colleges and universities is another hidden reason for high campus price tags.

Between rhetoric and action lies a maze of chasms and canyons, underbrush and dead ends, and undergraduates know it. So administrations mostly repeat what is, after all, true. Our students are adults. We must trust them to make responsible choices. Counseling services say, We are winning battles, but losing the war. Beer companies solemnly urge responsible consumption, then sponsor drink'n'raft bashes. Trustee boards say, What do you mean, we can't have drink trays on our carts when we play the university golf course? Students say, Get out of my face, or, I have a right to learn in peace. Parents say, How dare you arrest my daughter? or How dare you fail to safeguard my son? Placating is easier than confronting, entertaining easier than correcting bad sophomore essays phrase by phrase. Keep them distracted. Let them party. Bring on the new class. After all, some undergrads drink enormously and still get good grades. And in two or three years, most will have straightened out, gotten bored, turned toward the daylight world once more. But the human wreckage is real, too.

In the end, in the dark, the underpaid security people offer the most consistent witness to the night campus. I talked to one

Rutgers guard, a moonlighting sociology graduate student who found his job professionally instructive, like a duck blind set in a flyway. At twenty-six, he knew he was already too old to understand a lot of what he saw. The strange new music, the unchanneled energy, constantly amazed him.

"Frat row can get very scary," he pointed out, "but in fairness, they aren't the only problems. You get these calls from the science dorms: Naked guy running around with rubber doll. Or: Women screaming in dorm room. That one was a ritual initiation of female scientists, where the group brandings got *way* out of hand."

He thought a moment, moving his fork in precise parallel strokes through the remains of Himalayan chicken tikka and bamboo-shoot curry. We were in a campus restaurant at twilight, and groups of students kept coming to the window and squinting at its hand-lettered menu—papri chat, dal bhat, kothay, seven-bean soup. Some made ape faces, then drifted toward a nearby sports bar. Others brightened at the clean hot scent of lentil chips and jasmine tea, and came shyly in.

"For undergrads in general, the worst time is the first week of fall term, when they don't have enough to do, and the week following midterms, same problem," the young guard said. "I learned one thing very quickly on this job. The kids with green hair and nose rings are totally normal. It's the ones who are weird up here"—he tapped his forehead—"that you need to look out for."

FALL BREAK:
Through the Groves

Not all colleges schedule a fall break. Public campuses often march straight through to the end of term, fifteen unbroken weeks of academic slog, but a lot of instruction for not much cost. Private schools relish a pause in the autumn semester. Break lets professors catch up on midterm grading, suggests that campus minds, like overheated carburetors, need therapeutic time-outs. The most expensive schools have the shortest semesters. Only at this midpoint of the first fall term do bill-paying parents, now less dazzled, start doing basic math. At $28,000 for twenty-eight weeks of instruction, a full load of four courses per term means college costs $1,000 per week; at $250 per course, every class meeting skipped equals eighty-three dollars torn up and thrown away.

But you learn more outside the classroom than in it, undergraduates patiently explain. Some take Spanish dictionaries to Florida during break week, where their campus Christian-service groups will help migrant laborers harvest citrus and cabbage. Others hammer siding for city rehab projects, count hawks for the Nature Conservancy, join geology-class field trips to the southern Rockies, hit the beach at Cancun. Perhaps half those at private schools fly or drive home at break, importing dirty laundry across state lines. Others cannot afford a bus ticket to the next town. Many U.S. scholarship students will not see their families until the winter holidays. Undergrads from Malaysia or Venezuela may stay on campus till graduation day. A few are invited to American homes for break week; far more wander a deserted campus or hang disconsolately around the dorms, trying to study.

As the airport vans pull away from campus on Wednesday afternoon, or at the latest Thursday morning—only the sternest faculty schedule midterm exams on the Friday before fall break—many of the first-years are smiling. After eight weeks on campus, they not only know about genomes and Chinua Achebe and the philosophy of technology, but have acquired dazzling technique in poker and search engines, Nautilus, and fabric softener. This college ordeal, they are beginning to conclude, is not so scary after all.

Campus founders have known that for centuries. It isn't hard to create an American college. Today you pick a name, and a typeface; acquire voicemail; rent a motel room for class meetings; hire as faculty four or five of the nation's one million unemployed Ph.D.s. You put up flyers in supermarkets, announcing a registration open house. You announce that your board has decided to wait for current accreditation controversies to die down before finalizing the institution's official status.

And you choose academic robes, a surprisingly hard task. Long black gowns, tasseled mortarboards, and color-coded hoods and stoles have been ceremonial dress on U.S. campuses for only about a century. During the 1880s, a young drygoods wholesaler in Albany talked a few eastern schools into trying medieval dress-up, but commencement outfits grew so outrageous that a commission on academic wear was convened in 1894, to keep campus heraldry in line. The Intercollegiate Bureau of Academic Costume is still at work in upstate New York, deep in oak-leaf lace, scarlet silks, and leopards couchant. The world's campuses have invented some eight hundred degrees, so the expert eye must quickly sort M.B.A. robes for the University of New South Wales (old gold, kingfisher blue, and cream) from the doctoral colors of Newcastle-upon-Tyne (scarlet, rose, palatinate purple) yet also know universal color codes—arts and letters white, engineering orange, the gold and silver of mining schools, podiatry's nile green.

When overseas observers view the U.S. higher education landscape, they are most astonished by its freebooting quality and—except in heraldry—its relative absence of rules. Some thirty professional associations, like the American Association for Higher Education and the Association of Hispanic Colleges and Universities, cluster in a single Washington, D.C., office building, but they are far less powerful, singly or together, than the American bar or medical associations—and more distracted, for domestic terrorism has turned One Dupont Circle into an anxious fortress of security challenges and metal detectors.

Compared to colleges and universities abroad, the governmental hand on higher education is still very light. We have no ministry of higher education, no one strong tastemaker or directing force or dominant school. As nonprofits, neither operated as businesses nor regulated like government agencies, campuses pay no property taxes, though many make donations to local governments. Unlike any other industrialized urban country, the United States divides its education efforts into fifty separate state systems. Public institutions are the more regulated; state sunshine laws compel many to announce committee meetings and publish budgets. All colleges and universities must report (often quite reluctantly) their graduation rates and crime statistics. But so long as great stacks of federal compliance forms are filed concerning asbestos removal, historic preservation, and handicapped access, private campuses remain exactly that.

The onslaught of campus choice exhilarates some outsiders, baffles others. They find it hard to accept that the U.S. system of higher education is not a system at all, but a mixed grill of colleges on horseback and colleges at sea; colleges that relentlessly make you over, train you in the uses of power, then stamp "Grade A" on your forehead (most famously the Ivies, and the service academies); and colleges that favor benign neglect, like the vast sweet-tempered campuses of the Big Ten. Some schools are monocultures, like Juilliard or the thoroughly Baptist Baylor or Maine's Portland School of Neon Tube Design. Others have course timetables like phone books, with nearly as many campus lives to try on and discard. We even have ghost campuses such as the University of Deseret, founded by the Mormons in 1840s Utah, and imaginary institutions like H. P. Lovecraft's sinister Miskatonic University, or Rocky and Bullwinkle's hapless Wossamatta U.

The cheerful aggressiveness of American collegiate life can disconcert—the synchronized-swim squads! the champion mine-rescue teams! the marching bands!—and the exuberant possessiveness of campuses startles, too. The University of Alabama–Birmingham may have cornered the market on Proust papers, but the University of Louisville boasts the globe's largest Tarzan collection. Clark excels in geography, New Mexico in anthropology, East Carolina State and Texas A&M in marine archaeology, Indiana University and Minnesota's St. Olaf College in music. The University of Georgia shelters the original Confederate Constitution, the University of Florida maintains the International Shark Attack file, Kent State protects the planet's largest collection of hearing aids, the University of Nevada–Reno sponsors the world's sole institute for gambling studies. American campuses love statistics wars. Penn State leads the nation in campus Greeks, with fifty-eight fraternities and twenty-five sororities. Berkeley uses 190 miles of athletic tape yearly in its sports program. But its Golden Bear mascot looks staid beside the University of Delaware's Fighting Blue Hen, or the Fighting Banana Slug of UC–Santa Cruz.

Mostly, educators from other lands look at the daily round of an American campus and see a bouillabaisse of cultural production bubbling and boiling: poetry readings, lectures, chalk talks, symposia, open mikes, live concerts, improv sessions, art exhibits, master classes, radio broadcasts, technical demos, brown-bag discussions, editorial collectives, proseminars, keynotes, slide presentations, Q&A's. They marvel at how energetic it all is.

And how stubborn. Higher education is the last great American institution, except for presidential campaigns, to dodge systemic downsizing and reform, mostly because it *has* no system, no market laws, no set constituency to please. Manufacturing, the military, the health industry, the mainstream religions, even Congress, have all painfully acceded to change. The campus world claims privilege, resists accountability, fights limits of any kind. People from overseas universities find this bewildering. They do not understand why the American campus remains so torn between serving power and serving people; why it is so ambivalent about its role in undergraduate lives, probing and fussing one minute, ignoring and denying the next; why a majority of its faculty sit in state-of-the-art labs and excellent libraries and claim they do not feel free to research or speak as they wish. Especially, visitors wonder why the American college campus is so driven to be everything to everyone; why it seems so familiar, and yet so alien.

Almost no one, local or visitor, remembers that American campuses—even the Lakota-speaking ones—are distant and estranged cousins to all the rest, slow to alter, slower to adapt, transplants attuned still to a different sun and soil. Five hundred years is nothing, in higher education. Even the noun "campus" is borrowed, and the idea for it, too. The first modern use of "campus" occurred at eighteenth-century Princeton, whose flat treeless college grounds reminded an instructor of the Campus Martius in Rome, where imperial legions once practiced maneuvers. The usage held, and spread. (Harvard and Yale kept the older term "yard," as the University of Virginia has remained "the Lawn" and Tennessee's mountaintop University of the South is "the Domain.") By the 1870s most Americans thought of "campus" as somewhere evocative and apart, both the whole college property and the spirit of place embodied in buildings and grounds.

The genealogy of the campus begins in the stony hills above the Aegean. When we speak of the groves of academe, the phrase is a very old echo, but true. Akademia was an olive orchard two miles outside Athens, where Plato founds his school about 390 B.C. Here the idea of campus also rises—a community of people, slightly removed from the world of affairs, who make and share knowledge. Not too far removed: Academy and city stand together against the wilderness as places of reason, not feeling; of culture, not nature. From the beginning, academe is divided, self-doubting, self-seeking. Faculty are incorrigible talkers, students often too worldly for serious scholarship. Few of his clients attend lectures for sheer love of learning, Plato admits; most seek only professional advantage. Half the faculty claim reason and logic should be supreme. The other half believe that power stems from language. Neither philosophers nor rhetoricians are terribly sure what the point of the academy should be: To perfect the self? Train leaders? Create intelligent citizens? The arguments will span millennia.

Imperial Rome proves an excellent market for roving academics. Greek tutors educate its ruling class, Greek secretaries keep its records. But in matters of law the Romans devise their own higher education; Roman youths learn jurisprudence largely by arguing lurid hypotheticals, strong on pirate kidnappers, ravished maidens, and fiendish fathers. Critics soon declare such studies frivolous, treasonous, or both, since they encourage neither plain speaking nor practical skills. When Rome falls, formal knowledge seeks refuge at the edges of empire, in the new Eastern capital of Constantinople, in the Arab world—the Al-Azhar University in Cairo dates to 970—and in the isolated monasteries of Ireland and North Britain, too cold to conquer, too poor to covet. Over seven centuries, the classical heritage is recovered piecemeal, slipping again into Europe by assorted back doors, particularly Spain and Sicily. A booming medieval economy badly needs lawyers and administrators to handle its diplomatic affairs, its international trade, its property battles. Supplying a professionally literate class means organizing Europe's informal bands of scholars and students, who tend to travel light and leave town often, but by 1200 scholarship is a licensed industry. From Sweden to Siena, buildings and benefactors are acquired. Administrative routines emerge. Written exams and formal degrees develop to certify students in a set of courses called the trivium (grammar, rhetoric, and logic) and quadrivium (music, arithmetic, geometry, and astronomy).

Inventing a culture of learning comes harder. Medieval scholars try various teaching methods: first lectures; then formal debates; then fast, rowdy bouts of repartee known as *quodlibets,* or what-you-wills. Since students and masters at any school might come from dozens of linguistic regions, since scholars like to wander, a common tongue is essential. Speaking Latin becomes mandatory in the university world, a rule enforced around the clock by eavesdropping teams of language police called *lupi,* wolves.

At first professional behavior is also rule-bound. A medieval protective guild was called a *universitas:* merchants and craftsmen began them, law-course enrollees at Bologna formed one for students, but early professors had no such protection. Students contracted directly with scholars for services, and insisted on their money's worth. Before leaving the district, faculty often had to post deposits or swear to cover the advertised syllabus and lecture right to the bell. (As consolation, professors cite each other, whenever possible, as Doctors Invincible and Irrefragable.) But scholarly privileges soon arise— subsidized food and housing, exemption from most civic duties, the right to commandeer a horse, the right to quiet study. Any *studium generale,* as early universities are called, provoked bloody town-gown clashes. But to harm a professional scholar is sacrilege.

By the 1300s, a constellation of campus problems emerges. Undergraduates major in drinking and hazing, or cling to their own ethnic groups and fight all the rest; student riots can last days. Faculty specialize in vicious tenure struggles and recruiting wars, rely too much on teaching assistants, moonlight as wine merchants, hire thugs to intimidate students into signing on for expensive lecture courses. Critics still abound: they claim that universities only encourage a parasitical lawyer class; that lucrative civil law programs push aside the traditional high-minded canon; that faculty harbor heretical ideas. Before granting degrees, some institutions begin demanding loyalty oaths, a precursor of the modern alumni-fund-drive pledge. Admissions controversies arise. Gentlemen's sons discover higher education in the late Middle Ages, chiefly as an excuse for parties and peer bonding; a two-track college experience results, frustrating and durable, of struggle for the scholarship student and subsidized indolence for the rich and social.

If the university begins as a trade union, the college is invented as a safe place to sleep. Street crime and sordid rooming houses drive early scholars to attempt communal living in rented hostels or halls. At Oxford and Cambridge, a quadrangle enclosing dining hall, chapel, study areas, and dormitories proves an efficient plan for keeping young men supervised and aggressive townies at bay. A more impersonal model, in which colleges offer instruction but let students run their own lives, takes root in fifteenth-century Scotland, France, and Spain, then leaps the Atlantic to Latin America. The Spanish seed universities from Lima to Mexico City a century before Harvard opens in 1638. (Rhode Island Colony seems to have founded a slightly earlier college, which closes when the entire student body is erased in an Indian raid.)

The Massachusetts Bay Colony is better defended, and well-stocked with alumni of Cambridge University's fiercely Puritan colleges. They retain the alma mater's familiar schedule of fall and spring semesters. (By the mid-seventeenth century, Cambridge and Oxford switch to the three-term calendar they still follow, but the much older fall-spring pattern persists on most U.S. campuses.) A proper college quadrangle is deemed too expensive, too reminiscent of isolated monastery life. A three-story wooden building goes up instead, where some fifty students and faculty will lodge, study, and worship at very close quarters.

Along the Atlantic seaboard more colleges appear, ancient forms of higher education mutating briskly in the New World air. The colony of Virginia suggests in 1693 that chartering the College of William and Mary will aid in saving souls. "Souls! Damn your souls!" the Crown's attorney general cries. "Raise tobacco!" But in a pattern repeated across the continent for the next two centuries, a college rises in the wilderness, and a town grows in its wake. The sponsors of William and Mary are Oxonian Anglicans who understand comfort, unlike the Puritans to the north; by the time Thomas Jefferson is an undergraduate, the college resembles a baroque country villa, dignified yet domestic. As part of Williamsburg's ambitious urban design, a broad avenue links college and town, and undergraduates are encouraged to explore both worlds (lest they prove, as one student speech warns, "meer scholars, which make a very ridiculous figure").

All colonial colleges struggle to fulfill a fourfold task: to produce clergy and civic leaders, to combat barbarism, to contain high animal spirits among the students. Most of all, to fund-raise. Cotton Mather smoothly assures Elihu Yale that having his name on a college is even better than having it on an Egyptian pyramid. Want ads in a Providence newspaper, seeking college patrons, attract one Nicholas Brown. Colleges are the seedbed of revolution, and of political careers: a New York mob plus a nineteen-year-old student activist named Alexander Hamilton drive the president of King's College over the campus fence in his nightshirt and onto the safety of a British warship. Yet well into the early Republic, a distinctively American style of higher education stays elusive. The national university repeatedly proposed for Washington, D.C., is never funded; without an aspiring Oxford or Sorbonne to dominate the market, campus-founding spreads like buckshot. Since colonial campuses had received public funding, government oversight is built into American higher education from the start, making the concept of state universities easy to accept. North Carolina's legislature calls for one as early as 1776. By 1816, the network reaches west to Indiana and south to Georgia.

The next year, laying out his University of Virginia by hand with pegs and twine, Thomas Jefferson invents something quite new. He calls it an academical village. His vision of free-standing college buildings around a small-town green becomes a powerful campus model for the rising nation. But nearly as strong is the social and architectural urge to class colleges with prisons and insane asylums. When the University of South Carolina builds new dormitories in the 1820s, all have separate fireproof entries, to foil the student vandals and rioters assumed to lurk in long college corridors. Except for this useful tip, campuses shun innovation until the eve of the Civil War. Pigs and cattle wander muddy grounds, faculty censor student mail, college presidents personally whip both students and instructors. In 1800s slang, "college" means the state prison; itinerant daguerreotypists and bordello piano players revel alike in the title of "professor."

Half wardens, half camp counselors, early college faculty often live among their charges, and endure having their heads drenched in ink, their benches tarred, their horses shaved. "Bisket, tea cups, saucer and knife thrown at the tutor today," a nervous Harvard professor confides to his journal in 1788, and three generations later conditions for unmarried instructors have scarcely improved. At mid-century most of Dartmouth's filthy rooms are officially declared unlivable. At Princeton, so many chamber pots are emptied from windows each morning "that the lower floors smelt to high heaven," a young professor of Greek recalled.

Except for communal meals and daily chapel, students mostly stay in their rooms and study. Faculty pay house calls to quiz them on their progress, or lecture by reciting fact after dry fact till the hour is done, then herd classmates into cold, dark recitation rooms, draw names from a hat, and force the victims through stumbling line-by-line translations of Homer and Cicero. College libraries open only one or two afternoons a week, and book borrowing is strongly discouraged. Desperately bored, some undergraduates take up dueling; others revivalist religion; still others begin to organize debating nights, literary societies, and science clubs. This alternative, unofficial college life is known collectively as the extracurriculars. The most popular diversions of all are fraternities and other secret societies, which sweep U.S. campuses from the 1820s on.

At the start of the nineteenth century, England has only two universities—Oxford and Cambridge, both in poor condition, physically and intellectually. America has no true universities yet, but almost too many colleges. In an era of romantic expansion, of canal building and gold mining, every town and territory craves a college. Having one is an indisputable mark of culture, like a pianoforte in the parlor. Hundreds spring up, hundreds die. In the New World, unlike the Old, simple, natural campus settings find many admirers. Thoreau visits Williams in the 1840s and approves its inspirational Berkshires beauty. "It would be no small advantage," he exclaims, "if every college were thus located at the base of a mountain." (Melville disagrees, saying a whaling ship was his Harvard and his Yale.) President James Garfield even defines the perfect campus as Williams professor Mark Hopkins at one end of a bench, and a student at the other. Hopkins's teaching style baffles colleagues; he talks to students as if they are human beings, asking them to discuss readings and ideas, not merely recite. Many of his peers still lecture in high-medieval style, though American Latin has turned decidedly shaky; when dogs wander into nineteenth-century classrooms, professors tend to say, "*Exclude canem, et* shut the door!" (The charismatic Hopkins was no intellectual; he once admitted he never could fathom the *Critique of Pure Reason,* leading later academics to suggest an even better educational arrangement might be Mark Hopkins on one end of a bench and Kant at the other.)

By the 1850s, American builders are reviving Greek and Gothic forms, and campus marketing takes full advantage of the period rage for instant history. Administrators want campuses that encourage "tendrils of memory and affection" in graduates. The college on the hill becomes a sentimental icon, aided by promotional prints like the 1850 image of the infant College of the City of New York as a castle in a forest glade, though the school actually stood at the crowded intersection of Lexington Avenue and Twenty-third Street. As the frontier moves west, college builders keep pace; in Michigan, in Illinois, in Iowa, formidable master plans go up piecemeal in country still half-wild. The small-college model replicates across the continent like a virus—first Oberlin in Ohio and Carleton in Minnesota, then Colorado College, Whitman in Washington State, and southern California's Pomona—as New England and New York pioneers impose familiar townscapes on pine and sagebrush lands.

The Civil War leaves southern schools in ruins, but galvanizes northern higher education. Reassured by the success of two tax-funded "people's colleges," Penn State and Michigan State, the 1862 Morrill Land Grant Act sets aside a public lands allotment the size of Switzerland for states loyal to the Union. Many of the new nonsectarian schools flounder, fight one another for public money, overinvest in agricultural and technical courses, and have trouble attracting students. But in theory, the land-grant institutions mean campus advantages are no longer for the well-to-do, or for ministers in training. Large-scale federal support of learning becomes an accepted feature of the educational landscape. So does consumer choice. In upstate New York, Ezra Cornell confidently announces the founding of an institution "where any person can find instruction in any study." The president of the new University of Minnesota claims to be interested in everything from Plato to hog cholera.

For these proudly practical schools, the designer of Central Park invents an entirely new look. A public campus should be a planned suburb, Frederick Law Olmsted tells Cornell's development committee; open, picturesque, and full of pleasure drives. At Iowa State, at Berkeley, at Massachusetts, he promotes informal groupings that recall tidy prosperous farming villages, or English country estates. Olmsted's bucolic visions spark a national taste for rambling campuses. But competition soon trumps charm. By 1870, school colors and songs are already popular; by the 1880s, campuses everywhere are energetically manufacturing traditions, from senior proms to Maypole dancing. College sports are such a national craze that the red-and-white design on the Campbell's Soup can is inspired by Cornell football jerseys. From 1890 to 1930, in a frenzy of beautifying and regularizing, over a hundred giant stadiums (plus innumerable fieldhouses, gymnasiums, and natatoria) will rise on U.S. campuses, and imposing new libraries and dorms as well. The sweet rural village look is swept aside in a rush to grandeur.

Inside the fine new buildings, faculty and administrators are painfully rethinking every aspect of campus life. Slowly, grudgingly, students receive more freedoms. Elective classes and big survey courses replace the drone of recitation rooms. Nationwide the number of faculty quintuples. Professors gather into programs and departments—biology, history—rather than stay independent operators or hired hands. They plan ways to get and keep power. Some wonder openly if a good library is not more use than a postcard campus, others try to make higher education a true public service through summer sessions and extension courses. Municipal colleges like New York's Hunter offer no-frills education, including night classes for working people, an urban parallel to the land-grant experiment. Private urban campuses also arise—the universities of Rochester and Buffalo and Syracuse and Pittsburgh, Kentucky's University of Louisville. Schools that once survived nicely with a bursar, a provost, and a dean or two discover that the price of ambition is an administrative cadre determined to run the campus like a corporation, all bottom lines, boosterism, and bustle. Lawyers and economists, not clergy, begin to fill presidential chairs.

Defining higher education's mission still agitates everyone. Is the point of college to build brains, or character? To expose undergraduates to ideas, or to the right ideas? German universities advocate a businesslike, stripped-down operation where pure scholarship reigns. Johns Hopkins and Clark agree, revamping into research-driven schools. But Oxford and Cambridge continue to treat academe as a nursery for those who will someday run the world. Eastern private schools are torn: they can continue as self-assurance academies for their regional rich, or they can try becoming genuinely national forces. Yale even flirts with the idea of becoming a land-grant university. On more and more campuses, in the late nineteenth century, the obsession with science grows; academics struggle to be pure, rigorous, incorruptible, promoting inquiry for its own sake, creating a cathedral of knowledge brick by brick. As struggles begin over accreditation and standardized entrance exams, educational critics declare that the frenzy of expansion gives faculty an excuse to isolate themselves and shamefully ignores undergraduate clients. Give young people personal attention and moral guidance, as in the earliest colleges, they argue; keep the campus cozy and magical; let the world wait.

The debate plays out in stone and steel. Columbia deliberately links its buildings to the urban streets, following the lead of the City Beautiful movement. Advocates of Collegiate Gothic counterattack. Their romantic confections (quads and towers built of steel-reinforced concrete with a handcrafted skin of stone turrets and pinnacles) are a perfect style for trustees made nervous by the machine age. Prepackaged medievalism spreads from Yale to the Rockies. Plutocratic money underwrites a rash of fantasy campuses, each plusher than the next. Stanford is a self-sufficient university city, arcaded, ordered, monumental. John D. Rockefeller orders up a Middle Ages-by-moonlight campus in a Chicago marsh. Duke is also heavily Gothic, Vanderbilt a bric-a-brac mélange, and Emory vaguely Renaissance, because the architect felt that Atlanta's climate resembled northern Italy's. Administrations everywhere decorate dining hall rafters with the flags of ancient foundations like Padua and the Sorbonne; or write away to Oxford and Cambridge for souvenir stones, the more battered the better, then cement them proudly into dorm and library walls. But the crisis of values persists, never to retreat.

Nearly all American campuses are still run by men, largely for men. Oberlin had welcomed black and female students since the 1830s, building on revivalist convictions that God views all as equal and independent. Western schools fuss relatively little over the presence of women on campus: Colorado's earliest professors include female academics; at Iowa State, women students of the 1880s rejoice in their own military drill corps, complete with seven-foot pikes. Eastern education remains serenely masculinist (though anxious debates recur over proper terminology for female students—Protomathian? Novian? Girl-graduate? Maid of philosophy?). Women may attend science courses at Harvard only if they sit in lecture-room closets with the door ajar. MIT often insists on sex-segregated labs; some professors hand their mending to early female undergraduates. The first women's colleges choose their architectural subtexts with special care, trying to seem both feminine and intellectual. Smith houses its students in cottages, to simulate family life in a New England town; Sarah Lawrence picks a reassuring suburban Tudor; Radcliffe fades deprecatingly into the Cambridge clutter, declaring itself a mere Annex. Only Bryn Mawr boldly co-opts the collegiate Gothic of the most powerful male schools.

World War I levels old walls that separate campus, politics, and commerce as scholars adapt their skills to the national defense. Chemists perfect nerve gases, political scientists advise in Washington, historians turn out patriotic editorials. (Professors of German, like instructors who oppose the war, often find themselves unemployed. In the new campus economy, faculty are still disposable. They know it, resent it, and push for lifetime contracts, an idea they dub "tenure.") The genteel Edwardian course catalogue is swamped by full-credit classes in telegraphy, typewriting, canning, and phys. ed. When the war ends, vocational studies cannot be ousted. Business and home ec programs spread like kudzu, and so do two-year or junior colleges. Many campuses design watered-down "general colleges" as holding pens for immigrant, older, and untalented students until they take the hint and leave after a year or so, an academic track tailored for "graceful failure," as one university president puts it, but also institutional profit.

Defining a good education worries Jazz Age schools. Some, like Bennington, turn experimental and modern, trying to close the gap between learning and life through independent study, internships, and interdisciplinary seminars. Others, eager to apply scholarship to public needs, thrill to the progressive Wisconsin Idea, that the boundaries of the campus are the boundaries of the state. Many newer universities push the department store or service station model; the University of Chicago counters with a stiff course of Milton, Locke, and Sophocles. Faculty care enormously about such debates, students very little. Postwar admissions policies are still pleasingly loose. E. B. White recalled that at Cornell, "I knew two men from Hawaii, a girl from Johannesburg, a Cuban, a Turk, an Englishman from India, a Negro from New York, two farmers, three Swedes, a Quaker, five Southerners, a reindeer butcher, a second lieutenant, a Christian Scientist, a retired dancer, a motorcyclist, a man who had known Theda Bara, three gnomes, and a lutist."

By 1924, nearly a million men and women are on campus. To be an undergraduate is suddenly glamorous: there are college movies, collegiate souvenirs, collegiate clothing lines, collegiate dictionaries. A sportswriter invents the term "Ivy League." Campus novels and exposés lead best-seller lists, from *This Side of Paradise* by Princeton dropout F. Scott Fitzgerald to *The Plastic Age* by Brown instructor Percy Marks (whose chronicle of students dazed by heavy petting and corrupted by cynical professors both inspires editorials and sermons nationwide and convinces Brown's library to keep its copy in a locked case). Most administrators resist pop culture's invasions of campus life. "Every university official," darkly announces one Princeton dean, "knows of many cases in which the sum of human happiness would have been increased had a father bought his son a ranch or farm, instead of a college degree."

The 1930s strain and disrupt all the campus cultures. Complacent faculty encounter a wave of refugee intellectuals from the Continental universities, and learn the hard way that American scholarship is in many fields an oxymoron. Some Depression-era undergraduates still dress for dinner twice a week. Others work three and four jobs and sleep in their cars. The four-years-and-out pattern weakens as some students desperately prolong campus stays. Antiwar politics flourish. Expensive chapels continue to be built, monuments to a dissolving ideal of the Christian campus, but Greek life is fast replacing religion as a student interest. (In 1921, one undergrad in seven belongs to the YMCA or YWCA; in 1940, one in thirty.) A new campus figure appears as well, the dean of student life, charged with organizing, chaperoning, disciplining, counseling.

By V-J Day, the Thirties campus will seem idyllic. During World War II, many institutions double as flight schools or officers' training camps. Students and faculty join up, retired professors are recalled to teach. Administrators everywhere fret over the Servicemen's Readjustment Act of 1944. The GI Bill of Rights will entitle men and women with three months in uniform to three paid years of higher education, five hundred dollars a year for tuition, seventy-five dollars a month in living expenses. Many educators loathe the idea, warning that America's campuses will become educational hobo jungles.

Often they look that way, as flimsy married-student housing and Quonset hut classrooms bloom at school after school to accommodate nearly 2.5 million returnees. Between 1946 and 1949, enrollments at many campuses double or triple. Professors of the day remember GI Bill enrollees as fully adult young people with old eyes. A college education from the government is a modern Homestead Act, and they know it. Many outstudy and outthink their more privileged classmates; before such hunger and impatience, prewar traditions like the well-mixed cocktail or gentleman's C falter and fade. Campuses begin to shed their familylike nature, and with it two centuries of assumptions about who should and should not sit at table. Catholics and Jews begin attending traditionally Protestant schools; working-class eighteen-year-olds are slower to say, "College isn't for people like me." In 1900, 232,000 Americans were on campus; by 1940, 1.4 million; by 1946, 2.4 million. In 1960, 3.2 million. In 1970, 7.5 million.

Every school that can takes advantage of a Cold War economy, and will for decades. GI Bill money leads to defense-research funding and then to even more federal largesse, especially in the sciences and social sciences, millions for the asking with very few apparent strings. An academic-military-industrial complex helps underwrite multiversities—the supercampuses—that emerge in the 1950s and 1960s at universities like Maryland, Massachusetts, Michigan State. Huge new buildings house just-invented programs in aerospace and computing, classes grow larger and larger, chairs who once knew everyone on campus cannot recognize all members of their swollen departments. The entire giddy operation is held together, administrators whisper, only by allegiance to the central heating plant.

Campuses begin to view themselves as independent cities, secular, professional, credential-driven, with urban problems to match: high density, conflicting land-use patterns, the clashing interests of a varied population. At mega-schools like UT-Austin or the University of Illinois at Champaign-Urbana, students need a bus system to get from class to class. Some universities install their own landfills, others their own airports. Straining for space, flagship campuses set up branches and satellites, then absorb junior and teachers' colleges, creating immense statewide systems of higher education for the era of regional consolidation and interstate highways. The Scholastic Achievement Test reduces more and more high school seniors to two crucial numbers: math score and verbal score. Massive science buildings crowd campus skylines. Humanities majors regularly denounce their slablike façades and concrete plazas as technocratic and alienating; resident geologists or engineers shrug, and return to their slide rules. Some schools try disguising raw new real estate with ivy and Georgian columns. Others fling themselves into modernity. Walter Gropius designs Black Mountain College in North Carolina; Mies van der Rohe plans Illinois Tech. Eero Saarinen recasts parts of MIT and Yale. Frank Lloyd Wright creates Florida Southern. Skidmore, Owings and Merrill produces the Air Force Academy in Colorado Springs.

As campuses are invaded by the car, parking lots claim huge

acreages. Students and faculty commute by freeway to the University of California–Irvine. UCI resorts to ring roads, UCLA to jokes. ("This is a four-year school, five if you park in Lot 32.") Some schools resemble the new shopping centers, islands set in concrete; others take care to harmonize new and old, from the University of New Mexico's pueblo-style architecture to Stanford's insistence on a campus of red tile roofs. A small-is-beautiful movement arises, too, as counterbalance; the utopian University of California–Santa Cruz, planned in the years around 1960, scatters its low modern colleges in a hillside redwood forest, Jefferson's academic village transplanted to our farthest shore.

But this time around campus purposes need no footnoting. A generation beyond the first GI Bill, mass higher education has become indispensable to the daily workings of society. The campus is the training ground for every skilled occupation, gatekeeper to the professions, engine of sci-tech advances, patron of artists and scholars. But the questions that troubled Plato's grove are still unanswered. Who owns academe—the students, the professors, or the administrators? Is knowledge neutral, or is it really about power?

Freeze frame. The campus world of 1960 or 1965, just distant enough for nostalgia, looks better and better to middle-aged faculty and alumni. Cultural commentators on the right yearn for an era when, they believe, the golden chain of memory and tradition had not yet snapped, when high modernism and scholarly rigor proceeded hand in hand. Advocates of the left remember a time when the bourgeoisie could still be shocked, when the long dream of social progress might, any minute, become fact. Gas was nineteen cents a gallon then, of course, and one summer's hard work paid for the next year's tuition and expenses, even at private colleges. Upon finishing a degree one said to major corporations, "You may employ me now," and generally they did.

But go back. Walk around. What might catch a time traveler's eye? At many schools, the central campus would still look entirely familiar, a basic eat-sleep-work constellation of prewar dorms and dining halls, classrooms, and offices. Peripheries of campus change much faster than cores. The extreme austerity of a mid-century campus would startle the contemporary viewer. No Pei or Venturi rehabs here, no Pizza Hut and Reebok outlets in the student union, only steel desks and straight chairs, clanking radiators and dingy tile floors, genteel, threadbare, institutional-drab—and in session six days a week. Until the mid-1960s, many American schools scheduled classes Monday through Saturday, mostly to keep freshman and sophomore men busy and on campus.

In this vanished world the reading loads for English and history courses would appall today's undergraduates—three hundred pages a week, at least—but the science assignments seem childish, and lab conditions Victorian. Faces at the podiums are overwhelmingly male. Professors carry expandable brown-leather briefcases with white stitching and square brass locks, and wear tweed jackets with suede elbow patches, briar pipes upturned in chest pockets. The shooting-party-in-Norfolk look reigns as academic uniform from Wilson's era to LBJ's, though a few official eccentrics insist on sandals, or spats, or come to important meetings in disreputable sweatshirts, Einstein-style. Faculty members drive old cars or bicycle to school out of necessity, not ethics. Though a few privileged or entrepreneurial souls are already contracting their services to government and private industry, faculty salaries are dreadful. Most professors share offices and do their own mimeographing, but compensate by insisting on dignity and distance, addressing all students gravely as Mister or Miss. (Some older men even recall a time when students rose to their feet as a professor entered the room.) On research trips beyond Calais, American faculty carry formidable letters of scholarly intro-duction, gorgeous with learned flourishes and red and gold seals. Deans, archly amused, refer to these creations as dago-dazzlers.

The mid-century campus is full of astonishments. Female residence halls schedule weekly hose-and-heels tea parties, re-quired lessons in gracious living. Men attending land-grant schools must often endure two years of military drill, a relic of charters granted after the Civil War. Mandatory chapel is a fading custom, but even at public campuses, students some-times recite grace aloud before meals. Faces in seminars and stadiums are largely pink; African Americans in the South at-tend segregated colleges and remain curiosities at most north-ern schools. What else? Fountain pens. Square glass ashtrays in every office and classroom. Clean, quiet bathrooms, not an alarm strip in sight. Campus infirmaries where the all-purpose cure is one large brownie, eaten slowly, and a lie-down on cool white cotton sheets. Library reading rooms so quiet you can hear people breathe, no clatter of laptops or ringing portable phones or music leaking from headsets, only the rustle of pages and, in hot weather, the purr of oscillating fans. Coeds who knit during lectures. Coeds. Jokes about creeping bureau-cracy. ("Do not fold, spindle, or mutilate" is a common laugh line; in this lost world computers fill small buildings, and run on punched cards.) The semicovert drinking, and very covert sex. The jovial readiness of administrators to suspend or expel. The wild popularity of student film societies, and also of sar-donic folksingers like Tom Lehrer. The reciprocal scorn of so-cial independents and the Greek or club world; an easy condescension by both toward day students and commuters. Junior-year-abroad programs strongly favor destinations reach-able by turbo-prop aircraft: Avignon, Amsterdam, Mexico City. But the greatest single loss between this time and ours is

the vanished deferential army of extremely smart women—
faculty wives who quietly revise and index husbands' books,
departmental secretaries able to replace any dean—whose
iron-willed management skills free even small poor colleges to
indulge an air of cultured certitude.

In the course of fall break, October becomes November. The
counseling-services appointment book fills more swiftly as students in difficulty, academic or personal, begin going under.
Faculty work later, already polishing talks for their winter conventions. Even at Gulf Coast or Florida schools, the life of the
campus moves indoors. From Hanover to Berkeley, committees convene for lethargic discussion of the educational mission, and the sorry state of the endowment, and how the two
might be reconciled. Inside and outside the walls, theories on
what a campus is, or should be, pile up like cars in freeway fog.
A rite of passage. A right of passage. Meritocracy. Nation-
in-miniature. Culture hearth. Cultural landfill. Seedbed for
the overclass. Incubator of unlabeled eggs. Fantasy amplifier.
Aging vat. Marriage mart. Theme park. Postmodern plantation. Day-care center. A place that makes people safe for ideas.
A system for telling students what not to think about. A corporate enterprise, with educational subsidiaries. Club Med,
with a little light reading.

As always, what you see depends on where you stand. The
campus is a classic contested site. On their good days, administrators feel like sluice keepers in charge of a thousand resource
streams. Corporate contracts and crates of canned goods flow
in, paid invoices and students with diplomas surge out. Engineers look at a college campus and see chaos with feedback;
physicists, a barely contained chain reaction. Oceanographers

see calm on the surface, reefs below. To those who stay behind and pay the bills, academe can seem linked to the working world by the U.S. mail, and not much more. Campuses may look to one another like bright islands set in darkness, but to everyone else they can seem mazelike and a little sinister, unpredictable, unsupervised, uncontrollable.

At the dawn of the twentieth century, Harvard president A. Lawrence Lowell felt the undergraduate years most resembled a ferry ride across a wide river "with little to mark what is really happening, and when the farther shore is reached, the transit, in retrospect, seems short indeed. But the passengers are not the boys who came aboard, for although they have the same names and the same class numbers, they are quite different people." A generation later, the built-in contradictions of the American campus enchanted the Swiss architect Le Corbusier. It is a green city, he said, a temporary paradise. Some inhabitants refuse to cast any campus as a *locus amoenus,* a sheltered pleasant place. To ecologists and geographers, clipped lawns bordered by exotic trees can seem monuments to fungicide and artificiality. If more schools let a forest grow in their main quadrangle as Indiana University does, they claim, we'd all be better off.

Traditionalists in any discipline recall that Cicero, asked to define happiness, replied, "A library in a garden." Exactly, they say. It is the duty of the campus to guard heritage from barbarism, to prescribe a program for the life of the mind. To conservative eyes the Nineties campus, struggling loudly with change, seems a grand country estate trashed and subdivided, some parts gone wild, others thoroughly to seed, still others overbuilt. This vision pleases biologists and environmental historians, too, though for another reason: they study transformation, and to them any campus is a food web of people and ideas, consuming and remaking, an endless shimmer of populations in time and space.

WINTER:
Important Minds

For academics, September is the month with no money. Professors do get summers off, but many eat a lot of canned soup before the first of their ten-month salary checks are issued, four or even five weeks after classes begin. October is the month of ceaseless committee assignments: rules and procedures, outside appointments, library, student discipline, alumni relations. By November, both junior and senior faculty are surreptitiously scanning the latest job listings, looking for chaired professorships at rich sunny schools. All through December, America's 800,000 college and university instructors bring semester or quarter or trimester courses to a smooth close, like bus drivers delivering loads of tired passengers to the curb.

Along any corridor of faculty offices, as fall turns to winter, the intellectual entrepreneur is trolling for hot gossip, extra reviewing assignments, new grant money. In the next cubbyhole, the born researcher is happily sorting and baling fact. Just beyond, the conscientious teacher gravely asks his tenth student visitor of the morning what she plans to do with her life.

In every academic department, one or two faculty doors are always shut. These professors won't turn up for *anything*. "I don't come to campus Monday, Tuesday, Thursday or Friday," they patiently tell angry deans—who may reply that other senior faculty stay at the office past midnight, six days a week. Some academics teach wonderfully but rarely publish; some write constantly but hate to teach; a few possess such intellectual rigor that they send copies of new work to their worst enemies and demand critique. Everyone is convinced, *convinced,* that they are ignored, unappreciated, misunderstood; professional thinking, they mutter, is harder than it looks. Most of the year, faculty members labor alone in library or lab. But in many disciplines, December through March is the season for displaying fresh intellectual wares, an annual flurry of symposia and conferences, self-promotion and self-doubt.

In my second undergraduate winter, I took a course with an archaeology professor who lived at a low rolling boil of discontent.

"I was born in one of New England's most ancient towns," he informed our first class meeting, flicking syllabi right and left at sophomores born in Oconomowoc and Wauwatosa. "And my most rewarding days, alas, were spent on the banks of the Charles." In his case, that meant Tufts. But he carried a green Harvard bookbag through all the years of his inland exile, like Odysseus his oar, and loved to lecture on the great chain of being as shaper of days and ways.

"Imagine a ladder of virtue descending down all creation, first the angels, then only a little lower, man thinking, then down and down to animals, and plants, and 'stocks and stones and worse than senseless things,'" he would intone, looking hard around the room, so we would know in what category we fell. I thought he would levitate the day he got a Guggenheim grant. The money was nice, of course, but what really counted was knowing his name would soon be enshrined in the little cream-colored brochure of foundation honorees, publicly, permanently, deliciously anointed as a sensibility that mattered, an important mind.

Though in theory any professor may pursue any intellectual interest—a musicologist retooling as an urban-studies expert, say—most U.S. faculty find, plow, fence, and defend one small intellectual plot throughout a career. The drawback can be spending half a century with a very few competitors who know you much too well. The advantage lies in truly knowing a subject, be it Roman coins or kidney disease. After a while, you either feel you own a field, or *are* a field. Edit Herbert Hoover's papers long enough, and you can write his speeches better than he did.

For scientists, social scientists, and humanists alike, most of faculty life is comfortable routine: conference papers given, midterm exams graded, departmental reports issued, professional journals scanned. But certain tests of vocation almost no contemporary academic escapes. Dealing with the competition. Offering one's knowledge to the outside world. Breaking into a closed intellectual circle. Adjusting to changes in your field. Should fame and success suddenly arrive, they can prove the hardest challenges of all.

The transcendentally talented, like the transcendentally self-ish, will always thrive on campus. Unfortunately, argues anthropologist Clifford Geertz, the mental map of the American professoriate is strongly center-out, not top-down. All academic disciplines share a peculiar career pattern—the exile-from-Eden syndrome. Unlike the clergy or the police, where you start a career at the bottom of a ladder and move up, in academe you train for professordom at the best school you can, always knowing your future probably lies lower down, farther out.

• • •

Despite leafless trees and swaths of dirty snow beneath the evergreens, the Connecticut salt air is soft, the pale wintry sun nearly warm, and on a stone terrace beside the Yale University art museum a hundred of the world's best Renaissance scholars embrace like angels in a triptych; air kisses, brilliant smiles, and elaborate cries of welcome in English and Italian. These are among the very few people anywhere who could survive, even prosper, if dropped tomorrow in Medici Florence. They live there most days anyway, happier in the 1590s than in the 1990s. After a brief, ugly tussle with the main door latch (humanists are not very right-brained), they surge toward the museum auditorium, where their Renaissance-studies conference is about to begin, chattering all the while.

"We all know who she knew to get the Getty—"

"On a Richter scale of disastrous talks, a 7.5—"

"—and then he started telling leper jokes to the trustees—"

"Pay no attention, he always claims we need a new Raphael catalogue—"

"She'd crawl over broken glass to get that job, and you know it—"

"—thinks Leonardo was bisexual, on what evidence I don't know, she says she doesn't *do* evidence—"

"—just as well he didn't come, his idea of dinner conversation is, 'I've got you in a torture chamber, see, and you're completely right-handed, see?—'"

"—my newest scheme is a line of cards for academics to send anonymously: 'Your work is boring and derivative.' 'Your department chair hates you.' 'We know you steal office supplies.'"

"How can she whine for money to the dean when she wears two-hundred-dollar shoes?"

"All the *pezzi grossi* are here now. We can start," says a junior professor from North Carolina, as assorted bigfeet, sultans, rajahs, dragons, and satraps settle tenured waistlines into red-and-silver auditorium seats. Around each distinguished mentor, current and former graduate students gather to gaze haughtily about, like little Italian Renaissance courts. Academic families can be closer than real ones, just as affectionate, just as quirky, just as cruel. They reunite only once or twice a year, at massive annual learned-society meetings, or else at small specialized conferences like this Yale gathering. A scholar's loyalty is first to the discipline, then to the campus. Intellectual compatriots are rarely at the same school: a humanities professor is hired to be a representative for a distant (or dead) constituency, a curio in a cabinet. Some don't mind; they're introverts anyway, and enjoy feeling like cosmopolitan outsiders, resident aliens. But for others (living five hours from the nearest good research library, local colleagues on cruise control, students dull or aimless), a specialists' conference is water in the desert.

Talk follows talk. Vasari's Florence: Artists and Literati at the Medicean Court. The Inventory of an Art Collection in the Vasari Household. Vincenzo Borghini and Cultural Politics of the Gran Ducato. The Precedence Controversy Between Florence and Ferrara. Marathon listeners, the Yale attendees follow all the arguments with eyes half-lidded, or murmur shorthand countertheories. "Barolsky says—" "I know, Freddie does, too." A young professor up for tenure mispronounces the name of the keynote speaker, then refers to him twice as "Doctor." This is not done. He should have said Professor, or Mister. This Grave Tactical Error, or GTE, raises eyebrows all over the room. One junior colleague ostentatiously licks a finger, and draws a tally mark in the air.

When these hundred scholars tour any great museum, each painting's tiniest detail—an egg, a cap tassel, a wine-colored reflection—calls up decades of subtext, the personal and professional hopelessly tangled: frenzied quarrels over forty-year-old journal articles, celebrated clashes of rival footnote police, stale gossip, fresh scandal, eager cabals. Of the older scholars in this elegant room, some have sued one another's universities for jobs, some helped save monuments of Renaissance art from the great Florence floods of 1966, some (claiming the work and the life are obviously separate issues) leaped to defend the British art historian Anthony Blunt when his decades of treason were revealed in 1980. Professors with Mayflower fortunes defer to professors who fought their way out of slums from Boston to Miami. Many academics, in all fields, are born to working-class or lower-middle-class families. But after decades of cocktails together at the Florentine research retreat I Tatti, and years upon years of spring receptions at the Frick Museum talks in New York, this company of scholars all have the same voice, a swooping transatlantic accent of no known provenance, studded with meaningful pauses. "Your . . . *remarkable* . . . paper is a decidedly toothsome amalgam." Or, "His analogies all seem a bit . . . *undigested.*"

Younger crowd members—untenured instructors from around the nation—watch them somberly. As University of Iowa economics professor Donald McCloskey recently pointed out, "Most of the teaching in American colleges is and will be done by non-Ivy, non-elite graduates: forty-year-old nurse-supervisors going back for Ph.D.s in nursing at UT-Austin, late bloomers who became professors of history by way of Case Western after the army, Ph.D.s in accounting from Louisiana State with backgrounds in English from Southeast Missouri." Usually, such faculty teach moderately ambitious people at moderately ambitious schools; regard a dozen articles as a decent lifetime output; prefer a pleasant, balanced life of coaching kids' soccer and weekend cabins to competitive scholarship and fame-lust.

Those at Yale today are the other sort. The academic way is everything to them. The life, they call it. You give up a lot, for the life. They know all the bibliography, all the names; they fall on the *Zeitschrift für Kunstgeschichte* and the *Art Bulletin* like *People* magazine. ("Look, Janet Cox-Rearick. *Dynasty and Destiny.*" "Gino Cordi the paleographer is right across the aisle.") Most yearn to be *pezzi grossi,* and have mastered many of the requisite skills. They can compose a gracious memorial for a deceased colleague, snipe at rivals' junk degrees, usher students out of the office in under two minutes. They practice the high art of one-word intellectual critique ("What did you think of his paper?" "Sad."). They search colleagues' mailboxes after hours, and can reel off one another's mentors and career itineraries like baseball statistics. He did a postdoc with X. He was Y's assistant. She was at Z, you know, before coming here. But even these violently ambitious younger scholars may get their first real jobs at forty or forty-five. One bargain used to underlie all academe: suffer, wait, and one day you, too, will rule. But for twenty years now, a dwindling job market has forced Ph.D.s in all fields to play musical chairs for the very highest stakes they know, leaping from two-year post-post-doc to three-year replacement, sinking ship to sinking ship.

• • •

Scholarship used to demand extreme feats of memory, endurance, and concentration, the researcher as intellectual athlete, or even martyr. "Every time I remember the name of a student, I forget a fish," said an early Stanford academic, and he was right: traditional scholarship meant caring passionately about the placement of a ganglion or the tertiary derivation of a verb; willingly, eagerly turning yourself into a human card catalogue, cross-indexed in four languages. Error, not accuracy, was the benchmark, completing a perfect bibliography perfectly typed a minor triumph, discovering a tiny flaw in a competitor's work, to pounce on and magnify, a major one.

But the digital revolution turned such monopolies obsolete, and the assumption that order is good or necessary began looking shaky, too. The old dance of explanation and objection remains—Why do you say that? How do we know?—but trends in thought could not be more different. Collage and flux and doubt, irony and playfulness, eroding and destabilizing privileging, praxis, liminal, metadiscourse, cohort accumulation, the academics and critics in mid-passage pronounce, and watch the faces of their elders freeze.

Fairness in scholarly discourse, saying "This is not my taste, but I want to understand your way of approaching the material" is exceedingly rare in any field. In the past, scholars would leap academic borders to solve a specific problem, then retreat. Now, disciplines themselves are morphing, and genres melting. Biology merges with physics and chemistry, anthropology borrows from literary theory and feminist studies, economics mixes with cognitive psychology, political science checks out mathematics and law, Renaissance studies soaks up semiotics and social history.

In every academic field, generational transitions are bitter, dinosaurs against impertinent puppies. But in the humanities, especially, the World War II and Korea generations are only now leaving the scene. Many went into history, art history, languages, or literature on the GI Bill, wanting to redeem horror by teaching civilization's cleansing glories. Seeing the postwar campus in armed-services terms seemed logical and just: tenured professors were senior officers, assistant profs the lieutenants, graduate students noncoms, undergrads the enlisted troops. But today's restive heirs are professional mandarins, who entered the campus realm at eighteen, and never left. High academe becomes their biosphere, a suburban mall walk an expedition to Mars. *Illiterate people, eww. How real.* Give up, you old-boy powermongers, they murmur. Their elders brood: we endured Depression, saved the world, rocketed the American campus from storefront to conglomerate. *You're* our legacy? *Eww.*

By Monday the challengers (those with jobs) will be back in seminar rooms across the nation, facing politely restive students accustomed since high school to postmodern angst. They want something more now, something novel, to make their own. Let's talk ethics, the postcontemporary ones say, historical context, the hard realities of a multicultural nation. Those at the head of the table, still pleased with themselves for surviving Yale's whirlpools and undertows, will pay no real attention. Clearly, their charges are too young to know their own minds.

After the first day's papers have all been delivered, the Renaissance scholars head to the Beinecke Library for a reception, grumbling vigorously at the four-block walk. ("What is this, a nature hike?") Yale's rare-books library glows softly in the twilight, a modernist box of translucent marble, granite, and bronze rising from a stony courtyard where in-line skaters play fierce silent roller hockey. In atrium and mezzanine, Yale's Gutenberg Bible and the elephant folio of Audubon's *Birds of America* dream in their illuminated shrines, ignored. Some scholars want to corner the conference organizer and scream at him for leaving their books and articles off the official bibliography. Others nip up handfuls of sausage rolls and mini-pizzas. A great glowing glass rectangle, four stories high, dominates the interior of Beinecke. Within it stands a massive column of books. Their buckram and calfskin bindings, crimson and forest-green and russet and tan, provide the only real color the building has, and all it needs. The Renaissance experts walk slowly round and round, hors-d'oeuvres plates in hand, like workers in an atomic plant circling the power core.

All academic events are public performances, and the reception is as important as a panel or a paper. Higher education is one long performance, for students often, for peers always. Sometimes the stagecraft can be extremely simple. When scholars still had typewriters, a keyboard's constant rattle behind closed office doors could impress and intimidate— though in at least one case the professor was typing the same sentence over and over and over, for years. Scholarship has no annual profit-and-loss statements, only the ceaseless struggle to tell posterity whose ideas have value, and whose shall be neglected. Peer gossip at campus receptions can nudge one interpretation into the mainstream, another into the dustheap. You have to get in there and fight.

The talk rushes on.

> "Photo permissions are over a hundred dollars apiece now, just how are we expected to cope?"
>
> "—do excuse me, I need to return an international phone call—"

"At the Bibliothèque Nationale, the librarians told me, 'The books you want are not necessary for your research.' At the British Museum, they claimed my material had been lost in the Blitz. It's a book from 1975, I said. They didn't care—"

"—*all* artists are magicians. We accept Vasari as fact but he's actually closer to historical fiction, a fantasy entertainment of the first water—"

"My romantic status? I think that topic has been sufficiently thematized—"

"—and he's been sitting on that damn research for thirty solid years—"

"So, what are you working on?"

Outside, as I walk away, late-winter dusk is moving over New Haven, but the weather is fine still, with only a few backlit streaks of cloud to the west, rose and red in a hyacinth sky. In the courtyards of residential colleges, beyond the guard booths and electronically locked gates, undergrads wait for dinnertime. A few tap croquet balls across the inner greens, or pace beside locked dining-hall doors; most idle under carved and fretted archways, talking happily with friends. I cross the street beside the music school, and stop. In its lighted practice rooms, window after window has been flung open to receive the last soft air. Within one ground-floor studio, twenty students in T-shirts and sweatshirts are practicing Palestrina. The strong young voices rise, halt, redo one phrase, and another, then rise again. The students do not know it, but just outside, a dozen of New Haven's homeless are crouching quietly in the flowerbed. Hands folded in laps, canes and shopping carts and nameless bundles set tidily along the curb, they listen rapt in the half-dark to the sweet cascading song.

Voices from the faculty world, recorded on committees and on airplanes; beside the escalator at conventions and before the trifle at professorial dinner parties; in the brief adrenalized moments between one student conference and the next; and in departmental hallways after difficult meetings, the speaker looking anxiously about, and talking fast and low.

A Big Ten zoologist: Faculty life is communal but not intimate, like a penguin city.

A departmental secretary: Some intimacies I can do without. I have seen faculty trim their toenails with their teeth, right here in the office.

A southern dean: In 1992, a Texas A&M researcher accepted a $200,000 private grant to transmute lead into gold. Imagine, a practicing alchemist on the faculty. Did other scientists laugh? No, they all wanted grants, too.

A junior researcher: Funeral by funeral, science advances.

A western political science professor: Despite appearances, there are no radicals in academe. Everyone is a reactionary where their own field is concerned.

Georges May, professor of French, Yale University: The university is a daughter of the Church. We inherited from it the costumes, the vocabulary, and the concern for truth, and when the truth is at stake you may regard as a heretic one who disagrees with you.

A Berkeley transit official: We give out 55,000 parking tickets yearly. Only Nobel Prize winners have free reserved spaces. Vengeful faculty will video whole lots, then turn in the violators. Doctoral students in ethics forge parking permits.

A retired administrator: Hire obsessives, and get out of their way.

An Ivy League faculty member: I needed to look up a citation lodged somewhere in the 137 volumes of the *Patrologia Latina.* Going into the library, I met Peter going out. I explained my problem. He looked at the sky a moment, then told me the volume, page, *and column* where I would find my extremely obscure quotation from the Church Fathers. I thanked him, waited till he was out of sight, then rushed for the reference room. He was right.

———◆———

To civilian eyes, the life of the mind seems neither comfortable nor safe. Consider Archimedes on hands and knees during the sack of Syracuse, so absorbed in drawing geometric figures in the sand that he never sees the killing stroke. Or Budé, sixteenth-century librarian to Francis I, informed in the midst of a tricky translation that his house has burned down, who says only, Tell my wife. Tell my wife. I do not concern myself with domestic matters. In the Old World, historian Merle Curti once noted, a citizen upon seeing a professor tipped his hat. In America, he taps his head. (Old American academic joke: Professors Brown and Smith enjoy a pleasant home-cooked dinner. As the evening wears on, the guest shows no signs of leaving. Finally Brown says, "Harry, I'm sorry, but it's two A.M., and I must ask you to go. I have an eight o'clock class." "Tom," says Harry, "you're in my house.")

There is no theme so weird and wild that academe cannot domesticate it with invited panels, seminars, workshops, roundtables, footnoted catalogues, and annotated bibliographies. The section of the *Chronicle of Higher Education* devoted to upcoming scholarly meetings is a weekly roster of specialized marvels. Judicial biography. Organized crime in antiquity. Solar cooking. Silk proteins and spider evolution. Feline oncology. Social contexts of East Asian metallurgy. Ancient Greek erotic magic. Medieval textiles. Playground safety. Ultimate meaning. Bulgarian studies. Scholars at campuses famous and obscure constantly hunt answers to questions no one has yet thought to ask, about protein folding, molecular tweezers, women's roles in foreign policymaking, the evolution of aerobics as postmodern folk dance, even the best method for preserving mastodon meat (dunk in a very cold pond till spring, as it turns out). Forestry and aerospace professors may join forces to discover why green oak lumber is so hard on carbide-tipped saws; tannic acid in the wood, they conclude years later, eats away at the microscopic layer of cobalt gluing the carbide to the blade. Meanwhile, entomologists count Costa Rican short-horned flies, geologists and archaeologists ponder oxalate phytoliths of opal and calcium; shallow-water biologists map marine snow.

Nearly all academic fields require a doctoral degree for advancement into the permanent, or tenured, ranks of associate and full professor. Getting there was never easy, or made easy; now the intellectual training is often less arduous, but the road to a job, any job, extraordinarily rough. Top graduate schools may accept one applicant in eighty for a five- or six-year degree program that often stretches to seven years or ten. Of those admitted, easily half drop out or change their minds before receiving the Ph.D.; of new Ph.D.s (many now $100,000 in debt), only two in five get any kind of academic post. Some find only galley labor: part-time, or adjunct, work paying well under minimum wage. A fortunate few get hired on for full-time teaching, seven years, up or out. Harvard or Michigan Ph.D.s who once would have smirked at the prospect of jobs in Lubbock, Texas, or Greeley, Colorado, now plead for them; one $30,000-a-year opening at a nice small school like Macalester in St. Paul, Minnesota, or Northern Arizona University in Flagstaff may draw five hundred desperate applicants. At first-tier research campuses or designer-name colleges, one assistant professor in ten, or one in twenty, may receive the great prize of lifetime employment.

Professors must be based in academic departments, which can contain three people, or sixty. Some departments are happy, or at least collegial, some coldly formal, some like business offices (pick up mail, nod to office staff, vanish into cubicle), some chaotic. I have seen departmental gatherings where professors traded convivial jests in Latin, and ones where senior men urged each other to perform carnal acts with livestock. More often, a faculty meeting merely revives bits of fossil time: really good jokes from a 1953 graduate seminar; the summer day in 1969 when an angry young scholar (plump and well-mortgaged now) vowed destruction to a corrupt system; a rainy 1980 evening when a floundering researcher suddenly understood a new method and pledged himself to it, a promise sometimes more lasting than marriage.

Unlike its cousins, military and religious life, academic existence knows almost no set schedules save lectures and exams and the annual departmental photograph (canceled sometimes four and five years in a row, because no one can agree on a time and place, let alone the order of seating). Deans and chairs despair. A faculty is a society without rules, admits Henry Rosovsky, Harvard's faculty dean. Most senior professors act like volunteers, observes Milton Greenberg, former provost of American University in Washington, D.C. "At the very least," he notes dryly, "we should begin to view college or university employment at full pay as a full-time professional engagement." Administrators notice when faculty talk of teaching burdens, consulting opportunities. The outside conflicts, the personal-convenience squabbles, seem to academic managers endless, inflexible, irresponsible, a classic producer cartel.

But faculty aren't blind. They study the red Ferraris in parking lots behind materials science or molecular biology buildings, and suddenly the rituals of conventional academe, especially its discuss-it-to-death, nothing-must-ever-be-done-for-the-first-time meetings, start looking like pointless road bumps in the race to get rich, and be a star. Being a professor, on the other hand, remains at its core an act of conscience. The calmest faces in any departmental meeting room are often the isolatoes, the very few who, given perfect security and perfect freedom, are making things with it still, and helping others learn. The work of the mind is for them what the sociologist Burton Clark has called the absorbing errand. Nothing and no one can keep them from it.

But their common protracted ordeal makes all faculty think in sevens: seven years to the doctorate, seven tensely smiling years to tenure, when assistant professors become associate professors, seven more till you get—maybe—a year's sabbatical. Then the anxieties start again, in a higher key. Making the top rank of full professor. Scheming for the even more prestigious named professorships, so you can sign your mail as the Smith Professor of Electrical Engineering, or the Jones Professor of Pacific History. Becoming department chair. Staying sharp. Will I become a gargoyle or a grotesque? Will my mind shut like a clam at forty-five? So many do. And the winnow-

ing, the spoilage, have only begun. An unfortunate percentage
of these honed and cosseted intellects (maybe half of any
tenured group, say optimists; try three-fourths, murmur the
unkind) by age fifty or sixty are assumed by peers and deans to
be deadwood faculty, or at least estivating faculty, turtles sunk
deep in mud.

After tenure, a campus asks only one thing of its professors:
keep your brain alive. But many do not, will not, cannot. Very
few tenured faculty refuse outright to help undergraduates;
being out of touch with one's field is the far commoner sin.
The greatest human problem in academe is not the calculating
user or the intellectual sadist or the professor who plays fa-
vorites but what used to be called a Notes & Comment man,
the kindly colleague in the slow lane who can't produce, or
else writes very, very slowly, fussing for years over tiny points,
reading the same lectures year upon year from yellowing notes.

Career officers in the armed forces, or senior business executives, may not be noticeably more productive. But for seven
centuries the campus has asserted that there is more to life than
fighting and money. Being held to the higher standards the set-
ting daily proclaims can badly startle some professors; after
years of hearing the obedient rustle of paper whenever you
say, "Three important points on the exam will be," it is easy to
forget how many people want to cast you not as the great scientist or critic but as secular clergy, each classroom a parish.

Disciplines age out at different rates. Mathematicians tend
to have their best insights very young, historians late—or
never, if early passion for a field evanesces. To divine who will
plod and achieve, who will squander their thirties but blaze
at forty, who will write again after years of wandering and
silence, is harder yet. Tenure committees agonize. Can they
grow with the field? Will they? Can we stand to live with
them meanwhile? The tenure process has no way to cancel

its mistakes. Compulsory retirement has been itself retired; if you decree, your school must pay and feed and water you until you die.

The rarest gift in academe is a productive old age. I remember sitting on a wooded ridge in western Wisconsin with a retired university geologist, dropping rock after rock onto his rough veined palm as he reconstructed from a handful of gravel the world before the glaciers came, distilling a lifetime of learning into language a child could follow. Once at Princeton I saw the great Byzantine expert Kurt Weitzmann lecture about his work on the illuminated manuscripts of the Monastery of Saint Catherine at Mount Sinai. His party of German adventurer-scholars had arrived there by camel just after the First World War, fighting bandits and sandstorms all the way, and he explained what they found and what it meant with lucid mastery. At eighty-three, he spoke for over an hour without one note. I remember, too, a University of Wisconsin neurologist, a former U-boat captain, who reported to the campus teaching hospital till he was nearly ninety, carefully keeping up with all the research journals. His last diagnosis was his own. He sat down hard one morning, paused thoughtfully, then said to his students, "I have just suffered a fatal heart attack. There is nothing to be done in such cases. Please observe the symptoms with care." He died later that day.

———————

All academics soon locate themselves along a human-contact continuum. At one end is the hermit-scholar, content to work alone. Then come people who function best in labs or research institutes, doing pure investigation, unbothered by undergraduates and their creative excuses. The university is meant to be a company of scholars who can also do classroom work. Colleges stress teaching. Community colleges, like corporate education centers, are teaching-only. Beyond them stands the tutor, coaching and polishing one private client, and now the instructional computer program, too, tireless at drill, needing neither parking space nor dental plan.

On any campus, the bystander quotient is high. For the last twenty-five hundred years, some academics have been wanderers, some opportunists, most stay-at-homes. But even the tenured can turn restless. They start feeling like performing seals: kick me in the leg, I lecture for hours on Dryden or dendrites, and who really cares? Some try to be public intellectuals, explaining over and over what people on campuses do, and why. But often the public resists, viewing academics as very bright people with no common sense. Many professors now hire out to industry as professional refuters: impassioned academic critics of the evidence for global warming turn out to have taken hundreds of thousands of dollars from the petroleum and coal industries. Others dive into the commercial mainstream. Yale classicist Erich Segal horrified colleagues by writing lucrative potboilers like *Love Story;* historians like the Tulane-trained Newt Gingrich and tenured professors of economics like Texas A&M's Phil Gramm ran for Congress. Hundreds of academic economists keep the day job but also manage hedge funds, do econometric forecasting, play the global currency markets.

Campuses talk a lot about public service. Yet except for state extension efforts at the land-grant schools, faculty outreach to the larger world tends to be individual, sporadic, quixotic. San Francisco State professors and student teachers form an academic SWAT team to save an urban grammar school in trouble, bringing test scores up and discipline problems down. Auburn architecture specialists turn hay bales into handsome low-cost housing. Faculty-student teams from the University of Illinois tour the state in a mobile van, advising struggling firms. "Everyman, I will go with thee and be thy guide,/In thy most need to go by thy side," promises the character of Knowledge, in the fifteenth-century morality play *Everyman*. But between the active and the contemplative life now, the tensions only grow.

Professor Roger Shuy of Georgetown University sits in his tiled Washington, D.C., sunporch, fiddling with a Nakamichi tape deck, then leans back in his swivel chair of varnished oak, fingertips steepled, listening hard. Male voices fill the air, urgent, confused, overlapping.

> *Police officer:* "You knew he was going to shoot him, didn't you?"
> *Suspect:* "Yeah, he was talking about it, he wasn't saying, you know, I'm going to shoot this guy, and I was like, well, hey, man, it's your choice."
> *Officer:* "You said, go ahead?"
> *Suspect:* "Uh-huh."

Shuy hits the pause button. "Notice that uh-huh. Does it mean 'I knew he was going to kill' or does it only mean 'I hear you, keep talking'? The guy may be guilty, but the prosecution's tapes don't prove it. When you really examine the structure of this conversation—the response strategies, the topic initiations—you realize it's the interrogator, and not the defendant, who keeps bringing up murder."

Shuy (pronounced "shy") is not a criminologist but a linguist, a specialist in the structure and function of human speech. Neatly inked labels on file drawers chronicle a few of his current research interests: Arson, Drugs, Sex Abuse, Trade Secrets. A Sony digital recorder, Mitsubishi video machine, and padded AKG headphones wait nearby. Behind Shuy's head, reference books crowd the shelves: *Law of Confessions, Pragmalinguistics, Telling Lies.* His basement is crammed with crime. Transcripts of testimony from money-laundering cases fill furnace-room shelves. To reach the cabinets marked "Bribery" and "Murder for Hire," Shuy must step over his daughter's rocking horse. "Toxic shock. Libel," he murmurs, reading files. "Perjury. More libel. Say, would you like a copy of my paper on 'Linguistic Analysis of a Murder Confession'?" He hands me an offprint from *Historiographia Linguistica* (vol. XVII, no. 1–2, 1990) and begins excavating another paper-packed drawer.

Shuy is the country's most active expert witness on language crime. Where most linguists may be offered a case every other year, he averages one visit to the stand every eight weeks, and charges $1,250 per court day. Professor Shuy specializes in taped conversation. From thousands of hours of recorded talk, he teases out meaning word by word, then maps the complex speech acts—threatening, admitting, promising, agreeing, offering bribes—on which many civil and criminal cases turn. Exchanges are frequently garbled or hurried, the sound quality often poor. Sometimes he studies a single segment a hundred times.

"When I listened to my first murder tape back in 1979, I was thoroughly shocked," Shuy says. "I had never heard a discussion about killing people before, and it frightened me." But soon he was on the stand in the so-called Blood and Money trial of a Houston oil millionaire, where his three-day testimony about covertly taped murder solicitations helped win unexpected acquittal. In the Chicago judicial-corruption sting known as Operation Greylord, he gave evidence on verbal entrapment. After Shuy testified to a Senate panel that conversations between federal judge Alcee Hastings and a Washington, D.C., attorney employed a partial vocabulary code, government attorneys persuaded the panel that Hastings was involved in an extortion scheme. Impeachment quickly followed.

In a litigious society where courts often set public policy, more and more multimillion-dollar settlements hang on precise interpretation of a sentence, a phrase, a single word. "You'll be hearing from our linguist!" has become, in U.S. legal circles, a serious threat. With audio- and videotaping so prevalent, many attorneys want an academic linguist on the stand to interpret crucial exchanges. For juries (and some judges) it's the difference between visiting a museum alone or with a trained guide. In an accounting malpractice suit, what exactly does a contractual promise of "accuracy" imply? A professor of linguistics can document all possible meanings. Was the captain of the *Exxon Valdez* intoxicated when his oil tanker ran aground in Prince William Sound? A linguist provided an expert opinion on the phonetics of drunken speech. When a reputed mobster muttered enthusiastically on tape about "leg-breaking," Florida prosecutors rejoiced—till a linguist versed in context analysis noticed that as he spoke, the suspect was dining on boiled crab.

Two days later, escaping a cold winter rain, Roger Shuy hurries into the immaculate granite-and-beechwood precincts of the Tarrant County Justice Center in downtown Fort Worth, Texas. His plane from Washington was very late, the jury trial in Courtroom 348 already under way. But Professor Shuy is prepped. His pin-striped navy suit was custom-made for court work at Saks Fifth Avenue, its jacket cut extra-full, to drape easily even when he raises his hand for the oath. The acuity of his hearing has been freshly certified, since opposing counsel often demand the date of a language expert's last hearing test. Shuy is lanky, affable, and hard to shake; lawyers appreciate his neat consecutive mind, juries like his flat Ohio accent and his ability to translate academese into clear but not condescending explanation.

Today's pivotal evidence is all written. The plaintiff, Mitchel Bien, is a deaf man in his thirties who visited George Grubbs Nissan to price a car. Bien alleges that for four hours the sales staff held him there against his will, first persuading him to write a $4,000 earnest-money check, then hiding his car keys and refusing to return his deposit, despite increasingly desperate pleas. Eighty notes scrawled on scrap paper and computer printout, snatched by Bien as he fled the building, form the central evidence for charging the auto dealership with false imprisonment, emotional distress, fraud, gross negligence, deceptive trade practices, and violation of the Texas human resources code.

"I find the plaintiff's sentences extremely straightforward," Shuy tells the nine-woman, three-man jury as he unrolls yards of multicolored charts. "In fact, you can't get much more direct. Mr. Bien complains nineteen times, defers buying seven times, rejects the offer ten times. Sentences such as 'Give me back my check!' 'I'm hungry,' and 'Let me go home!' show no evidence he wanted to buy the car." Two weeks later, a jubilant plaintiff's attorney phones. The jury has ordered the Nissan dealer to pay the deaf plaintiff $6 million.

Give me back my check. Let me go home. Why import expensive professors to explain the obvious? Courts are now wary of junk science, of new science, of any science. Some refuse to let linguists testify, saying their evidence is potentially confusing to juries. Or not scientific enough. Or else too technical. Unfortunately, if you put a linguist under oath and ask, "Are you a scientist?" the answer might be "Some days," or "Define scientist." American linguistics grew out of anthropology research early in the century, and is still a loose confederation of subfields and specializations. Deciding where to house the linguistics department on campus can make strong deans blanch. Its acoustics experts work in labs, like hard scientists. Language historians link with English departments. Theoretical linguists talk most readily with mathematicians and philosophers. Psycholinguists and sociolinguists draw their research methods from social science.

The ancient principle that language is the province of the court, and only the court, dies hard. Word meaning in law is traditionally a common-sense issue. "Lawyers and judges say: 'Why bring in a linguist? We all speak English!'" says Judith N. Levi, associate professor of linguistics and assistant dean at Northwestern University, a small, energetic woman with curly salt-and-pepper hair whose office is filled with Asian art. "To which academic linguists reply, 'Just because you speak a language doesn't mean you understand how it works.'"

Yet many academics view court work as for-profit betrayal. Though court testimony is always restricted to language issues, never directly addressing innocence or guilt, scholars who venture into courtrooms often endure colleagues' envy, bafflement, or rage. Administrations rarely object when faculty are expert witnesses—UCLA's year-end activities report even has a space for court testimony given—but fellow scholars can become extremely agitated. To them, the scholar's duty to speak truth to power is best done from a distance.

"Why do you want to help criminals get off?"

"The legal system is such a mess, why mess it up more?"

"Don't you already have a decent salary?"

"Why get your hands dirty with something so *practical?*"

"Putting linguists on the stand tests how much of our theorizing is relevant and how much is academic grandiosity," says Levi tartly. "You're made to stand by your research, in public, under oath. Not all faculty are comfortable with that idea."

At the annual meeting of the Linguistic Society of America, the decibel count is soaring. Beside the escalators of a downtown Philadelphia hotel, morphologists battle semanticists. ("I never *heard* such tacky verbs!") Instructors from California crowd into the lobby, shaking snow from umbrellas, excitedly pooling local field research. ("My cab driver actually said, 'We're glad youse come'! A genuine and unambiguous marking of the second person plural!") Linguists from a dozen campuses perch on planters in the lobby, eating box lunches and discussing dissimilation in Chinese secret languages and zero allomorphy in copula constructions. "Here's a list of things I dislike about my latest paper," says an assistant professor in an orange poncho, producing copies and passing them around.

In a meeting room nearby, Judith Levi, Roger Shuy, and other legal linguists are sharing tradecraft with an attentive crowd. Levi—who credits her equanimity on the stand to ten years of practicing meditation—explains how training in semantics (the study of meaning) and syntax (the study of sentence structure) recently helped her interpret the insurance-contract phrase "sudden and accidental" (as in "sudden and accidental release of pollutants") in a chain of Environmental Protection Agency/Superfund cases. The typical accident, she hypothesized, is a car accident, fast, unexpected, unintended, harmful. Are there not-fast accidents, in common speech? Yes, "historical accidents," say. At stake: who pays billions in cleanup costs at twelve hundred polluted sites nationwide.

"You do a chart, you explain it in plain language," she says, "and you make the jury say, 'By God, it *is* ambiguous.' Small victories are all you hope for. But words change lives."

So do vowel sounds. William Labov is a professor of linguistics at the University of Pennsylvania, an authority on American phonetics and dialectology. He once helped resolve a bomb-threat case through testimony on regional accents. Pan Am had charged a Long Island–born cargo handler with making a threatening call, which ran in part: ". . . There's gonna be a bomb going off on the flight to L.A. . . . and I hope you die with it." No one witnessed him making the call; the only evidence was the language on the recording.

"To a Los Angeles ear, East Coast accents all sound alike," Lebov reminds the crowd. "But as soon as I played the tape, and heard those low back-rounded 'o's,' I was sure the accused man was innocent. New Yorkers use a high, over-rounded, ingliding 'oh' in 'off,' a lax 'ae' in 'that.' No Long Islander can fake, can even *make,* the Eastern New England vowel sounds the person on that tape produced." A hundred language experts chuckle at the very idea, then nod proudly at the verdict: acquittal.

The topic of sociolinguistics—how language and society interact—releases a flood of forensic war stories. Should citizens with limited English get special Miranda warnings? Whose language rights are violated when a teenager comes to school in a T-shirt reading "Drugs Suck"? Phonetics expertise helps in many trademark cases. Is Cache-Cache too close to Cachet? Will consumers confuse the radio station call numbers WVEC and WVEZ? When Quality Inns International announced plans for a budget lodging chain called McSleep Inns, the McDonald's corporation promptly sued. It was the first time any business has claimed rights over an English prefix. Quality Inns commissioned Roger Shuy to prove to Baltimore's U.S. District Court that the prefix "Mc" has entered the language to denote convenience and economy.

"By searching newspapers and magazines through a national clipping service, and using the Nexis computer database, I found them a remarkable range of citations," mourns Shuy. "McLube. McBagel. McHairpiece. McNews. McSurgery. McFuneral. McWidgets. I identified an entire thriving subculture of parody. 'McMeditation—over 5,000,000 Mantras Served.' I found them McTooth, a dental practice. I found them McMania, a drive-through therapy clinic. The presiding justice even announced he hoped he would not be considered a McJudge. We still lost. McDonald's *owns* that prefix."

———◆———

The linguists are meeting in midwinter because winter in academe is high season for conventions. From late November through late February, many scholarly disciplines hold their major professional assemblies in cities across America, preferably the warm ones. History and sociology, chemistry and mathematics, literature and languages, classics and philosophy all love and dread these annual migrations. Departments go to interview job candidates, faculty to deliver papers and moderate panels, graduate students to see friends, politic, and gossip.

Even small underfunded departments reserve hotel suites for their convention interviews. Whole committees will live in them for the next four days, twelve and sixteen hours straight, grilling candidate after candidate. Applicants scheduled early in the hiring process encounter dignified faculty intent upon delicate issues of methodology. Those slotted for the last day can discover committees sprawled on floors and beds, thumb-wrestling for the last room-service nachos. Pillow fights are frequent, and so are Freudian slips. "Leave us your dossier updates," chairmen boom, "so we may be rid of you as soon as possible—that is, so we may inform you of our decision in a timely fashion." Along all the hotel corridors, you see unemployed scholars patiently pushing their résumés under door after room door, hoping one of them contains a perceptive chair of a search committee from Harvard.

On my way to the Modern Language Association convention in Chicago, I notice a delegation of mathematicians in an

O'Hare waiting room, off to their own winter meeting. A mathematician plus a housing form can drive landlords and hoteliers wild. No smoking, no children, no pets, they will insist, no noise, no music, no room freshener. No sunlight. This is a group of fifteen, all men, generically disheveled in plaid shirts and glasses mended with black electrician's tape. In my first year at graduate school I lived next door to a quad of mathematicians who slept in their clothes on the floor, ate only chili cheese dogs, and played the accordion at 3:00 A.M. I sit watching with modest nostalgia as the group in the airport talks loud and fast of plug-and-chug, bifurcation, and confluence. A few older models lounge nearby reading *Scientific American,* but the ones aged twenty to forty are in warp drive, rambling from window to window to criticize the aerodynamics of passing aircraft, or cackling over the latest issue of *Wreckreational Math,* "published bioccasionally on a singular point" by the University of Toronto math department.

"Let A and B be 2x2 matrices with integer entries such that A, A+B, A+2B, A+3B, and A+4B are all invertible matrices whose inverses have integer entries. Show that A+5B is invertible and that its inverse has integer entries."

"No problem."

"Too easy, man."

They pore over the Math Humour column ("How many letters would this question contain if the answer wasn't already seventy-one?") and admire the Cool Prime Number of the Day, 739397. ("Not only is this number prime, all numbers obtained by truncating on the right, 73939, 7393, 739, 73, and by truncating on the left, 39397, 9397, 397, 97, 7, are all prime! In addition, the cyclic permutations 393977, 939773, and 773939 are prime as well!") Lots of people have done well in math, or majored in math. Leon Trotsky. Florence Nightingale. Art Garfunkel. Lewis Carroll. Wittgenstein. Michael Jordan. Professor Moriarty. But these are the pros.

There are other math pros, too, less numerous, or loud. I remembered an afternoon six months before at the Institute for Advanced Study in Princeton, the sacred grove of twentieth-century mathematics and physics. Founded in the 1930s, underwritten by the Bamberger department store fortune, it is the American answer to Oxford's All Souls, a restricted society of scholars, the ultimate academy. For years, almost the only women on the grounds were secretaries, wives, and cleaning staff who tidied the offices of demigods: Einstein, Godel, Oppenheimer, von Neumann. Institute offices are simple, the amenities not. Mosaics from ancient Mesopotamia adorn the modernist dining room where resident and visiting scholars placidly investigate roast pheasant and shitake risotto, zabaglione and hazelnut torte with double whipped cream; the wine cellar has 5,000 bottles.

The institute has begun co-sponsoring a national mentoring program for women in mathematics, to let them get acquainted before heading to the larger Park City mathematics institute, held in Utah each June. Men dominate engineering, mathematics, and the physical, life, or computer sciences; over three-fourths of those who earn undergraduate degrees in these fields are men. Only five of 305 tenured professors in the top ten American math departments are women. The number of American math faculty who are female has actually declined since 1940. For the last fifteen years, in math as in all academic fields, male professors have consistently been paid about 30 percent more than female professors.

For math women there are not many role models, and most come to bad ends. Hypatia of Alexandria, the fifth-century mathematician and philosopher, was dragged from her carriage and torn limb from limb by a Christian mob. Then came a long gap until Mary Somerville, a nineteenth-century British mathematician with a strong interest in natural philosophy. Her book on celestial calculation became a required text at Cambridge University, an institution neither she nor her daughters could attend. To honor her mathematical insights, her bronze bust was placed in the Royal Society's Great Hall, but Somerville herself, like all women, was barred from membership, and from the building. One of the first Oxford female colleges is named for her, and the word "scientist" first appears in a review of one of her books, but she died at ninety-two believing that to be a woman working in mathematics is a bitter, self-doubting fate.

Academic scientists like to have it both ways. We are cultured, they remind the rest of the campus; we read, we are musical, *and* (unlike you) not at all terrified by numbers and machines; no one from Media Services has to come to *our* lectures twice a week to push Play on the video. Scientists' mental maps are rarely predictable; ask them about great events of the 1860s, and they may talk excitedly of the benzene ring and the periodic law, not necessarily the Civil War. After that, commonality breaks down. Years ago, C. P. Snow wrote that the great campus problem is the gulf between its two cultures, the humanities and the sciences. But social scientists who study the professions insist there is no two-cultures problem. There is one humanities culture, and two hundred science cultures. (Nobel laureate J. Michael Bishop has ruefully recalled solid-state physicists who cannot define a gene, prize-winning chemists who never heard of plate tectonics, biologists who believe string theory has to do with pasta.)

All first-class academic science, whatever the field, is a team sport. Science may be a self-correcting, checkable method for finding out about the universe, but it is also intensely collective. Papers in the humanities are the fruit of solitary struggle; in the sciences, dozens of authors may receive credit for a single publication. Of all the scientists who have ever lived, half are alive today. They need to produce at an extremely fast rate to stay competitive; little time can be spared for fishing expeditions, or deviation from plotted trajectories. Knowing where to get money, where to set to work to get results, are crucial skills; inducting neophytes is an up or out affair, graded always on a steep curve. Good scientists tend to grudge every minute away from computer and lab. They know they might miss something. They know that if they don't keep inhuman hours, they will be forgotten. All teams have stars. The urge to know is strong in academic scientists, the drive toward fame stronger still.

Yet another new reality of higher education is the enormous phone bill, the harried weekends of hugs and laundry, the report card faxed cross-country. Every academic field has two-career commuter couples; many can't find jobs in the same city, or else one has a post too good to leave. More and more commuting scholars are mothers as well as scientists. Lab, bench, field, and clinical science keep the most daunting hours of any campus calling, their competitive work binges utterly incompatible with family life. And even sympathetic male professors are unsettled by female colleagues who request more than one maternity leave, or post a "Studmuffins of Science" calendar on the office door.

At the Princeton summer conference the lectures by women mathematicians focus on nonlinear wave phenomena, which has applications in heart monitoring, aerodynamics, and weather prediction; the science is interesting enough to make many mathematicians and researchers who are men turn up, too, but the more important task is getting women in the field acquainted. Under the oak trees by the institute duck pond, I find thirty math women, college-aged and middle-aged, looking dubiously at their souvenir T-shirts, embossed with the official Institute for Advanced Study seal, on which a nude woman represents Truth, and a draped one Beauty. But soon they spread striped Hudson's Bay blankets across the new grass, or perch on Breuer chairs liberated from the dining hall, watching the warm wind turn over the pale undersides of leaves, slapping away flies, scanning for fire ants.

"New Jersey *has* no fire ants."

"I'm sure to be the case that serves as the pattern proof."

For this panel discussion on How I Became a Mathematician, four professors assemble on the sunny lawn; another, Karen Uhlenbeck of the University of Texas, a conference organizer, ash-blond and sturdy, sits nearby to monitor and encourage.

"I suppose we may as well begin," says a middle-aged faculty member from the University of Illinois at Chicago, soft-voiced and dignified in navy and pearls. "I was at University College, London, on a particularly grey gloomy day, and thought, 'How nice to go to America!' So I applied to MIT, thinking it the science arm of Harvard. I met my husband there, at the very first math department tea." The undergrad women bunched around her feet rustle and giggle; one is asleep, one peels red polish from her toenails, but a few listen so hard they forget to blink.

Professor Susan Friedlander riffles her bangs, thinking back. "I was the only woman in all my classes. The first woman to get a Ph.D. from my department. In math, you had best always expect to be the only woman in the room. Expect other things, too. If a group of mathematicians is talking, and a woman comments, her idea will be ignored. Five minutes later, a man says the same thing, and it is enthusiastically picked up, and incorporated into the discussion straightaway."

Oh, yes, says Barbara Keyfitz, of the University of Houston, who lectured the previous day on nonlinear hyperbolic partial differential equations. "And early influences are very important. My father was a math major who exclaimed to me 'Maybe you *are* a genius' whenever I said anything mildly intelligent from age three on. And I read a lovely kid's book, *Mathematician's Delight,* which thrilled me. And I had an iconoclastic University of Toronto professor who told me, 'You should be writing papers that raise eyebrows.' How that inspired me! I say it now to every student I meet!"

She looks hopefully at a brown-skinned student nearby, who nods slowly, then returns to her mango Snapple. "Do you have any questions? What can I tell you that will help?" No questions. Keyfitz turns to Fan Chung from Taiwan, who has an extremely soft, small voice, and a gaze of steel. She, too, was encouraged by her father to do math, and now teaches at the University of Pennsylvania but worked for years at Bell Labs. Remember, she tells the young women, math is universal language. I can read software and engineering papers, but they can't always read mine. Her best advice? "Go to colloquia! I met my husband at one, but they are good for other reasons. You learn the problems that matter, learn if you love the work." Questions? No questions.

Janet Talvacchia from Swarthmore College speaks next; she is younger than the rest, dark-haired, bouncy. "My parents are immigrants, they never went to college. None of my cousins had college. After a misspent youth, I got a scholarship to Bryn Mawr. It's very, very important to have undergraduate teachers who really train you, or else you'll never compete. At Penn, in grad school, I did geometry. Jobs were very tight, postdocs, too, so I went for a teaching post. Was my advisor horrified! He said, 'Undergrad teaching will mean the end of your math career!' Then on day one at Swarthmore, they tell me, 'You have to fit in here. If we don't like you we won't tenure you.' So far, it seems all right. There are lots of paths, you know.

And often a subterranean nice-people network to counteract the awful people. Adapt, live with less, be straightforward, don't be discouraged, satisfy the math part of your life."

Questions? No questions. Really? Not one? Surely there's stuff you want to know, that we can help you with. All the women faculty start to talk again, in fits and starts; like many mathematicians, they are not especially articulate, but to warn their professional daughters away from time-consuming, spirit-sapping, career-destroying errors, they are willing to try. Our professional world looks the same as ever, they tell them, but underneath it's changing drastically. For one thing, there are no jobs. For another, the men won't give you an inch. "Don't wait, don't hang shyly behind, don't expect to be given things." "Stay alert to departmental politics. Protect your time."

Love the work, and it lets you survive the life, they insist. But the girls are silent, their faces blank. "Do we get the Fermat video tonight?" one says, at last. "I loved *The Joy Luck Club,* I cried and cried." They wander off in twos and threes, talking about going dancing, about tickets for shows in New York. The senior math women remain for a moment on their Breuer chairs, in the shadow of the institute, looking depressed. They're better on paper, one tells me, apologetically. I say they don't seem very energized. Uhlenbeck shoots me an irritated look. "They're here, aren't they? If there weren't a problem, they wouldn't be."

Are you encouraging them too much, being too upbeat about the road they face? I ask. A pause, then antiphonal sentences float onto the summer air as they try to put into words an innumerate stranger can understand the struggle to make a half-life a whole one.

"This is a very small community."

"We do what we can with what we have."

"With what we can carve out, lay claim to."

"You get so sick of being the only one in the room without a tie."

"But really, there's no one to help. The senior men are literally from a different world. 'When I was a graduate student . . . ,' they say. They're so protected, they can't change. Selfish is their middle name. Not cruel, just self-centered. Blind."

"And the older women, the ones who broke the way in for us, are still very afraid. We must do better work than the men, they tell us, and not make any waves."

"Women may be better treated in math than other sciences, actually, because there's not enough of us to be a threat."

"But men in math have always been judged on aggressiveness. Monomania. Women in math keep believing they can work their way to greatness."

"But they don't get in there and work the contacts. They disappear. When you're 10 percent of the graduate student population, you can't afford to be maybe 1 percent of the faces at colloquia and department teas."

"This mentoring program gets women knowing each other early on. The East Coast network is pretty strong. But elsewhere the isolation is continual, awful. We're trying for vertical integration, the high school teachers, the undergrads, grad students, faculty, all math women."

Inflated expectations *are* a problem with some of the younger scholars, says one professor quietly. They want a nice office on a nice campus, or nothing.

A little silence falls. Then Uhlenbeck says fiercely, "Look. There is always a way. You can teach algebra to Alaska pipeline workers. You can go find a community college; it pays better than McDonald's. Whatever it takes to do the work. Always, *always,* do the work."

———————

Chicago in December, the one hundred eleventh convention of the Modern Language Association. I was here in the early Nineties, when the profession of literature study was feeling glitzy and brash. Then, many practitioners thought they had managed an intellectual revolution, but today only the literary lesbians riding the Hyatt's long escalators retain any of the old swagger. They lean against the handrails, arms linked, or wave to friends in the lobby below, admiring one another's spiky crewcuts and ochre toreador pants and pale yellow platform shoes, audaciously retro cat's-eye glasses shimmering with rhinestones, pink and blue.

Everyone else is wearing grey, or seems to be. After fifteen years of struggle for the soul of literary study, progressives and conservatives are equally dispirited. The Chicago convention hotels are like a battleground at nightfall. Budget cuts on every American campus have made sworn enemies, for now, into sullen allies. At more and more schools, administrators have begun floating a disturbing new concept: condensing English departments, comparative literature departments, language departments, and creative writing programs into one utilitarian Department of Literature. This is like telling IBM to go into typewriter repair. The twenty-six thousand members of MLA

have fought for decades to make the study of literature specialized and theoretical, to invent for it a convincing narrative.
Knowing they may soon be forced into teaching Business
English or English as a Second Language or even Freshman
Composition is a stunning loss of prestige. Like all the humanities, literary specialists are victims of intellectual-capital flight.
Only yesterday, it seems, to be elite meant being able to take
apart a text, any text, with passion and flair. But suddenly
the print culture has lost its cachet; all the smart kids are
majoring in technology, or environmental studies. In 1970, 20
percent of undergrads wanted to study arts and letters; in
1995, 8 percent do. The party has migrated to other campus
zones, leaving behind bruised egos and devalued career invest-
ments.

The 1995 meeting draws some nine thousand registrants,
but overall this is a very young MLA. Experienced hands endure the interviewing grind, go out to dinner with old friends,
then head for O'Hare as soon as seems decent. Crowds wandering between the Hyatt and the Marriott are chiefly graduate students, untenured faculty, and the enormous backlog of
Ph.D.s produced in the hubristic Eighties, now either under-
employed or unemployed. The formal convention program
offers 775 learned panels, but compared to the flamboyant in-
surrections of other years the topics are very tame; Poe the
Pundit, Byron's Narrators, a knowledge industry grinding on.
In the Marriott lobby, terrified candidates for language jobs
endure twenty-minute interviews in French and Italian, talking carefully to strangers about favorite restaurants and favorite
syllabi. Two escalators away, a Teaching of German session is
packed, and fretful. ("The kids are definitely not as verbal as
they used to be." "Many of us can't cover in four terms any
more what used to be material for three semesters, or even
two." "We have a tough sell here, a subject eighteen-year-olds
think is hard.")

In the Hyatt hallways, thousands of dispirited literary critics mill about, trading rumors of jobs in Pomo and Poco (postmodern and postcolonial literature). Some play with the $500 Plagiarism Screening computer program in the exhibit section, or read the scanty job advertisements, wincing. *University of Alaska, one-year replacement position, must teach four courses per term, valid air pilot's license required.* Hundreds more quietly abandon the annual round of author-society cocktail receptions (populated by gloomy, self-doubting Melville scholars, rakish Keatsites, jolly Twainians) and tiptoe instead into workshops on real-world survival to learn how literary Ph.D.s can turn dissertations into screenplays, write romance novels under pseudonyms, or moonlight as content providers for the on-line services.

"Remember, *The Bridges of Madison County* was written by a dean at Northern Iowa, who became independently wealthy with a single book," says a professor from Indiana who writes historical mysteries, and beside me a woman from Northern Alabama gasps, then wriggles all over in delight. At a panel on new forms of publishing, a California professor of screenwriting absolves novice entrepreneurs of lingering guilt about taking the system for a ride. Our overlords owe us big, he says serenely. Outside deals are the way to go. Charge top dollar, then add a few zeros. It's not like your school is going to care. "As we say at my campus, the administration pretends to pay us, so we pretend to work."

The recreational professoriate is here in force. Most academic meetings now have a spectator contingent of Ph.D.s. They are the lost generation of scholars, close to fifty now, squeezed out when the job market first went bad in the Seventies. Many did drive cabs for a while, then got into software, or law, or advertising. We like keeping a toe in the field, they say, and fervently discuss the lack of quality prose in the business world, the need to maintain standards even in environments hostile to scholarly instincts. ("Many's the time I've been tempted to employ a semicolon or even an unnecessary emendation, but I always resist." "Stout fellow.") Many still dream, now and again, of returning to the life.

When Oscar Wilde visited America, he watched a full moon rise over Charleston's harbor. "How lovely!" he exclaimed. His hosts only sighed. "You should have seen it before the war," they told him. From a corporate campus, or a corporate cubicle, academe's perks seem as lustrous as ever: the afternoon peace of the faculty club, the grace-and-favor house deals for senior faculty, the low-interest tuition loans for faculty kids. The medical packages, the gym and library privileges, the special concert rates. The free review copies of new books, the free computer time. The free time.

Some faculty lagniappe is a holdover from more genteel days, some incentive to keep valued employees from defecting. (If you want an interesting experiment, say academic cynics, cap professorial salaries at $60,000 and make all outside consulting *pro bono.* Then watch who stays.) But just as experienced professors claim that undergrads only come in four varieties (smart ones who work, smart ones who don't, dull ones who work, dull ones who won't), so most faculty fields can be categorized as hard and applied, hard and pure, soft and applied, soft and pure. Good people in the hard/applied world (professors of medicine, business, law, molecular biology, engineering, and computer science, especially) must be kept sweet with bonuses, perks, and special deals, for their salaries would double or triple on the outside. The hard/pure crowd has learned to bargain: give me a new atom smasher, or I call Berkeley. (Such tactics may backfire: 30 percent of Berkeley's faculty have accepted golden parachutes in recent years, including 40 percent of the tenured physics faculty; the money saved buys young experts in emerging areas like theoretical particle physics or nanostructures.) Soft/applied fields are, like all academe's niches, at least 25 percent overpopulated; still, the commercial world, or other nonprofits, or government, continue to absorb a fair number of rural sociologists, development economists, and professors of advertising science.

Like classicists and art historians, literature specialists are a hundred years behind the market, soft, pure, and in alarming oversupply. Departments accept humanities grad students as degree candidates to claim the prestige of a doctoral program, faculty then use them as cheap labor for teaching and research. But the leap to the tenure-track ladder is longer each year. We never promised you jobs, say campuses, when their products complain. You said on the application forms that you loved literature for its own sake. No one put a gun to your head and said, Get a Ph.D. This MLA makes those who have left the field grateful, at long last, for anchorages outside academe. The semiotician heroes of the Eighties are now doing market-research consulting for whiskey and phone companies. Avant-garde spokesmen like Duke's Stanley Fish calmly announce a midcourse correction: sorry, but there is, after all, no road to political power from the English department. Some new books in the publishers' booths are as specialized as ever—*Our Vampires, Ourselves; Solitary Pleasures* ("the first anthology to take masturbation seriously")—but publishers' reps say an unusually high number of display copies are being stolen by people who look them in the eye, then snatch and run.

The MLA delegate assembly that used to pass spirited resolutions on fetal-tissue research or intellectual freedom in Central America now only struggles to find a place to land. Every town wants the rich conventions, or the polite ones—doctors and librarians are welcome everywhere—but only four cities will still accept the MLA: Chicago, Houston, Toronto, Washington, D.C., perhaps Las Vegas. New York no longer bids to host this scholarly conference ("They found we're bad tippers," says one delegate, bravely), San Francisco is out because of California's opposition to affirmative action, and the MLA will not meet in states where sodomy is a crime.

Flashes of the old defiance pop up still. A sarcastic manifesto goes round on rules for literary criticism in the 1990s: no unfamiliar language, no politics, no controversial ideas, no sex, no weird paper titles, no irony. ("The lesson is clear. Employing irony, speaking tongue in cheek, talking wryly or self-mockingly—these smartass intellectual practices give our whole profession a bad name . . . nobody understands your ironies but you and your theorymongering friends. . . . So just wipe that smirk off your face. Try the following topics: Feminism—Threat or Menace? Why Poets Are Just Regular Folks. Poems to Treasure Always. How Literature Can Make the World a Nicer Place.")

But the members' lounge is full of sober, defeated conversation.

"Eventually, enthusiasm turns to cynicism. I never thought I'd say so, but . . ."

"I'm beyond cynicism. I'm into despair. Not one interview. I'm forty this year, my contract is up, and I'm moving back in with Mom and Dad. Better to be unemployed in the family than unemployed in Georgia."

"Where will you be next year?"

"God knows. You?"

"Getting out. Looking for some other profession."

"Any ideas?"

"No. All I can do is read and write."

At a packed session on the future of tenure, the provost of Illinois Wesleyan is on her feet, explaining to desperate young Ph.D.s the view from the other side of the desk.

"Lifting the cap on retirement has caused real problems. Academic freedom is not the issue. Do I want to get nasty at the end of someone's career? No! But a fourth of our physics department, a fourth of poli sci, a third of French should be out of there. I don't know what to do. According to my lawyer, it's illegal even to talk to them about it."

A grey-haired professor turns on her. "On my faculty of eighteen hundred, maybe a dozen over seventy are still teaching. That's age discrimination you're talking, economics over principle. Why not fire people because you don't like their religion, or their sexual habits?"

At the panel table, the general secretary of the 44,000-member American Association of University Professors, Mary Burgan, shakes her head. "Legislative attacks on tenure are rising so fast it's scary. Arizona, Pennsylvania, Minnesota, they're all trying to do away with it. Market ideology rules."

"Faculty have to be able to read a budget," protests an Ohio professor. "We don't train our grad students to be professors, only scholars. By the time they get tenure they're completely unsocialized."

"What's your advice then?" calls a grad student.

"Downsize your expectations," the senior man replies. "Smaller colleges. Regional schools. Think local. Think community colleges. Don't obsess about tenure. Some schools have had a so-called moratorium on tenure for ten, twenty years now."

"And it dilutes the quality of the faculty in an awful way," says a professor from a small local school.

"Persist. Persist. People die, you know."

"Assassination is good, too," the graduate student says.

All through the session on tenure, as people arrived and left, the door of the conference area kept catching on the Hyatt's carpet, letting a roar of hallway talk into the hot packed room. People in the front glanced around, irritated, but those at the back stared them down. A dozen junior and senior academics stood just inside the threshold, and a dozen more just beyond. Not one, in the course of an hour, would reach over a hand, or move one step, to shut the balky door. And though contemplating the death of tenure made faculty from across the nation rage, rationalize, choke back angry tears, and mutter about social justice, the great taboo of the profession is never broached. No one says, Maybe some of us should go teach high school English.

Instead, the debate surges on. "My university has a huge managerial class, dozens of new vice presidents," a stout woman in a fringed coat is shouting. "They have to—the senior faculty have abandoned self-government for personal convenience. And what about the adjuncts? They have no health care, no travel money. They haven't got *offices*. We use them and disappear them. We should be ashamed."

"Let's not get into the adjunct problem now," a California professor says repressively. The many adjuncts in the room begin to hyperventilate.

"If not now, when?" mutters a disgusted Florida part-timer, tossing her convention program into the air.

In the last thirty years, faculty faces in mainstream academe have changed enormously. Far more are Jews, Asians, African Americans, women. Outside the sciences, quite a few more are openly gay. Italian, Irish, and Central European names are still rather rare on faculty rosters. So are working-class whites, Hispanics, conservatives, the openly religious, those with military or big-business backgrounds, and people from heartland states at campuses on the East or West Coasts.

But American academe is really two faculties. The tenured ranks are heavily male and middle-aged, and within them you find an astonishing range of ability: professors who have founded whole fields in their garages, working nights and weekends, and professors who include letters to the *New York Times* as official scholarly publications in their year-end reports. Below them lurk the tenure-track faculty, full-time but not yet permanent. On a parallel road to power are academics who take on administrative duties as a way to bring up a salary, lighten a teaching load, or make an honorable exit before tenure committees notice they can't produce even one small scholarly article in seven years. (A great secret of academe is that while jobs are very hard to get, tenure—except at the very top schools—is quite easy. Of those up for tenure at the University of Massachusetts–Amherst between 1990 and 1993, 96 percent were granted lifetime employment; nationally, the figures are a little lower, but odds remain excellent. Academics hate to judge one another in public; people are often kept on because their personalities fit existing departmental psychodramas, or because their records are acceptable and nonthreatening, not necessarily because they are outstandingly creative, productive, or smart. Administrations can kill funding for positions, but otherwise have no say in the process; only faculty hire other faculty.)

The highest-paid professor in America is a Cornell heart surgeon (male) who gets $1,779,730 in annual salary and benefits. For people with advanced degrees, professors nationwide are not wildly overpaid. A full professor at a small college averages $53,000. One at a good state university may get $65,000. At research campuses, most teach some form of three and three, campus shorthand for three course preparations per term; at liberal arts colleges, four and four. But operating beside and below this professorial cosmos is the shadow world of the adjuncts: all the campus instructors given the courtesy title of faculty member in return for handling much of the actual undergraduate teaching. For adjunct faculty, $1,000 *per course* is not unusual. Adjuncts are often female. They have no job security, and few benefits, except at the rare campus, like Rutgers, with an adjuncts' union. Many schools ban them from regular departmental faculty meetings. Their office is a bookshelf or file drawer. Often they have no computer privileges, no voicemail. They hold student conferences on the lawn, on the curb, in the cafeteria, in their cars. They teach and run. Freeway flyers, they call themselves, since so many drive daily between two or three or four adjunct appointments, in different cities, or even different states. Adjunct faculty handle undergraduate writing courses, language drills, discussion sections for large lecture courses, all the low-status, labor-intensive, high-contact aspects of turning raw confused adolescents into presentable young adults.

The academic value of a college credit is the same whether the course is taught by a full professor or an adjunct. It's also the same price. Adjunct faculty are thought to account for 40 or even 50 percent of all face-to-face undergraduate teaching now, as opposed to 22 percent in the early 1970s. But the industry does not really know. The AAUP does not really know. No one bothers to track such instructors. They are the temps and day-care workers and field hands of academe, hired sometimes the week before classes start, segregated thereafter into basements or separate buildings, snubbed by the tenure-track people, invisible to real faculty. Adjuncts try to feel real, too, and can be passionate about helping their students improve, but all know not to get too fond of a school. After six and a half years, deans and legal departments invariably usher them out the door, for fear they will sue for tenure, and maybe win. So many desperate Ph.D.s remain on the market that any dissident can be replaced in half an hour.

To save even more money, many campuses let undergraduates teach. Peer coaching and peer tutoring can be excellent ways to help college students learn. But in math and econ and writing and language courses, students are now often in charge of the classroom, running discussion, correcting problem sets, giving tenured faculty time for other work. Even professors so blocked that they can't write letters of recommendation are still inundated with advisees, tenure reviews, visiting-dignitary luncheons, manuscript-review requests, committee meetings, talks to community groups and alumni. At cash-strapped institutions, senior faculty have to clean their own offices, take out their own trash. They are in no mood for extra student contact, no matter how much legislatures grumble. Why *not* let undergrads teach each other? It's good experience, administrators say, smiling. As you will note in our brochures, we've always said our students are very bright, very capable. Collaborative skills are important in the new economy. We consider this an opportunity, not a problem at all.

Solutions to the adjunct problem abound, in theory. Upgrade their status, give them long-term contracts, and pay them part-time salaries based on what full-time faculty get. Or create massive numbers of new full-time positions, hire experienced adjuncts to fill them, then reduce adjunct ranks to a more rational 15 percent of instructors, not 40 or 50 percent. Or fire them all, and make tenured faculty teach five big classes a term, as they did forty years ago. Should professors protest that teaching Intro to Philosophy is a monumental bore, tough darts; a Pennsylvania court has just ruled that increasing the teaching load does not violate academic freedom. Some administrations, watching their campuses hemorrhage cash, have another suggestion: give up the dream that real college classes are taught by real college professors.

But academe remains rich in dreams and nightmares and collective memory. The campus utopia is always somewhere else: Plato's grove, or a Paris where Abelard lectures wonderfully beside the Seine; a golden homoerotic Oxford before 1914; or Bletchley Park in 1943, full of dons saving civilization through math skills. The paranoid style also remains alive and well on campus. Land-use economists comb colleagues' CV's for evidence of CIA funding; political scientists carefully document McCarthy-era pressures from alumni and trustees to force out faculty with unorthodox views; historians are haunted by the righteous collaborations between German academics and Hitler's ministry of propaganda, and the book burnings that came after.

For tenure-ladder faculty, the greatest nightmare of all is the suggestion that tenure's time is past. Ninety-seven percent of four-year campuses offer tenure to their faculty. Before 1915, none did. Maybe, some say, none should now. Tenure is bad for academic freedom; it discourages risk-taking and innovation. Tenure rewards the useless and punishes the useful. Tenure is the equivalent of welfare, in the public mind. Tenure, employers tell college presidents, cheats the undergraduates: they arrive at first jobs full of theories and techniques twenty years out of date.

But alternatives to tenure assume faculty can or will turn out scholarship like any other product. Healthy fear, some administrators comment, does wonders for one's output. We're not flipping burgers here, professors retort; we can't be creative on demand. Metaphor wars flourish. Faculty are like a string quartet: you can't push for efficiency without adulterating quality. So lengthen your season, and play more concerts, suggest the many professors who are consistently productive. The tenured faculty is the campus investment portfolio, administrators say; a diverse portfolio is good strategy, but we should have the right to sell off nonproductive holdings. Meanwhile, deans quietly debate three-year or five-year creativity contracts as one possible tenure-substitute, or rolling appointments regularly reviewed. Shorten time to tenure to three or four years, perhaps. Go to fixed-term appointments. Insist on post-tenure reviews. Form a national union for faculty. Let people choose a research or a teaching track. Let good teaching be a bigger factor in tenure, as it was in the Forties and Fifties. At Minnesota's Carleton College, research publishing is less important than what your students say: a hundred letters from current and former undergrads go into every tenure folder there. If we don't police ourselves, others will, some faculty warn; the Texas state legislature's education committee has already cleared the way for campuses to fire tenured faculty who receive two consecutive years of low performance ratings from students and peers.

But campuses are viper pits, say those who want to keep the system intact. Change faculty hiring to a five-year contract, like that of any corporate executive, and contractees lose all freedom of speech. Deans and committees can punish the tenured, with dismal offices, or no raises, or vile committee assignments, but they can't keep them quiet. The freedom to speak and write is so very fragile, doubters and dissenters so often later proven right, intervention attempts (internal or external) so very frequent in campus history. Tenure may be wasteful and cruel, its defenders observe, but it protects the compact with the public to preserve one place in society where people poke into odd corners and make odder connections, for reasons not immediately obvious. Tenure protects innovators from academics.

•   •   •

Near the Hyatt meeting rooms, I look on the Who's Where board to find Sherry Young, but she has not come to MLA. After raising five children, Young earned her doctorate in Romantic poetry from the University of Dallas at forty. In 1991, aged forty-five, she sent out thirty-three job applications but got no MLA interviews. Young was then a visiting lecturer at the University of North Texas in Denton. She augmented her yearly adjunct-teaching income of $16,000 by taking three other jobs. Rising each day at 5:15 A.M. to begin a hundred-mile drive, Young also coached business writing at various corporations, managed an office for an exercise-equipment company, and worked as an AT&T sales rep, all to stay with the literature she loved. "I can teach anything from Homer to James Joyce," she told me then, "but I'm dying of exhaustion. I won't leave the field. I won't. Literature carries compensations that are not monetary."

Five years on, I track her down at her old campus, the University of Dallas. Young has jumped to administration after all, and has no complaints about the lifeboat it represents. By adjunct standards she had been doing well, getting $1,100 a course at Texas Christian University, and keeping up all the other work, too, but in 1991 the University of North Texas had a 63 percent budget cut. All adjuncts were dumped, Young among them. She went to four more MLAs, getting to several final interviews, but ending always with rejection letters.

"I lost heart," she says now. "I felt rejected by the profession, abandoned by my school. Those were dark, angry days. All I had invested seemed lost. I divorced. The only job I could find was in a nursery, hauling plants in a warehouse, writing catalogue copy. I tried everything, anything, to keep my mind alive. At garden club demos, I would shower the ladies with arcana about Victorian topiary from my old grad seminar notes."

Finally, an old friend got a job at Dallas, and hired her, too.

"It occurred to me I was following the track of the Ponaroa, the comic hero in the classics who wins by unethical importuning. But at that point I didn't much care."

Now she is a director of external programs, running community seminars and marketing university trips abroad. Some years she leads the Rome Campus sessions; the University of Dallas owns a villa in the hills above the city.

"I even got to Greece," she told me, "and saw the burial place of Byron's liberation fighters. Such tawny skulls, perfect, intact—well, you know how Romanticists love bones and ruins." Good luck, I tell her, meaning it. Good luck.

One of MLA's most popular personalities could not attend the Chicago meeting. If he existed, which he does not, Manfred Mickelson would clearly be the sort of academic who updates his vita nightly before retiring: this elusive visiting professor with a Cornell master's degree claims forty papers given at literary conferences, articles under consideration at twelve scholarly journals, four books under contract with major publishers, and a whopper of a dissertation about sex-starved pirates in the Caribbean: "Commerce, Homosociality and the Engendering of the Body in Defoe and Wollstonecraft."

Eight weeks before this December conference, a real-life academic search committee, dazed from reading over a hundred actual folders for an actual eighteenth-century literature post, decided to invent the perfect job candidate. Then they decided to send out his application letter. Manfred is rumored to have received over forty dossier requests, and six invitations to meet with actual hiring committees. ("We still have not learned whether, despite being unable to show up in person for his MLA interviews, Manfred received any actual offers," his Internet supporters conscientiously note. "Manfred in any case belongs not to an age but to all humankind. Feel free to download, print, and circulate.")

On the way home, I encounter a distinguished emeritus literature scholar, a former Northwestern professor who recently managed his retirement with military dispatch, cleaning out the office in one long weekend. He decamped to a tower office in the library, leaving behind, he said proudly, nothing but a smile, like the Cheshire cat. How did you know it was time to go? I ask. Suddenly he is not smiling, not at all.

"When you go around turning off lights and closing doors each night," he says. "When the grounds crew saws a limb from a tree, and you want to rush over and fling yourself across, to keep the place the same as it always was. Then you must find the grace to understand that your days on campus have come to an end."

———

Back to Chicago, but this time in March, ten blocks farther south on Michigan Avenue, and at the zenith of Fortune's wheel. In the faded rococo splendor of the Hilton ballroom, wintry Lake Michigan light shimmers through rose-pink drapes, brightening the haze of cigarette smoke above round tables where a hundred MacArthur Prize Fellows and their families are lunching. Many MacArthur winners eat with great intensity, stripping grape clusters one-handed and flipping the naked stems to the floor, cramming whole rolls into their mouths. One swipes an imperious finger through leftover hotel gravy on a tablemate's plate. As tribute to a departing administrator, grantee after grantee stands to recount the effect of a MacArthur award on one's life.

> "You feel like an elephant fell on your head, but people return your phone calls so much faster."

"Most of us are extremely suspicious of the system; it's good to be among others who have bucked it and won."

"I was ready to quit, give up, give in, be a sheep among sheep, and then you people called."

Chicago's John D. and Catherine T. MacArthur Foundation, which claims nearly $3 billion in assets, is the nation's seventh-wealthiest nonprofit, thanks to the real estate and mail-order insurance successes of its eccentric founder. His equally eccentric son, Rod MacArthur, invented the foundation's Prize Fellows program, which since 1981 has tried to fast-forward the creative process. The controversial premise of these so-called genius grants: paying very smart people to do exactly what they like will, eventually, benefit all society. We locate superbly original minds, the anonymous selection committee says, then let them roam. A five-year, no-strings MacArthur award averages $350,000. You cannot apply; they phone you. Recipients have ranged from eighteen to eighty, and their first reactions are seldom very inventive.

"Oh, my God."

"Oh, my God."

"Oh, my God."

"Yes, I've been waiting for your call," said one writer, coolly.

"Can I call you back to confirm?" a political scientist pleaded. "I played this joke on a colleague of mine last year."

And once there was only a long silence, then a distant thump, the sound of a body hitting a Massachusetts laboratory floor as a winner fainted. Since a fat prize that frees you from paper-grading is every academic's sweetest private dream, and since nearly two-thirds of MacArthur winners are tenured faculty, I once arranged to attend the Fellows' secret conclave, held every eighteen months somewhere in Chicago, to observe the outcomes of this ultimate thinker's dream.

The day's planned entertainment is a series of symposia on creativity, but most fellows mill instead outside the conference rooms, sidling from group to group while consulting very expensive watches. They gossip about chemists who urinate in competitors' test tubes to throw off results, and about no-fail ways to keep rabbits out of the garden (tentative conclusion on both issues: There is no easy and moral solution). I wander from group to group as winners converse.

"We've obviously got to reconceptualize the whole framework of what we call human rights, I mean, is war official violence or what?"

"My agent tells me we can go $200,000 for the film rights, no problem—"

"At MIT you get tenured for just *citing* the economics literature—"

". . . total assholes at USC, wouldn't even consider our research proposals—"

". . . and sometimes I just think about myself, and how I was once an embryo, and how before that I wasn't there at all. Really mind-blowing. My parents, too, and all the way back to who knows what? Sometimes you wonder if animals—"

(A musicologist in a cream cashmere sweater sternly interrupts: "Other life species.")

—"if other life species have, you know, a comprehension of the flow of their overall achievement, their state of meaning, their moment in time—"

Nine tenured fellows fall raptly silent, thinking about this. An eminent cultural critic brightens.

> "Well, I saw this PBS documentary on wasps, and they went out and learned to sting their enemies really purposefully."
>
> "Right, like those assholes at USC."

Cautiously, I open a nearby door; color slides of fat, sullen seals eating wildflowers are flashing in a very dark room.

"These are seals from halfway up the eastern side of Lake Baikal. Next slide. No, not that one. Yes. This is a seal from halfway up the western side of Lake Baikal. They are the only freshwater seals in the world. There are many theories on how they got into Lake Baikal, all conflicting. Next."

Escaping the seal session, a cluster of archaeology-minded fellows regroup by the coffee buffet, to plan their assault on the best-seller lists.

"I thought we could combine Von Daniken's *Chariots of the Gods?,* which sold very well but had no sex and violence, with the old group-writing technique of *Naked Came the Stranger,* and produce a fantastic read."

"Hey, *Naked Came the Maya!*"

Three laugh. One ducks behind the sofa, and makes a careful note.

Romantic munificence attracts back-seat drivers. Critics of the fellows program are perennial, as are their questions. How do you pick these people, anyway? Why has the program no accountability, and no productivity requirement? Why so many male tenured academics? Some recipients do use the money to make their lives more unexpected, starting novels, taking up watercolor, learning physics or Greek. Some buy

Italian villas, others lots of books. Some give back, like California woodworker Sam Maloof and Chicago Hispanic-housing organizer Paul Roldan; both used MacArthurs to set up youth scholarships and education funds.

But most grantees keep traveling the same roads, only faster. The men go on as always, but women awarded MacArthurs often get much better jobs, right away. People in new or edge fields like environmental history or superstring theory win overnight respectability. The head of the International Crane Foundation can finally afford more trips to Pakistan and Siberia to save wild birds. Yet fifteen years after launch, no great books have come out of this creativity experiment, few scientific revolutions. Much MacArthur money has vanished into dead ends, temporary or permanent, from research-assistant salaries to an attempt to underwrite a public-television series on landscape to a dozen tentative theories that died quietly in the back lab. Millions of fellowship dollars have been mundanely spent, on patios and tuitions and silverware, on new cars and old debts. Prodigality, or long-term mulching? We don't know, the foundation insists, nor do we care.

The MacArthur's attempt to bypass the academic credentialing system and force creativity into bloom, like winter branches under a sunlamp, echoes in perfect miniature the riddle it set out to solve. When legislatures and parents and reporters fume at academe for lack of measurable product, they're not after freshmen or deans but the professoriate, staring for decades at bread mold or Mongolian verbs in what looks like subsidized ease. Whose autonomy is more important, the academic's or the university's? Faculty often seem to demand the perks and deferences of the show-business universe, appearing in the classroom nine hours a week at some schools, just four at others, abetting a world where adults act like kids and kids like adults. But a bad campus performance can run for decades on taxpayer dollars, impervious to bad reviews, or investor rage. There are three human species, students whisper, men, women, and academics.

By commercial standards, the campus taste for delayed payoffs and deliberate long shots seems astonishing waste and frivol: attic meets playpen. Academe saves everything, old star maps, vials of smallpox virus, outtakes of D. H. Lawrence novels. You never know, professors say, you never know. In the 1930s, Texaco money let the University of Texas–Austin sweep up whole file cabinets of drafts and correspondence from modernist writers like Eliot, Joyce, and Woolf at bargain rates. Today the smart money is on Third World political papers—especially ephemera like demonstration handouts and underground newsletters—and also the historiography of media and cyberspace, from "I Love Lucy" development memos to early software designs. Guess right, and scholars in 2098, or 2298, will be extremely grateful, and very busy.

But the campus penchant for slo-mo can also make formal research publication (the official conversation of mind and mind) like broadcasting to another galaxy, then waiting for reply. In the sciences, books are not necessary for advancement; articles are. The competition is enormous, the review process harsh and political but relatively quick. In the humanities and social sciences, no one takes you seriously without a book. A one-volume study may take years to research and write. When the manuscript goes out for review and comment, even friends may take six months to turn in a two-page opinion. Enemies will happily delay the process a year. If the project is accepted by a university press—many are not—authors or their schools often write the publisher a discreet and hefty check, a practice called subvention. All know how few copies will sell.

Three years beyond release, the first reviews appear in specialized journals. Two years more, and the seven people in the world who understand what you are trying to say may write convoluted letters to the editor, of censure or praise. You can post your work on the Web, and many do, but to hiring committees from the pre-chip age that form of information-sharing is not real publishing, being neither permanent nor peer-reviewed. From the first dim framing of a question to community critique, wise scholars count on five years, or ten. Fine, say critics, if only something came of it. Academic books are often outdated before they ever see print, yet literally hundreds continue to be published every day. Ninety-five percent of all research articles are never once cited after publication. Quite true, say scholars testily; go ahead, criticize capitalism because most businesses fail.

But a few contributions live on and on. A very few turn a field—or a world—upside down with casual brilliance. You see graduate students sitting cross-legged in campus library stacks sometimes, carefully adding their names to the blue-and-white sign-out cards pasted onto the back flaps of such books, the academic's chain letter. Ten, thirty, forty years before, other anxious unknowns—now great professors, or great dead professors—handled these volumes, drank from these wells. When we, too, become important minds, the grad students reason, some diligent intellectual historian will discover this thrilling skein of signatures, and be awed. Most libraries will have long since converted to on-line processing. But the devoted, and the ambitious, are never fazed.

SPRING BREAK:
Behind Closed Doors

Spring on campus makes everyone restless. Students pester instructors for parole: "Can we have class outside? Pleeease? We'll work twice as hard." Veteran faculty know they never do; undergrads released into pale chill sunshine can only talk about plans for the upcoming spring break. But in buildings all over campus, the college staffers that students never see are already thinking four and six months ahead. Groundskeepers order more fast-growing grass seed; the scuffed and muddy lawns must be perfect by commencement day. Admissions offices are deep in financial-aid negotiations. Faculty already know their fall teaching loads. By mid-March, campus grownups turn tired and snappish; one batch of product still needs finishing, another is already on the conveyor. *Over spring break, everyone vows, I must get caught up. I haven't been off campus since January, except to go home and sleep. Why live in a college town, if you never have time to enjoy it?*

All college towns are alike. But nearly every campus hones a distinctive in-house manner. At New York University in Greenwich Village, students in dark glasses and ripped black leggings shoot experimental videos in the elevators. In Dallas, sorority members at Southern Methodist University jog very slowly across campus at ten in the morning, wearing full makeup and pink warmup suits, pausing frequently under the live oaks to spray one another's perfect hair. Near Orlando, at lakefront Rollins College, tanned undergraduates water-ski between classes as friends watch from the student-center verandah, trading bites of black-bean fajitas and Key lime pie. Above the Pacific, the University of California–San Diego perches on a sunny bluff, its hot-weather architecture lightweight and functional, stairways exposed, plazas strangely bare. "Where are your students?" I once asked, walking under the rustling UCSD palms. My faculty guide smiled beatifically. "Up there!" he said, pointing over the blue-green ocean, and so they were, sixty or seventy at least, hang-gliding across the faultless California sky.

Some campuses are old enough now to be (as Henry James said of Harvard) a dense organic pile. Others are still feeling their way to confident solidity. But walk down any campus hallway, ease open its classroom and lecture-hall doors, and you will hear the steady drone of teaching. At Rollins the for-credit courses range from Personal Economics and Leadership Skills to Sunbelt Politics, Sociology of Kurt Vonnegut, Jr., Sociology of Paranormal Reality, Alcohol and Society, and What Is New Age? *1) Choose and summarize a poem,* instructs an assignment for World Literature. *2) Take notes while you read. 3) Write an essay about the poem. 4) Remember to include a thesis (a thesis means you say "I wish to argue that . . .").* At SMU, a poised woman in a Chanel-pink suit swiftly writes architectural vocabulary on a green chalkboard: soffit, Ionic, linenfold, six-over-six. At UCSD, two hundred undergrads watch a balding physics professor trot back and forth across the well of a lecture room, face screwed in thought, elbows flapping. "All right, everyone, imagine a black hole in a box. We'll have a more realistic example in a moment."

Teaching is academe's most secretive aspect, even more than salaries and budgets; it is also one of the few human activities (claims former Harvard president Derek Bok) that does not get demonstrably better from one generation to the next. One early Johns Hopkins president, asked why his campus had so vivid an intellectual life, knew the answer right away: we all go to each other's lectures, he replied. But that fine custom died long ago. On most American campuses, faculty may spend forty years together, and never once witness their closest colleagues dealing with live undergrads.

I started teaching on the college level at twenty-two, when I was younger than some of the seniors in my discussion sections, and had my share of problems: the student who got a D-, burned his course notes, and mailed me the charred scraps in a blood-red envelope; the perfect charmer who was removed from class by apologetic police and taken to an institution for the criminally insane; the wrestler who snored through a handful of classes he deigned to attend but wept at will in dean's offices. My best student ever was a trilingual Vietnamese refugee who wrote perfect papers and perfect exams, each one grave, balanced, intensely original. At twenty, he dropped out of school to work in a wholesale plumbing supply house. A younger brother and sister were still in the refugee camps, and he hoped to get to them before the typhus epidemics did. My worst student ever was the son of a household name, who wrote flaccid, disconnected essays blaming his father for spending more time with his bodyguards than with his children; that student, too, dropped out, and was given a corporate division to play with. The most idealistic kids I ever taught rented a car over spring break, spread their assigned texts on the dashboard, and drove like fury for ten days, just to say they had walked in Faulkner's woods, and watched the sun rise over Mark Twain's Mississippi. My most efficient student was a woman from Gloucester, Mass., whose family were commercial fishers. She sent home all her assignments every week; parents, cousins, and grandparents followed along in the evenings and mailed me businesslike essays to correct, with requests for further reading; six college educations for the price of one.

College teaching methods vary enormously. Some faculty are obsessive outliners, enumerating points A, B, C with agonizing slowness. Some practice one-liners in front of a mirror till their timing gleams. Some are boxing coaches: come on, come on, let's have a response. You. You. You. Here's a quarter, go call home, you'll never be a scholar. Some professors want to be ranchers culling the herd, others shepherds protecting it. Certain faculty build a lecture like a house, finishing in precisely fifty minutes. Others ramble on till students begin crawling out the exits on hands and knees. There are professors who bring lost worlds to life with love and skill, and professors who can make exploding galaxies dull. U.S. faculty lecture in academic robes over tweeds, in expensive business suits, in cutoffs and flip-flops, in black bustiers. A few begin bellowing while still out in the hall; quite a few, convinced undergraduate minds can absorb no more than three ideas per lecture, still orate in robust 1950s style ("Gentlemen, ladies, I submit to you the following proposition . . ."); others won't take questions because it wastes time; still others stand rigid in front of three hundred people, murmuring facts in a monotone, eyes shut. Some want to open minds, some to change them, some angrily call research "my real work" and classroom time "babysitting." Nearly all are trying to make even the most mercenary students think in new ways. Just once in their young lives, professors mutter, they should know it's possible.

Norman Maclean, who spent decades at the University of

Chicago before writing *A River Runs Through It,* thought teaching mostly biological, a reflex either present or absent: if you can do it, you get a little better over the decades, and then a few years before retirement you get a little worse; few academics at age sixty still enjoy entertaining nineteen-year-olds, and many feel it is insincere to try. I love teaching, but have never found a shortcut for socializing a class into wanting to learn. Some groups you can't wait to see depart; others are so lively and engaged that you want the term to go on forever. But by the fourth or fifth session, the human chemistry of this fourteen-week clan is usually clear. After the hour is done, all the students may begin heading to lunch in one amiable gaggle, and stay friends for years. Three or four may ally to bait a vulnerable instructor into tears or rages as the rest look on with clinical interest. Every college course or discussion section develops a corporate personality: there are dud classes, enigmatic classes, feisty classes, kind classes.

Early in my teaching life, a supervisor scheduled an observation visit just before spring break, to watch me run a freshman-sophomore writing seminar. I really, really needed that job. One day before the observation, flu turned to laryngitis. Desperate, I wrote out dialogue on file cards, and handed them round for the students to read aloud:

This is

Professor X.

He has heard of your brilliance,

And would like to see you at work.

I expected disaster. But the undergrads took over. Courteous, energetic, thoughtful, and only overacting a very little bit, they offered one another perceptive prose fixes, traded arcane bibliography, and posed question after stimulating question, keeping the discussion as vigorous as a good tennis match. From January to March, I had listened to their housing problems and family crises and life decisions, let them tell me about all the things on campus they found odd or shocking, made special appointments with faculty who could help with their research topics, given them phone numbers of alums offering part-time jobs, passed on ideas for summer internships and books to try, gone to see them dance and dive, forced the football player into sustained thought, kept the math major from driving us all mad, encouraged the shy smart one, hushed the chatterbox, sat on the snob. Now they were returning the favor. As the class filed out, backs to the supervisor, they muttered comments like prison-movie convicts. "Was that okay?" "Did we do it right?" "We want you to stay."

Even with a working voice, I could not have spoken. The supervisor said the class had gone well enough. "They seem . . . *interested* . . . in the material," he said, suspiciously. But I kept the job. If you keep the job long enough, a living-in-fairyland effect sets in; the students all stay the same age, and you get older, till one day you are teaching the children of your first undergrads, whose parents have told them to be sure and look you up. As kittens become cats, so undergraduates are future alumni. They make their views on educations received very plain in the end-of-term course critiques, which frequently focus on the professor, rather than the material taught.

Eurobore.

Needs new wardrobe.

Cancels lots of classes.

Never let this man near students again; his hobby is general condescension.

Some reviews are deliberately mean, some pan performance and ignore content, some are heartfelt and perceptive, notes tossed over a very high wall. Few campus adults in power take course comments seriously. Who cares what the students say? The greatest of all campus secrets is passing time. Wait them out. They leave, eventually. We stay. *You can't allow students to dictate in the classroom. No one is going to tell me what I can or can't do in my own courses.* That students can have sharp eyes and definite opinions is a concept very few institutions grasp. Year upon year, schools underestimate their customers on an industrial scale, wondering always why alumni giving is such an uphill battle.

College students today seem immature in some ways, very old in others. Male professors used to marry female undergrads at a great rate; now women on the faculty can recount their own authority-versus-friendship crises, or at least twinges. "These *incredibly* cute boys come into my classes and call me ma'am," a fortyish female professor at Cornell University explains. "And I'm standing there in my grown-up shoes thinking, 'Hey, where were *you* when I was nineteen?' A sophomore turned up for office hours last week with a bottle of excellent sherry and two glasses. I'm afraid he'll ask me to Barbados for the weekend next."

Most undergraduates have no time for interspecies romance, for they already maintain exhausting double lives: partier, activist, skater, bass guitarist, emergency medical technician, parent. Their prejudices are strong. All hate academic red tape. Many hate print. For most it slows and daunts (if you want a shock, ask undergrads anywhere to read aloud a passage of nineteenth-century prose). Elizabethan English is now like

Sanskrit; Shakespeare courses rely heavily on in-class movies. Most students under thirty-five, in fact, know human life and culture largely from the screen, not the page. An impressive number can identify "Gilligan's Island" episodes from a single isolated fragment of dialogue. But other references confuse and agitate. What's a Zeus? they demand. Who is Guadalcanal? Nonreaders are handicapped from the start, and often never catch up, no matter how forgiving their instructors. More allusions that baffle, reported by faculty at a dozen campuses with selective admissions. Zen. Sisyphus. Sacramental. A house divided. Red-letter day. Land-office business. Draconian measures. Pyrrhic victory. Judas. Harriet Beecher Stowe. The Sphinx. Martin Luther. Martin Luther King. They've never heard of any of this stuff. Their exams and papers get very testy.

> Why doesn't Nora in *A Doll's House* just go to law school?

> The governess in *The Turn of the Screw* is a weird and quite uptight person due entirely to male-dominated society.

> In the novel *Paradise Lost* the poet expresses the depressed feeling of the overtired worker. The poet is thinking he (the worker) has lived his life to the fullest and though there are some challenges remaining he is basically content to pack it in and die.

They are not fond of impractical challenges, or taking chances, or dark alleys. "Aren't we making too much of this?" and "I don't know what you want me to say" are constant classroom cries. In 1968, 85 percent of American undergraduates expected college to help them develop a philosophy of life. Now less than half do. At these prices, speculating and exploring are not cost-efficient. At these prices, students expect the college experience to be foolproof, or at least of consistent quality. Besides, professors often don't like it when you think for yourself, rather than regurg. Some undergrads are on campus for the bottom line, others to pick up gloss and confidence, but like students always and everywhere, they take care to be sternly leftist with the Marxist instructor, sweetly liberal to the liberal; to imitate Attila when writing papers for a conservative, then turn rigorous and anal in lab reports.

When they slip—which is not often—faculty are always stunned to learn how unimportant the life of the mind is to most college students, how anxiously they groom their résumés, how strong remains their urge to help improve the world, how rich their collective lives, how firm their misconceptions. Many cannot name all fifty states on an outline map, and harbor strange ideas about other American regions, unself-consciously asking students from California at what age they became promiscuous, inquiring of Kentuckians when they plan to marry their cousins. Undergrads are visually liberal, aurally conservative; any accent—urban black, Texan, Brooklyn, European—that diverges from the local norm, or from broadcast American, sets a class member instantly apart. Some late-adolescent speech is national, and contagious: dignified senior professors can find themselves announcing that a departmental policy is "Totally random! Grossiola!" But if a student does not sound right, the others grow uneasy, formal, distant.

Caught in the backwash of great change, they develop pragmatic social formulae: "Were your parents together, when you were growing up?" In 1961, Columbia English professor Lionel Trilling lashed out at the middle-class students who attended his lectures, looked politely, as directed, into the dreadful abyss of modern life, and took good notes, in order to be well-rounded. Today students are often *from* the abyss, and

know more of its ways than any academic. You get students
from expensive suburbs who have never had to make a bed, or
a deadline, and students from dying city slums whose parents
literally kept them indoors all through adolescence, studying
for the SATs: *One of us is going to make it out of here, kid, and
you're elected.* They are the heirs of social revolution and global
migration, doing the best they can: the Bangladeshi sorority
sister; the born networker who still translates gas bills for his
Korean parents and plans to be the first Asian-American president; a fourth-generation Puerto Rican, pressured into joining
the Hispanic student association although she speaks no Spanish; a tense, jokey pre-med, half black and half Minnesota
Swede, the child of a long-dead civil-rights romance who
knows he makes both sides of his family uneasy.

But oh, the excuses. Fancy schools yield fancy reasons for
work undone. I had a callback for a Broadway musical and left
my report on the plane. My therapist says I can't come to class
because I have incipient claustrophobia. My roommate the
Prince got another terrorist kidnapping threat. I went to Paris
for the weekend and the Concorde broke down. My father
was indicted by a federal grand jury; we stayed up all night
burning his investment files.

Students at public campuses have other explanations. I was
in detox. I work three jobs, and fell asleep at the wheel. My
grandmother died (sometimes twenty-five or thirty grand-
mothers expire just before finals, in a class of 250). Some excuses even turn out to be true. My cat had kittens and I am her
coach. The police impounded my car, and the term paper was
in the glove compartment. I need to take the final early because the husband of the woman I am seeing is threatening to
kill me. I missed the final because I walked in on a convenience store robbery and was locked in the basement with the
clerk all night.

What is the core of the undergraduate experience, its center of gravity? Faculty assume it is the classroom. Students usually say the campus. College condenses and intensifies: in spring term, especially, near-misses and chance connections seem to haunt every day of every undergraduate week; they brood on summer jobs, on next year's housing, on loss and waste and luck. If only I had taken that year off. If only I had talked with her earlier. What if I hadn't walked through the wrong door that morning, and found my life's work? In class, if a student is ready to hear, if a professor still loves the material, odds for happy change improve—but even then, say faculty glumly, we are intellectual mechanics, filling heads; gardeners pouring fertilizer on plants that may or may not thrive.

Why learning occurs is as profound a campus mystery as it was in 1400. Despite the liberations of the Net, most undergrad instruction remains startlingly late-medieval: lecturer, lectern, listening faces, pen and paper for note-taking, a window to look out of, when bored. Campuses grew up in the first place because scholars congregate around books, and students around scholars. You pay to watch someone think. Then they watch you think. After all these centuries, the unavoidable core of college is still people in a room with the door closed, struggling toward that moment when the faces change. Oh, yes. I see. I do see. I think you're wrong. I think that's right. Let me tell you why.

Is it better to stuff students, or to stretch them? No one knows. Consistency of campus product is always hard to prove. Mentoring from faculty radically improves the odds either way. An academic advisor who sees a pattern in a sophomore's interests that the sophomore may not is an excellent start; an instructor who takes time to match students with internships or research-assistant jobs fosters both career training and personal development; a professor who invites a whole class home for blueberry pancakes teaches her undergrads more than Japanese verbs or quadratic equations. Ensuring that students are active learners, not stenographers, means extra work for faculty: it takes hours and hours to organize paper-draft exchanges and policy task groups, to persuade outside experts to visit a class for free, to stay late because the seniors need a pre-exam course review, to buy sixty bamboo poles so your two-thirty lecture can reenact the Battle of Actium—knowing all the while that if you could bill by the hour, like the doctors and lawyers these kids may become, you would now be very rich indeed.

It hardly matters whether the course topic is rainforest botany or introductory Arabic, small-business strategies or history of medicine, contemporary film or Caribbean lit. No subject can survive a bad instructor, or an instructor who cannot remember what it is like to be a novice. Having academic stars on campus looks good in the brochures, but for the average undergraduate the educational effect is rather like moving to Los Angeles, knowing that Robert Redford lives somewhere in town. Professors who love their fields, like professors who make students do the work, are far better campus assets.

Time and quiet to think and read and explore, a critical mass of people as smart or smarter than you are, being asked to do things you never thought you could are all—probably—what make college work. In the last several decades, thousands of studies on achieving academic quality on the college campus have appeared; a 1991 review of twenty-six hundred of them by Ernest Pascarella and Patrick Terenzini, *How College Affects Students,* concludes that the factors most fervently advertised by schools (institutional prestige, selective admissions, state-of-the-art resources) indeed help people get higher-income jobs but do nothing to ensure development of mind or character. For that you need personal attention from faculty, a rich flexible curriculum, and lots of involvement in campus life. In the end, an undergraduate education is not so much a pile of notebooks moldering in the bottom drawer, but learning to talk in front of a group, to read and to summarize, to reason on demand, to push yourself late at night. To live and work with people you might never speak to in ordinary life. To think against the grain. To manage time. To not be afraid or rejecting. To not say, every other sentence, "In my high school, we . . ."

Try as you may to deal with them all as individual souls, after years of teaching some students look like trouble right away, and some like great fun. Engineers tend to be wonderfully organized and responsible; like students from Commonwealth countries, they have the high school training that makes college work a pleasure, not endless desperate catch-up. Older learners are a delight. College, they love to announce, is wasted on the young. Undergrads with strong families behind them can be just as determined to wring every bit of value from their classroom hours. Students with hangovers are tiresome; those with SAT hangovers, hard to deprogram. "Perambulating the verdant enclosure," they tell you proudly, "I impacted an arboreal structure." Poets and pre-laws can have egos like elephant hide. Born-agains are difficult; like students who want to write about race and gender oppression, only one topic interests them. Athletes are always falling asleep in lecture, because they are so tired, or else leaving class early, to get to practice.

The very worst are students who are in school for the wrong reasons, or don't want to be on campus at all. A considerable number (faculty tend to estimate 40 percent, students 30) seem glad to get as little as possible for their money. They cheer when lecture is canceled, grumble at makeup labs, chafe at any mark less than a B. "Perhaps I'd better meet with your department chair to discuss why you have a problem with raising my grade. I didn't pay good money for this course to be abused." Sometimes a mutual nonaggression pact develops between lazy students and lazier professors: "I won't bother you if you don't bother me." Some of the best students to be with are those who wake up one morning and realize they have a brain; or those who understand, in five years' time, that the struggle was worthwhile. The very best are those who discover, while still in school, that they are hungry for learning, in class and out of it. They roll and revel in the campus like young horses in a spring field.

SPRING:
The Imagekeepers

Before Judge Alexander M. Sanders, Jr., became the nineteenth president of the College of Charleston, he used to eat fire in the circus.

"I also swallow swords, juggle, and ride elephants," he says absently. "Excellent training, *excellent,* for my current job." Sanders is bent over his wide mahogany desk, signing the day's first correspondence. Spring sun brightens the plaster roundels on the high office ceiling, dapples a slate fireplace flanked by blue sofas. Nearby are shelves of disarrayed law books, the college flag, a globe, and a basketball autographed by the New York Knicks, who arrive today for playoff practice in the campus gym.

Sanders's assistant Elizabeth Kassebaum, daughter of Kansas U.S. senator Nancy Kassebaum, arrives for a schedule check. "I'll be a little late for that student-leader luncheon at twelve-thirty," says Sanders, still signing. "Better tell them to eat silently till I get there. And find someone from Zeta, black sorority Zeta, not white sorority Zeta. I want them to be sure and turn up."

On a humid Charleston morning late in April, red roses twine the wrought-iron fences on this campus of verandas, courtyards, and brick walks. Spanish moss shrouds the live oaks beside the administration building, Randolph Hall. Founded as a private institution in 1770, reorganized as a city school in 1837, the College of Charleston (enrollment 8,000, plus 1,700 graduate students) is the oldest municipal college in America. But it never appears in the annual *U.S. News* rankings of best campuses, never broke into the name-brand national market, nor cares to. Instead, it serves a city, Charleston, and a South Carolina region, the Low Country—the dozen flat rich counties spreading from sandhills to sea islands, a hundred miles of tomato field and cypress swamp laced by the curves of the Edisto and Santee rivers that flow wide and slow to the Atlantic. The two-block view from the president's bedroom window includes a dozen restored antebellum mansions, an all-black public housing project, a high-rise nursing home for aged Episcopalians, frat row, and the city jail.

College of Charleston applicants come from fifty states and sixty-seven nations. The school just imported six Serbian and Croatian undergraduates from Bosnia ("Three of each, and they haven't killed each other yet," says Sanders, ebullient). But most C of C students are South Carolinian, or at least southern. The school is one-third male, two-thirds female; C of C women frequently date military cadets from the nearby Citadel. Diminutives abound on class rosters and dorm doors: Tori, Jodi, Brandi, Ashley, Suzi, Tiffi, Maci, Tazy. Tidy but not luxurious, the school harbors decades of donated furniture, and two ghosts.

Even on the state level, the college struggles. The average square footage per student in South Carolina is 250 feet; the College of Charleston has 110. Half its undergrads work while in school. The four-year graduation rate is 65 percent. But

Charleston has become (like San Francisco, Santa Fe, or Vermont) a desirable place to spend college years; the city has the Spoleto arts festival, good restaurants, nearby beaches, barrels of historic charm. Recruiting white students is easy, black students not. About 8 percent of the College of Charleston undergrads are African American, still a coup for a campus all-white until 1970.

"It's hard for us to get to critical mass, because historically black South Carolina State is only fifty miles away," Sanders explains. "We need them, they don't need us. I recruit 'em like sports players, see, I keep folders of prospective students who are black on my desk, and when I get a minute I call 'em up and explain why they should come here. But even the architecture looks unfriendly to them. I believe it's all these columns."

At fifty-seven, rumpled, grey-haired, deceptively informal, Sanders has a lawyer's baritone that he plays like a cello, able to move in mid-syllable from sweet to cold. He makes $110,000 a year, lives in an august four-story Georgian house that comes with the job, and has just signed a second five-year contract, an unusual feat. College presidents these days have extremely short shelf lives, their average time in office just 3.6 years. In the national Rolodex of campus-driven businesses—the Atlanta firm of academic lawyers who specialize in tenure and grievance cases, the Illinois detectives who perform background checks and credential searches (many academic job applicants routinely lie about degrees)—a rent-a-president agency now thrives, too.

Administrators are the designated grown-ups of higher education, its liaisons with the outside world, its strategists and architects, moderators and enforcers. They are the prose of academe, as faculty are the poetry and students the drama. For all campus managers—presidents and vice presidents, provosts and deans—spring is the bad season, a blur of grants due, admissions figures due, trustee reports due. Spring is also the traditional student sit-in season: undergrads sweep into presidential offices, impound schedule books, then issue E-mail manifestos for ethical investing or more Asian studies courses. Administrators used to end student takeovers by refusing switchboard and bathroom privileges. But postmodern protestors arrive equipped with cell phones, sleeping bags, omelette pans, and fifty-pound bags of cat litter.

Successful academic management these days means discouraging big, expensive ideas, encouraging small, practical ones, and perfecting a dozen pleasant, neutral ways to say, "Don't be ridiculous," "Figure it out for yourself," and "Yes, you have to work for a living." The apex of the administrator's art is to rise in a meeting, say calmly, "Nothing to report," and sit down again, mess-free. It's not easy: academic managers mostly see humanity as lawyers do, tear-stained, defensive, demanding. As campuses become less informal, less social, and more like business offices—"I signed on for a calling, and got a corporation" is a common plaint among administrators as well as faculty—problems once worked out over a glass of adequate wine now end up on the administrator's calendar, or else in court. State and federal auditors are turning tougher (the president of William and Mary was recently cited for serving afternoon sherry to staff members on state time) and students more litigious, charging schools with breach of contract, fraud, misrepresentation, or negligence. Pace University undergrads recently sued their school because they thought a computer course was too hard, and got a tuition refund plus $1,000 damages; one Albright College student sued because life with a party-animal roommate drove him into costly therapy.

Being a campus administrator means having everyone mad at you, all the time: senior art majors caught trying to counterfeit currency on the color copier; animal-rights sophomores who liberate rhesus monkeys from psych-department cages; same-sex faculty partners seeking tuition rebates; home-schooled hockey players demanding extra athletic eligibility; fraternity brothers who see no fire-code problem in keeping a can of gasoline, a carton of vodka, and a stack of hay bales in the same small room. A delegation of townspeople may arrive to argue leash laws, or protest bacteriological research on campus, or insist that the school donate more to local government. All are told: "Your ideas are refreshingly innovative, and certainly deserve further study."

But not right now. Before lunch, a campus administrator may need to inspect a dozen human brains in formaldehyde jars, discovered by first-year tunnelers in a dorm sub-basement; soothe an assistant professor vowing to go on hunger strike after a tenure turndown; confirm that the soccer team may not terrorize janitors by pursuing them on bicycles through the locker room; nod gravely when a professorial delegation announces that faculty morale is at an all-time low (faculty morale is *always* at an all-time low); then go watch fine wire strung around property borders to make the entire campus an eruv, or approved enclave, so Orthodox Jews can move more freely between buildings over the Sabbath.

The phone calls crash in like surf. A reporter asks why public funds pay campus scientists who then sell their time to private corporations; a junior professor is caught dropping rare books from a library window; a senior member of the economics department reports his sex-change operation, then hints a gender-discrimination lawsuit is on the way; a Washington bureaucrat insists that a site-visit memo be issued *immediately* to determine if campus salary and wage reporting is in compliance with OMB Circular A-21. If a faculty collective arrives to demand funding for a conference series on third-wave feminism and the homeless ("Let's build them all portable geodesic domes!"), then outside the window, in the marvelous spring sunshine, other seasonal rites are surely being enacted: undergraduate women dance around a freshly dug Mayhole (Maypoles are unacceptable phallic symbols) while just beyond a picket line of footsore women staffers, average salary $18,000 a year, agitate for an improved health-care package that the institution cannot possibly afford.

Nine-thirty A.M. Provost Conrad Festa, a trim middle-aged executive brandishing a double handful of paperwork, appears in Alex Sanders's doorway. College presidents handle foreign and domestic policy, give inspirational speeches, twist arms, kiss babies. Provosts work behind campus scenes, marshaling space and managing budgets.

"Good morning, Judge," says Festa, offering a sheaf of papers. Sanders scrutinizes, signs, scrutinizes, signs—then hears another "Good morning, Judge," from the office threshold; two catering representatives from Aramark want to discuss how the college can produce income from the nine-hundred-acre plantation it's just been given. The buildings are in bad shape, the land glorious. Rent it out for weddings? Set up a second conference center? Sanders spent the previous week-end on another fine waterfront acreage, recently purchased by a local African-American couple, she a lawyer, he a stockbro-ker (and College of Charleston '84). The Ku Klux Klan spray-painted trees and dock, then left a burning cross; the college asked students to help an alumnus clean up. They hoped for a dozen volunteers; a hundred came.

The morning's first crisis: Recreational services and student activities offices are clashing over rights to space in the gym. Accreditation teams from the all-powerful NCAA—the National Collegiate Athletic Association—are wandering the campus on a three-day inspection, so Sanders's ruling is swift. Building Services must (gently) extract the Knicks from the gym and move in tables for the health fair, then move out health-fair displays and set up swiftly for this evening's sports-awards banquet.

"Don't do this confrontationally, we've got to deal with each other another day," Sanders insists. Before taking this job, he never cared about sports. "I used to think all basketball games should start out 87 to 87 with three minutes to play. Initially, I tried to contain athletics here. I was wrong. Sports are enormously important to students. We have no football, but in basketball we even beat Tennessee, which spends $2.4 million on its basketball program, versus our $130,000. Our coach comes from the New Jersey Nets. He wanted a backwater school to take it easy in, but went out and won the NAIA championship anyway."

Born in South Carolina (his father a watchmaker, his mother an early advocate for black education), Alex Sanders attended college and law school at the state university in Columbia, a hundred miles away in distance, a thousand in outlook. He and his charming and efficient wife, Zoe (they met in kindergarten), will be upland outsiders if they stay in the president's mansion another quarter century. Back home, Mrs. Sanders observes, people move furniture to the middle of the room so they can bump knees and be cozy; in Charleston it's all pushed to the edges straightaway. Every January, Judge Sanders teaches trial advocacy at Harvard's Law School. If he could live anywhere, he says, he would pick New York City. Before accepting this campus presidency, Sanders spent fifteen years as a state senator, then eight as chief justice of the South Carolina Court of Appeals. More and more college heads, these days, are not academics: a former Bank of America head runs Michigan State, a public-relations executive heads Florida's Rollins College. Legal training also works. Sanders has had to fire two professors in five years, about average for a small school, dismissing one for bizarre behavior, one for intractable drinking. I ask, What if they'd sued?

"Sue, absolutely! I love lawsuits!" Three blond, ruddy male students suddenly bang on the office door. "Prez Sanders! Just wanted to say hi!" "Hi!" he cries in return; satisfied, they depart. Sanders wanders into the outer office to start work on tonight's sports-banquet speech.

"When was the last time I used the turtle story?" His administrative assistant checks a computer file.

"Rotarians, four months ago."

"Excellent. Turtle it is." He dictates changes as she edits on screen. " 'Every good athletic team is like a family. The children'—strike that—'the team members are the children, the coaches the parents—' " A worried young woman materializes in the doorway, clutching a daisy-painted backpack.

"Could you call the dean of that law school for me, puhleeze, President Sanders? I haven't heard a thing and I'm getting really, really nervous—"

"For you, madame, anything." They vanish into the sanctum. Half-revised, the turtle story hovers on the screen.

Two higher-education discontents are now colliding on every college campus—academic prestige-lust and consumer irritation at making an unreliable purchase—and the timing could not be worse. Is your product worth the price? It's a question colleges and universities have never heard before. The storms of the Sixties tore apart some campuses, but (like all tornadoes) spared many more. The Nineties money crunch exempts no one. Since Harvard's founding, U.S. higher education has grown every year, a three-hundred-sixty-year winning streak. Its problems have always been solved by adding programs, adding students, or both. Campuses in the past rarely worried about money. Either they did without, or raised tuitions, or intimated to their richest alumni that a new dorm would be most welcome, or calmly demanded more tax dollars on the grounds that investing in higher education kept America a force on the world stage.

Mostly, campuses used to go their own way because nobody cared enough about them; they were sweet, slow, protected backwaters that only a fraction of the nation explored, and their high-minded shabby gentility kept costs (and productivity expectations) low. For thirty years, campuses have played a public game by private rules, but alumni and corporate donors are less awed by the campus than they used to be, and (faced with professors who expect free state-of-the-art computers, or students who can't write an error-free letter) much less indulgent. Market saturation is on everyone's mind; one college graduate in five now works in a job that does not require a college degree. A third of Domino's pizza-delivery drivers in the Washington, D.C., area have B.A.s. A recent warehouse-supervisor job ad for The Gap is all too clear: "Bachelor's degree required, and the ability to lift fifty pounds."

Academic administrators everywhere talk fearfully of benchmarking, downsizing, outsourcing, re-engineering, centrality to mission, doing more with less. They know campus autonomy is under sporadic, uncoordinated but continuing attack, less from the public and the media than from government, and from families already on the educational conveyer belt, not happy to find campus services cut and prices raised. Wary fathers turn up unannounced to sit at the back of classrooms, taking fierce detailed notes; students sue over grades of B, claiming loss of future earning power. At the University of Illinois, parents recently sued over the size of an introductory economics class; an enrollment of 1,349, they argued, was not the intimate caring education advertised in the brochures.

You say costs are too high, campuses protest. But we have two big fixed costs: the physical plant, and the tenured professors. Define your terms. Discuss. Is the price of inputs (faculty salaries, or textbook costs) too high? Or are you really asking, "What has the campus done for me lately?" Is the university not serving up enough dividends to society? Or do you mean to say that tuition, not costs, is too high? When campuses petition Washington or state legislatures for revenue, there is no box on the quadruplicate forms for academe's other question to the world that underwrites it: *Why don't you love us anymore?*

Government officials keep asking simple, patient questions. How likely is it that a student will be graduated from your school in four to six years? How safe is this campus? Can a student in a wheelchair get to class? Intrusive and burdensome, administrations retort. You want us to act like everyone else, with an operating manual and five-year plan. We barely know who's on campus: at a large state university of thirty-five or forty thousand students, 10 percent of enrollees may be transfers from up to five hundred other schools. Besides, American campus governance resembles Thousand Island dressing—bits of authority in a fluid medium without precise boundaries, chaotically distributed.

Forty-three states are working for expanded oversight of higher education: they want to talk teaching loads, accreditation, exit tests, faculty quality. Congress has formally requested the General Accounting Office to begin hearings on the cost of college, public and private. Worried about collegiate tax abuse, the IRS has begun auditing higher education much more closely, sending teams onto campus to investigate income from bookstore operations, special credit cards often issued to alumni, tax-exempt campus bonds, technology-transfer revenues, the formidable salaries of many athletic coaches and college presidents. All are legitimate concerns: since 1994, observes a recent College Board study, American campuses are spending more on ads, public relations, and fund-raising than on teaching, libraries, and financial aid.

During the Civil War the College of Charleston was shelled by Northern forces but treated well in Reconstruction, since one of its presidents had been a Unionist. The great Charleston earthquake of 1886 damaged the campus severely, 1989's Hurricane Hugo only slightly. Many of its hundred buildings are historic homes refurbished; students scribble notes on African Poets or Marketing in French in graceful rooms the colors of Easter eggs, custard, peach, forsythia yellow, palest green.

A local essayist claims that Charleston is a city not restored but preserved, like figs. So is the college atmosphere, up to a point. Some courses use interactive video and Internet, but the 8:00 A.M. class lives on, too. The Latin and classical Greek requirement survived until the mid-Seventies. The college still requires math and hard science, and strains to keep the student/instructor ratio at eighteen to one. Everyone teaches here, administrators, too; as at nearly all small and mid-size campuses, the faculty has no research-only members. The largest departmental major is English. Recruiting internationals helps the balance sheets, but the school scrambles, always, for market share. Furman and Wofford will draw the state's best students; the Citadel is old and famous; Clemson and the University of South Carolina both vast and rich. The College of

Charleston charges less tuition than the competition, but gets less money from the legislature. It pushes liberal arts, and family feeling.

"We have some of the only residence halls in America with rules," says Sanders, dialing his attorney daughter in Columbia to ask for a phone number. "No overnights allowed. Men surrender a driver's license at the desk when visiting women's housing. Zero tolerance for drugs or drinking in dorms. I just threw five boys out of campus housing for having pot and beer in their rooms."

He lowers himself onto a sofa, brooding on management strategies. If campuses are perpetual feasts, this one is not a smorgasbord or a four-star enclave but a grandma's table, where you eat what's served.

"The best thing about the College of Charleston is the family atmosphere. The worst is the bad boys. Academic studies fall somewhere in between. It's highly illegal, but we engage in paternalism without ever admitting it, mostly by calling in wild partiers for stern talkings-to. These are nice kids, by and large, though not that many meditate extensively on the meaning of life. Instead they bring me cookies, and problems: boyfriend-girlfriend, financial stresses. They look like central casting. Their parents look like central casting. Every fall, Ozzie and Harriet bring their freshman down here, buy the notebook paper, hang the posters, hug all around, go home and *immediately* get divorced. The kid lands in my lap, a total wreck."

Out the door to a bank-board meeting, but slowly; in the ten yards to his car, Sanders hand-pumps six people, waves to the undergraduate daughter of Strom Thurmond, demands an update on calculus class from a passing sophomore, then detours to embrace three black food-service ladies as they chat on break in the humid hazy noonday sun under the oleander. ("Remember me, Judge?" "Now, now, how could I forget

you, of all people?") Two faculty pass us; one gives Sanders a
companionable grin, the other a correct unsmiling nod. Behind Randolph Hall, a gold Infiniti waits in the drive; we head
downtown at considerable speed. He likes the car very much.

"It's apparently an old South Carolina tradition to give college presidents a new car. They asked what I wanted; I said,
'Whatever costs more than what the president of the University of South Carolina has.'"

We tear down Broad Street past the Four Corners of Law
and the Cotton Exchange, the square thick-walled buildings,
trimmed in white, washed in citrus colors, reminding me that
Charleston is the Caribbean's north end. Sanders vanishes into
the First Bank of Charleston—"This'll take, oh, say, around
half an hour, maybe"—and is out again thirty minutes and
nine seconds later, making tracks for the Infiniti. Before the
twelve-thirty student-leader luncheon back on campus, he
must visit a golf tournament on the far edge of town, to cheer
on the school team.

"They asked for me," he explains. "I can't not go." We zip
around the Battery, past the restored town houses of Rainbow
Row, past the low hazy shape of Fort Sumter, then soar over
the skyway bridge west of Sullivan's Island, heading north.

I ask if he likes being a college president. "Harmless fun,"
he declares. "Harmless fun! I didn't quite expect it would be a
seven-day-a-week job. Nights, too: my calendar for last fall
claims I was out at some event or function sixty-three evenings
in a row. But with Mortimer Adler one day, an astronaut the
next."

Yes, he says, he is naturally extroverted. Yes, the faculty is
collegial. Actually, the 330 full-time instructors are collegial
with one another, not necessarily with their unpredictable,
parable-addicted leader. The younger people are very grateful
for him; some senior professors pointedly reserve judgment.
Sanders has a self-admitted reputation in South Carolina as a

flaming leftist liberal. ("Doesn't take much," he points out.) At thirty-four he campaigned for lieutenant governor on the Greyhound bus ("a real children's crusade"). As a college president, he tries to keep the students heavily involved in campus life, the alumni calm, and the faculty hopping.

"I make them do *advising*," he says with satisfaction as the car speeds past low groves of sand pines, shacks painted turquoise and pink, and roadside booths where black women sell baskets of coiled seagrass, woven in patterns as old as the seventeenth century, old as the oldest examples from West Africa.

"Our students, not unnaturally, want help with choosing courses. That's why we have the catalogue, faculty say. I tell them no, it should be more like going to Circuit City. The people who work there aren't called salespersons anymore, they're called advisors. They'll compare televisions and refrigerators till you're blue in the face. Going to college now is like walking into Circuit City, ready to spend $100,000. Should we say to these kids, 'Look in the catalogue, dummy'? You tell me."

Sanders trots up the wide country-club stairs and plunges straightaway into the air-conditioned dimness of a private dining room. He rounds the table, shaking hands, joking, complimenting, congratulating, remembering all the names, and then we are out again into the bright hot parking lot, running for the car, with twelve minutes to make the seventeen-minute drive back to campus.

"This is politics," I say, breathless.

"Of course it's politics! A third of our budget is state money, a third is student tuition and fees. We hustle for the last third. Technically, we're a state school, which translates to a state-assisted school. If the legislature gives us any less money, I tell them we'll be a state-*authorized* school. I'm out here cheering on the golf team because their coach is away in Columbia, performing his other function. He is our sole and very part-time lobbyist. The state's other campuses maintain *suites* and *regiments* of full-time lobbying professionals. Our guy gets a roll of quarters."

———————

The principal sources of campus support are tuition and fees, state and federal money (chiefly in research support and student aid), corporate support, gifts, and endowments, which are growing, but not as fast as programs and budgets. The endowment pool for U.S. higher education is over $100 billion, more than the gross national product of Belgium, but over 60 percent is firmly in the hands of the top fifty schools, and returns for all can swing from 4 percent one year to 15 percent the next. Money anxiety has tempted many schools into esoteric investment: leveraged buyouts, oil and gas, foreign currency, hedge funds, emerging markets like Brazil or Ukraine, nightclubs (Harvard put $10 million into the café chain House of Blues), Ponzi schemes, creative offers. Michigan State sells trading cards of famous economists. Michigan Tech has issued a gift catalogue organized by departmental wish list, from four-wheel-drive vehicles to computer monitors. Donate to the Texas A&M veterinary school $25,000 (if you own a cat or dog) or $50,000 (for a horse or llama), and after your death your pet will live stress-free at the campus Companion Animal Lifecare Center.

Development offices pull grants and gifts onto campus. They divide the work by source: corporate and foundation relations, annual giving (unrestricted giving by alumni, parents, and friends of the school) and capital giving, earmarked for physical plant and ongoing programs. Planned giving accepts largesse that is neither cash nor check, like real estate, fine art, trusts, or stocks. Offices of major or principal gifts concentrate on donors able to give over a million dollars (or over $5 million, at the richer schools). Development staffers learn to push the charitable remainder trust, the lead trust, the gift annuity, the gift of remainder interest in house or farm, the pooled income fund. In-kind bequests are less popular: when a will is read, a campus may suddenly acquire wheat fields in Washington State, office buildings in downtown Washington, D.C., cracked glassware, railroad cars, old church pews. NYU used to own a pasta factory, Loyola University in New Orleans a commercial television station, Augustana College of Sioux Falls, South Dakota, a bank. Vanderbilt University once spent weeks soliciting Winthrop Rockefeller for a major gift, so he gave them a herd of rare cattle, who ate their worth in feed and grain in the time it took to find a buyer. Some campuses hold discreet garage sales, shedding the boxes of mildewed books proudly donated by alumni to the library; others, like Utah, may give surplus volumes to campuses in Russia or Thailand. Sponsorship plaques adorn campus surgical suites, museum bathrooms, experimental flumes, garden benches, schools of music, swimming lanes, and fullbacks—USC's football team has sixteen named and endowed positions. (Endowing a Harvard research professorship takes $2 million now, though $600,000 nicely established the Burt Reynolds Chair of Dramatic Arts at Florida State.)

Few administrators care to discuss campus offices of development research. To sit in someone's living room and say "Give!" takes extremely thorough briefing. Dartmouth and Berkeley reportedly keep investigators on staff to track alumni fortunes; at a Yale, a Stanford, a Michigan, researchers may create detailed financial files on almost every graduate, with elaborate codings and rankings of giving potential. College giving operations have used many sources to estimate alumni income: classmate gossip, registrations, credit banks, ZIP code analyses, college financial aid statements, property assessments, divorce proceedings.

Alumni have begun to return the fiscal scrutiny. Gratitude and its cousins—sentiment, duty, the yen to see one's name on a very large fieldhouse—pay many bills in American higher education. Alumni donations run to $3 billion a year. Since private giving now accounts for nearly a third of some college budgets, the dance of donor and fund-raiser can decide a school's survival. Alumni are a deep pool of unpaid labor. (Princeton alone uses 8,000 alumni volunteers a year to run fund drives or pre-interview applicants). Some alums would also like to be a policymaking force. They scrutinize their old schools with proprietary care. On right and left, alumni-power movements try to buy campus change: more scholarships for gays or Koreans, more curfews and housemothers. The largest and loudest pressure group is the National Alumni Forum, led by former National Endowment for the Humanities head Lynne Cheney. The conservative NAF urges graduates to withhold funds from programs they dislike, agitate against administrators who resist alumni advice, reward schools with checks when they allow alumni to elect trustees—behavior modification by checkbook, exhilarating for graduates with money, worrying and frustrating for those without.

Alex Sanders hurries into a pillared boardroom, forty minutes late. All down two long tables laid with damask and silver, undergraduate leaders from the junior and senior classes look up from fried chicken, green beans, and iced tea to murmur greetings, three dozen attentive, pleasant faces.

At the College of Charleston, student protest means asking the administration for permission to plant a tree in memory of

Jerry Garcia. Today's reports on club activities are uniformly peppy: We had so much fun! Such a good time! We challenge you all to join with us in making next year even more of a success! A dark-skinned sorority president carefully straightens her special locket, a happy face embroidered over the African colors of black, red, and green, then rises to report on the newest pledges and their fund-raising plans. The Japan Club has held a terrific sushi party; the service club a darling Senior Prom for a local nursing home, complete with DJ and dancing. Phys Ed/Health majors yield to the college video newsmagazine, the entrepreneurs' club, the Fellowship of Christian Athletes, the student choir, the black arts and culture festival committee. A strapping student-body president tries to announce the senior class gift, a bronze cougar statue, but halfway through breaks down ("I guess I just want you to know, President Sanders, that this place has been a *true, true* alma mater to us all").

Sanders tells them sonorously that they reflect great credit on their generation, and on America. He thanks them again for the turnout at the KKK cleanup. "Someday, when your children ask you, 'What was the Ku Klux Klan?' you must tell them that you, yes, you, had a hand in wiping it out forever." The white students beam, misty-eyed. "Riiiight," says a black undergrad, through her best polite smile.

After lunch, students dart about the wide, columned hallway, exchanging summer addresses, preparing for life as alumni. "This school does not have, shall we say, the best reputation in the black community," the school's sole admitted radical tells me, levelly. "With this president, though—maybe. Maybe." "What do you think of President Sanders?" I ask a passing sorority head. "He's just so sweet!" she cries. A male athlete: "No comment." A female fund-drive organizer: "Like pouring ginger ale in warm orange juice."

The man himself, running on a few snatched bites of fried chicken and a half-gulped Pepsi, slips back across the hall to deal with student-appointment backlog. First in is a six-four weight lifter applying to med school; Sanders is hoping to get her into the region's Rhodes Scholar finals. Next, a distraught corporate communications major. Three credits have vanished from her transcript, but she badly wants to walk across the Cistern, as the graduation ritual is called, with her class. Sanders phones the registrar to intercede, leaning back until the big leather chair is nearly horizontal, staring out the window at a campus washed in soft spring light.

"Across the great sweep and scope of human history, sir, do you really think—oh, you do. Hmm. Hmm." The communications major, trying to maintain good posture on the slippery sofa, squeezes her eyes shut, praying. "Oh please please please please." Sanders sweeps her off to see the recalcitrant official. Compromise: she can walk, but must take a makeup course in the interim term called Maymester. A student delegation arrives to invite the president to a picnic. He accepts, gravely; they bound away, and Sanders collapses once more onto the sofa by the fireplace.

I ask him about crime. Two incidents in two weeks. An undergraduate woman was recently raped at two A.M. in an abandoned public housing project; what she was doing there is not yet clear. And just last night a twenty-four-year-old student, walking to his off-campus apartment, was mugged and beaten for twenty dollars. He resisted ("I remembered the pain and hassle of losing my ID card once before") and left the hospital this morning with fifty stitches in his slashed throat.

Says Sanders glumly, "I had a hard time getting used to the statistical fact that you can't protect them every minute. Over a year, inevitably, some get AIDS. Some just go bad on you. Some die. It's like having ten thousand children."

For the first time all day, Sanders looks tired and aging. The light has left the long windows. He sits in dimness and silence, then says heavily, "Let's go see those TV people." A half-step before Randolph Hall's main door, his shoulders lift and straighten, his head goes up, and he strides, smiling, toward a waiting crew from Georgia public television.

"I'm a grad," says the lighting person, shifting the big reflector he carries to offer a handshake. Sanders seizes his whole arm, claps him on the back.

"When? When?"

"'Ninety-one. And now look at me. My own piece of Styrofoam."

"Rolling," says the camera man. Sanders begins his standup. "Charleston is one of the great cities of the Western world, and the College of Charleston its crown jewel. As George Santayana once said—"

Cut. The sea wind is flapping his tie.

"Charleston is one of the—"

A plane goes over campus, low. Waiting for mike adjustments, Sanders gazes across the college green, where a dozen undergrads trade sandwiches, skateboard, kick hackysacks, or play blues guitar in afternoon sun. Beyond the central archway of the Porter's Lodge, with its chaste Greek inscription "Gnothi Saunton" (Know Thyself), a horse-drawn carriage clops slowly past. "The plaster of the earliest campus buildings was originally mixed with oxblood," drones the guide, "which gives this ancient and lovely architecture a characteristic rose-pink tone." Tourists in Hawaiian shirts lean out perilously to see.

Rolling. "I remember Charleston when I was a boy, the tumbledown houses by the harbor, the raw sewage on Broad Street," says Sanders, smiling into the lens. "This town took on a siege mentality after the Civil War. It turned away from the world. When an unfortunate whale entered the harbor by mistake at the turn of the century, Charlestonians went out in small boats and beat it to death. The skeleton hung for years right here on the college administration building, a metaphor for how Charleston treated visitors. Today the walls have fallen as they are falling all over the world. This college is the essence, the focal center, the crown jewel of a Charleston so cosmopolitan that to visit is a cheap trip to Europe. Come see us on campus, look around when you do at our vibrant young people, right out of central casting, deeply moral, for they are what make America great."

Freed of mikes and wires, he turns back toward his office, and manages ten steps.

"President *Saaaan*ders, I have a little legal problem—"

An earnest sophomore is at his elbow, flipping her long hair nervously. "My realtor says I can't move in because the people who had the apartment before me had a really big party and trashed the place so he's not going to let them out of their lease early like he said and so I thought that since you were a judge—"

Sanders holds up both hands to stop the flow. "Your realtor is a grad. I'll call him, then I'll call you. Promise never ever to have a party on the premises? Gonna be the world's neatest, nicest, quietest tenant?" A breathless nod.

"I'm a full-service president," says Sanders, dialing his office phone. "Yes? Yes? Alex Sanders here. I have a beautiful student, a fine leader of campus, with a tiny problem, and I'll give an honorary Ph.D. plus help on that antipartying ordinance if you solve this one—"

By the time he leaves a congratulatory message on the sophomore's voicemail a short, confident boy is shifting his weight on the neoclassical doorsill, wanting the judge to ask the mayor to ask the city council to close a street for a graduation bash. Sanders mock-scowls. "If he's recovered from last year's try at this—Maybe. Maybe. We'll see."

It's 4:00 P.M., time to go hear philosophy majors read their final papers, with lemonade and cookies to follow. The seminar room is modern, hot and airless; outside its sealed windows, live oaks toss in a fresh wind. As Sanders tiptoes in, one senior has just finished a presentation on feminism. Another, named Chris, advances to the podium, resplendent in a yellow power tie; he approves of Hume, Darwin, and E. O. Wilson, and sees no discontinuity between Kant and evolutionary ethics. Sliding assessing glances at Sanders, the faculty severely cross-examine. Is the circulation of the blood moral, then? Can you call behavior ethical if it is indeed naturally determined? Intrigued, the president joins in.

"Chris, would you accept that humans are more or less disposed to moral behavior? That a conscious commitment to moral behavior is as water to the flower?" Sweating but poised, Chris concedes that such conclusions would not excessively violate or contradict his thesis, and receives a patter of academic applause as he threads the desks back to his seat, glowing with relief.

———————

The College of Charleston provides its students with an increasingly rare undergraduate experience: the ad-free campus. Sanders will sell signage space in the gym ("I figure that's a lost cause anyway") but refuses to grant campus pouring rights to Coke or Pepsi. Penn State's provost may point to "our unseemly interest in revenue" as the main reason higher education is losing national respect, but even in his fourteen-campus system, Pepsi reigns. For enforcing one-product vending and advertising in sports arena and dining hall, Penn State will net $14 million in ten years. After state funding and tuition, PepsiCo will be its third-largest cash source.

Other schools also deliver captive audiences to the soft-drink industry. Coke has the edge, recently corralling Ohio State, Indiana, Texas A&M, and, in a $10 million deal, Rutgers. Coke campuses may sell only Nestea, Sprite, Fruitopia, and Minute Maid; the football team must douse coaches with Powerade, never Gatorade. Some faculty and alums hyperventilate. How can schools teach market capitalism yet permit monopolies? What if a liquor company made such huge offers to cash-strapped schools? But others point to one-product institutions like Emory (its endowment indexed to Coca-Cola stock) and Duke (founded and funded with tobacco profits); like churches, campuses have laundered questionable money for centuries.

But covertly, and claiming disinterested use. For undergraduates, the college campus was once a detox zone, sealed and self-sufficient, the world well lost. One enduring task of the college years has always been to wean students from the dominant culture—ecclesiastic, imperial, industrial, parental, commercial—then arm them to conquer, question or avoid it, as they chose; to be masters, not victims or tools. But for the inoculation to take, the babble of sponsored experience had to be kept at bay.

Campuses used to be colonizers—of landscapes, of student minds. Now campuses are the colonized. From Taco Bell to HBO, the consumer world follows millions of college students into gym, dining hall, activities center, classroom. Academe angrily debates arming campus police, but commercial intrusion receives mostly shrugs; now nearly all borders are permeable, all proprieties revisable. College students represent a $428 billion annual market in fast food, CDs, movie and concert tickets, sports equipment, clothes, cars. Many schools sell student lists to direct marketers for extra cash (though Middlebury fought in court to keep its directory private, even as it fought townspeople and faculty over the sale of college land for shopping-mall development). Salespeople on campus can be very persistent. A Notre Dame official found one vendor in the university chapel hawking coffee mugs, most credit cards accepted. More than 50 percent of college students have at least one charge card. Their annual income averages $4,000; their average card debt, $2,000, at interest rates of up to 19 percent. Credit-card counselor is one of the few campus jobs where openings abound; another is Residency Rambo, the staffer who checks student in-state eligibility.

Outsourcing campus services has become common and, administrators plead, necessary. Why keep a feudal army of custodians to shovel snow when a commercial service will do it better and faster? Do we really need to keep a master printer on staff, producing flawless concert posters one at a time on a shining brass 1910 Chandler & Price press, when a perfectly good Kinko's is right across the street? When Stanford's general counsel cut his staff by more than half and went to outside law firms instead, the university saved nearly $800,000. Marriott will service dorms and lunch line, Barnes and Noble gladly run the campus bookstore (they already manage three hundred, including the venerable Harvard Coop and the superstore at Penn). Pizza Hut has 114 on-campus franchises now, with Dunkin Donuts and Subway close behind. Faculty can be privatized as well. Few eyebrows arch at today's endowed-chair titles: the Mitsubishi Professor of Finance and the Toyota Professor of Materials Science at MIT, the Federal Express Professor of Excellence in Communications Technology at the University of Memphis, the Burger King Chair in American Enterprise at the University of Miami, the Sears Roebuck professorship in economics at the University of Chicago.

American higher education is now a mature industry, and an unstable one, its products and resources unevenly spread.

Private colleges still cluster in the East. California has 1,745,000 college students, Wyoming 30,000. Washington, D.C., New York City, and the upper Midwest have the most bachelor's degrees per capita (there are 800,000 college grads in New York City alone) and Florida has the least. Consumer restlessness has brought more open procedures to campus, more accountability, more choice. But it also obscures the ceaseless argument over the real point of a campus. Is it human development? Job training? Neither? Both?

In white papers, keynotes, and fund-drive kickoff speeches, campus executives try to sell new visions of the American campus. Like all college presidents, Alex Sanders has favorite lines he uses whenever he can: Tuition is the fastest-growing special tax in America. Global ties are a key to campus survival. Tranquillity is the hallmark of a great country club, not a great college. There is so much we do not know, pleads Charles Vest, the president of MIT: we still have no idea how to predict earthquakes, or use the sun's energy; where antimatter comes from, or why national economies grow; how our species learns and remembers; how cancer or viruses work; how old the universe is, what it is made of, what its fate will be. Surely, surely, this is reason enough to justify investing in the campus way.

In seven centuries, academe has confronted only three completely new ideas: letting in women, letting in computing, and allowing overt commercialism to seep onto campus. But commerce can mean global entrepreneurship, or it can mean yard sales and markdowns. The Eighties race to corner prestige lured too many schools into what ecologists call the too-much mistake: they overdeveloped, overpopulated, maxed out the credit card, ate the seed corn, invested in the academic equivalent of junk bonds, exceeded the system's carrying capacity. Between 1945 and 1987, hundreds of lackluster institutions vowed to be magnificent full-service universities; for a while, running on deficit spending and all-American nerve, some almost made it, crowding toward a fading revenue sun like seedlings in a forest of old tall trees.

Sustaining the calm, prosperous façade gets tougher each year. "You must not let in daylight upon mystery," said Walter Bagehot of the British royal family over a century ago; U.S. colleges and universities, last repositories of imperial habits on New World soil, instinctively agree. Who gets to come onto campus, and what they study there, have been recently democratized, but except for undergrad admissions and the undergrad course catalogue the root attitudes of the American campus, even a big state school, are still medieval, ecclesiastic, aristocratic, an extinct European world preserved in administrative routines and academic mind-sets like fossils set in stone.

Perhaps it is not such a bad thing (some administrators quietly say) to turn the student world commercial, the faculty cosmos entrepreneurial, and the administrative universe corporate, to let markets shape student life, faculty time, and administrative style. Romantic inefficiency pays few spin doctors, and fewer leveraged-buyout experts. Let the line blur between public and private spheres: that's where the intellectual action is, the lab findings that can be marketed, and the students, too. The president of New York City's Queens College frankly says his school should train its undergrads to fill the hiring needs of the private corporations that make campus donations. Faculty gasp, administrators look thoughtful. Both know that the campus teaches by example: how it treats the people within its walls, chooses its students, treats its faculty, deploys its money. Higher education is a product sold in a trust market, but two shoes have yet to drop, warns Gordon Winston, former provost of Williams College: deceptive accounting practices that can erase or create a budget deficit in an instant, and fast financial games played with citizen money, as colleges perfect interest arbitrage, sell tax-exempt bonds, and transfer millions from taxpayer funds to already-rich schools.

Exploiting student athletes is an even faster road to maximizing revenue. The nation's colleges generate $2.5 billion annually in retail sales of products bearing campus or team names, logos or mascots, outearning similar efforts by pro hockey and pro baseball—T-shirts, cologne, sunglasses, debit cards, and (for Michigan, Harvard, Notre Dame, and Penn State) novelty underwear. The University of North Carolina–Chapel Hill just signed a four-year, $4.9 million marketing agreement with Nike; the next step, some coaches worry, might be frankly corporate-sponsored teams, the Michigan Nikes, the USC Reeboks. Some institutions do take care to educate players for post-athletic careers. Duke, Holy Cross, Stanford, Colgate, Georgetown, Yale, Boston College: all have both high student-athlete graduation rates and winning seasons. Some campuses use and discard student players: at UCLA, 77 percent of all entering undergrads finish the degree, but only half the student athletes do. At Texas Southern, Texas Pan-American, Chicago State, Delaware State, even fewer athletes complete degrees.

Other campuses turn venture capitalist, backing in-house technologies and identifying faculty who can be groomed as entrepreneurs, a series of difficult calls. When a former $6.85-an-hour student programmer offered the University of Illinois fifty thousand shares in his new company, the university refused. The junior employee was Marc Andreessen, the product Netscape. But corporate research investment in universities is becoming very selective; the campus world is often not fast enough, or obedient enough, for business standards.

Yes, perhaps the definition of nonprofit should be rethought, administrators murmur, and with it the ancient academic squeamishness about being in trade. Do we admit limits to

growth, and to obligation? Or merely adopt a sprightlier letterhead, a more eye-catching seal? Deans, presidents, vice
presidents hesitate, agonize, form study committees. It is still a
very long way from the radical severity of Harvard's Puritan
"Veritas" to Hofstra's ads boasting "We Teach Success" or the
University of Northern Colorado's latest motto, "Quality, Diversity, Personal Touch."

———————◆———————

The roll of dead American campuses grows each year, little
noticed, little mourned: St. Joseph's College in California, the
University of Mid-America in Nebraska, Jordan College in
Michigan, Marycrest College in Illinois, Upsala College in New
Jersey, Nashville College in Tennessee, Griffin College in Washington State. Developers convert some into drug-rehab centers
or magnet schools; supermarket chains and parks departments
eye others. Academic history is powerfully local. Schools do
very little comparing of experience, or sharing of solutions;
each tower remains solitary. But even in distress, the campus
retains a few strong core myths. Faculty are unworldly. Students come for the coursework. Alumni are dumb but fantastically rich. Administrations know best. Campuses are very
good at being fortified enclaves, and at ignoring elephants
in the living room, very bad at explaining themselves to
strangers, worst of all at endings. The world of higher education has "a marvelous sense of fertilization," observes Jonathan
Cole, Columbia's provost. "We are experts at gestation and
early development, we know about maturation and expansion,
but we refuse to confront dying and death."

How might higher education best adapt, and best survive?
Students often propose recycling to lower costs; even a
medium-size campus of 10,000 may annually generate thou-

sands of pounds of hazardous waste, spend $6 or 7 million on utilities, and use a million sheets of copier paper. Faculty, administrators, politicians, and presidents emeritae (free at last to speak their minds) brim with ideas for change as well. A twelve-month college year. A Grade 13 year, Canadian-style, between high school and college. Better technical institutes and sophisticated trade schools, in the German manner. Reforming American K-12 education, for real; about half the first-years at California state campuses now take remedial courses. Enforcing equitable distribution of workloads by requiring all senior faculty to teach one undergrad course a year, and advise six actual students. Sending all eighteen- and nineteen-year-olds into a two-year national service program, so they come to college at twenty or twenty-one more focused and determined, like the first GI Bill students. Discouraging those who linger on campus by charging them higher fees. Making fourteen years of schooling the national standard. Reducing the number of required courses. Offering students a choice: the fully loaded college experience, or the no-frills version—schooling and basic lodging only—at much lower cost. More course credit by examination, substituting demonstrated competence in French or calculus for mandatory seat time. Declaring a major in the first year. Dropping majors altogether and teaching genuinely useful material instead: how the economy works, how to live in a democracy, how to deal with a lawsuit, or write a will. Working a full week, like everyone else.

Customer incentives help. Emory, Carnegie Mellon, Villanova, and Johns Hopkins use scholastic merit awards as aggressive recruiting tools. At some schools, twins may attend for the price of one; at Stevens and at Clark, any student can buy four years of college and—if grades stay high—get a fifth year free. Susquehanna and Clarkson are promoting a four-year degree at a three-year price; the University of Rochester awards

$5,000 to all New York State residents enrolling as freshmen. Michigan State, trying not to price higher education out of the average Michigan family's reach, guarantees its tuition won't rise faster than inflation. Georgia uses state lottery money to pay state college tuitions (though not room and board) for every student resident with a B average. At least thirteen states now have proposed or authorized prepaid tuitions, which allow students to fund college in advance, rather than pay off high-interest loans after the college years; the day the Texas tuition-fund office opened, it received four thousand calls from families anxious to join.

The American campus cornucopia means waste as well as choice. Too many schools invest in complex computing systems, then fire all the support staff as a cost-saving measure. Academic freedom often leads to academic overlap, as when three different departments simultaneously offer courses in feminism and technology, none aware the others existed, none willing to co-teach, reschedule, or cancel. "I often feel like I am president of Noah's Ark, with two of everything," says Gordon Gee, head of Ohio State. Intellectual consolidation, like restructuring, means awkward questions: Does the University of Kansas truly need an Institute of Haitian Studies? Why do two hundred campuses maintain varsity bowling teams? Downsizing higher education is even harder than welfare reform. In 1950, public universities spent twenty-seven cents of every campus dollar on administration; in 1988, forty-five cents. Nationally, in the 1980s, faculties grew by 6 percent, administrations by 45 percent. Not all campus officials are like Alex Sanders, hardworking and sociable. Downsize management, faculty tartly suggest, or else hire adjunct administrators—and remember that learning and efficiency aren't always the same.

Oberlin's former president S. Frederick Starr, like Stanford president Gerhard Casper, advocates a three-year bachelor's degree. Seventy-five percent of high school seniors endorse the idea, up from 42 percent in 1983. A three-year degree would create more alumni, and more potential donors; it also reduces the price of a Harvard B.A. from about $120,000 to about $85,000, a Penn State B.A. from $40,000 to about $20,000. Cal State's chancellor is all for three-years-and-out; he expects 700,000 more students before 2000, with no new financial support from California's legislature. To Arnold Weber, Northwestern's former president, campuses have a quasi-moral obligation to restrain price increases. Unlike profit-maximizing private corporations, he argues, campuses are tax-exempt; it's not fair to charge all the market will bear. But Vartan Gregorian of Brown thinks poor high school preparation makes a five-year B.A. the more honest solution. "If students [had already] received rigorous instruction in algebra, history, and the sciences, we might be able to consider the three-year degree. But they don't. We're trying to repair damage as well as further knowledge."

A conservative movement, determined, well-funded, would like to return the campus to 1960. Strip it down, they say. Fire all the hand-holders. No more special recovery housing for student heroin addicts, no more transgender coordinators, no gourmet wok stations in the cafeteria. A professor, a blackboard, and serious students are all any school needs. Educational conservatives think strategically: What campuses are ours? What foundations? Who can we surround, weaken, harry, topple? Organizations like the National Association of Scholars, which worked to end affirmative action on California campuses, or the Madison Center and the Intercollegiate Studies Institute, which support conservative student publications, or the District of Columbia's Center for Individual Rights, which spearheaded a crucial freedom-of-religion case at the University of Virginia, all receive money from some of the nation's largest conservative foundations: Bradley, Coors,

Olin, Scaife, Joyce, Smith Richardson. The same funds often support a growing counterworld of defiantly traditional campuses, some Christian, some explicitly conservative, many opposed to government aid, or scrutiny by accrediting groups, or both—Adelphi, Stetson, Hillsdale, southern Utah's George Wythe College, Jacksonville's Coral Ridge Baptist University. Yet some studies supported by such funding do suggest larger implications: a recent study of selective schools, conducted by the conservative National Association of Scholars, found that the number of class days during the regular academic year had steadily fallen, from 204 in 1914 to 191 in 1964 to 156 in 1993.

Another vision of higher education's future is the dissolving campus. What telemarketing and phone banks did for catalogue sales, QVC for home shopping, and ATMs for banking, some industry analysts claim, the Internet is about to do for distance learning. Arthur Levine, head of Columbia's Teachers College, even predicts that small residential colleges and research universities may be the only higher-ed institutions in business by 2050, the former because some parents will insist on sending their children away to school, the latter to groom aspiring researchers. If these vestigial campuses serve born scholars, the incurably social, and remedial cases, everything else will be in-home delivery of asynchronous learning, college education by modem. Older learners are the future market that higher education most covets, and they don't need to go to campus to grow up. Rather, they want tailored learning, a retooled brain. Distance education is hardly new: the Chautauqua movement blended traveling lectures and vaudeville acts with a program of home study in the 1870s; extension courses (and, in England, external degrees) are nearly as old. From armed-services courses to Sunrise Semester, working adults have long found off-campus learning practical, if not terribly picturesque.

Now it is profitable. The nation's twelfth-largest private university is the University of Phoenix. Its eighteen thousand students make it larger than Stanford, larger than Notre Dame. Founded and accredited over loud protests from Arizona State and the University of Arizona, UP has awarded sixty thousand undergraduate and M.B.A. degrees since 1980. The University of Phoenix has no dorms, frats, activities, library, or football team, only a toll-free research-desk number, and no campus either: classes meet in leased spaces only, office buildings, military bases, motels. Its twenty-one hundred instructors are all nontenured, receive no benefits, have no office hours (or offices), and receive $1,000 to $1,200 per course. Its on-line program, based in San Francisco, serves over a thousand students from forty-one states plus China, Belize, and Siberia. These undergrads never see their professors, and meet one another only when they fly to California for graduation. At a recent degree ceremony, Al Gore typed his congratulations via the Internet; CompuServe's vice president of future technology delivered the commencement address. The University of Phoenix is the nation's first viable for-profit university. Enrollments are soaring. So is its stock.

Another future beckons, too: the American campus as corporate accessory. George Mason University in Fairfax, Virginia, looks like a research park. The academic buildings on its main and branch campuses are named not Memorial Hall or Old Main but Module I, Node II, Unit III. GMU's newest, largest structure is listed on campus maps as The University Learning Center, but architectural critics tend to call it the Mall of Academe, and students simply the Mall. Its six-story atrium (gleaming, antiseptic, as placeless as a Hyatt or Westin hotel) is dotted with fountains, potted plants, frozen yogurt outlets, and fake Victorian streetlights. No unauthorized notices may be posted on its bulletin boards. Security cameras and foot patrols scan every stair and hall. Beside the ground-floor food court a hundred students—all ages, races, genders—wander silently like passengers in an airport terminal, window-shopping the simulated storefronts of the ground-floor perimeter: bank, patisserie, bookstore CD display, infobooth, bank. This is college as the ultimate individual experience: you come alone, sit alone, spend alone, leave alone. Student task groups do crowd the food-court tables, calculators in hand, wading through a course exercise about forming personal-trainer franchises— but with few smiles, little energy, less pleasure. Only when they talk of profits or power do these undergrads come fully alive.

"Shall we break the strategies and goals into paradigms?"

"First we need financial stats on user fitness trends."

"We have our own ideas."

"Worst possible approach. Fold objectives into the modeling plan."

"Go national."

"Go global. Your deliverable is a validation."

"We could make a stunning amount by staying open all weekend."

"What's your expectation of the numbers?"

"Big. Big. Big."

Two male undergraduates in the Taco Bell line are enrolled in college French.

> "She asks us to conjugate the verbs. We sit and stare. Her nerve breaks."
> "I remember. She goes, 'Anyone! *S'il vous plaît!* Anyone!' We gave her total nada, man."

Upstairs, the Mall's reading area has almost no books, but plenty of superterminals. I click on the GMU Web site and read the university goals statement. It is full of misspellings and typeface shifts, but the content is unusually frank. The purpose of this campus is student-oriented customer service. It is an interactive, on-line, entrepreneurial university with Harvard aspirations and a community college orientation, serving northern Virginia, an area where 40 percent of the population has arrived within the last five years. Eighty percent of George Mason undergrads work, 25 percent are from English-as-a-second-language families, 60 percent are transfer students. George Mason is proud of its new Patriot Center arena, a ten-thousand-seat facility programmed to realize nearly $500,000 of net income annually. Today the Patriot Center features Mortal Kombat II: The Live Performance, which is sold out. The mission of George Mason University is "1) economic development; 2) providing corporations with the ambience of serious inquiry."

At the edge of campus I find the old George Mason library, packed with students arguing in whispers about bird migration, oil and gas maps, German-American relations in the 1920s, and left-right handedness in same-sex fraternal twins. Yes, the Masterplots volumes are well-thumbed, and at least one scholar is ardently investigating the relation between deflated basketball diameters and self-esteem in high school sports, but after the sterile silent Mall, a library so crowded that people sit studying on bathroom floors is blessed relief. But they look so old. They *are* old: this lively campus counterculture of the bookish turns out to be chiefly graduate students, junior faculty, working adults serious about the college classes they're taking. Where are the rest of your younger undergrads? I ask a staffer, who rolls her eyes. "They rarely come here. Why should they? A lot of them are not exactly readers."

———————

Seven-thirty P.M. President and Mrs. Sanders pull open a side door to the Johnson Physical Education Center, hurrying to the year-end athletic banquet where six hundred dressed-up undergrads, alumni, coaches, and parents are tucking into shrimp, beaten biscuits, and spice cake. Most bat away maroon and white balloons between forkfuls; the decoration committee believes in patriotic excess. On the athletic-highlights video, the soundtrack fails almost immediately, in an amplified scream of static and feedback. The awards go on and on: Most Valuable In and Out of the Water, Highest Grade-Point Average, Best Student Trainers, Favorite Bus Driver, Fans of the Year, Most Improved Track Member (Female), Most Improved Basketball Player (Male). Sanders sneaks a look at his watch; he would dearly love to get home and see the last episode of "Murder One," but with eleven teams to go, chances are fading. Once on the platform, he keeps it short.

"When my daughter Zoe was three years old, her pet turtle expired. To distract her from desperate grief, I explained that to celebrate the passing of our beloved friend we would have a party, with ice cream and cake and candy and ponies to ride. Just as her tears dried, we looked down at the bathroom floor. Lo and behold, the turtle was waving its fat little legs. 'Do you know what this means?' I whispered tenderly. Zoe nodded. 'No candy,' she said. 'Daddy, *let's kill it.*'" Parents and alumni laugh.

"Well, Zoe didn't understand the principle of unselfish devotion, that much was clear. But all of you do. Remember, the opposite of love is not hate, it is indifference. You are not indifferent. You are all winners, over pain, pride, uncertainty, discontent. Every good athletic team is like a family. The players are the children, the coaches the parents. Together, you make miracles. You are my heroes."

A male athlete sticks a finger down his throat; teammates smother laughter. But adults all over the room are nodding, smiling, rapt. The women's golf team rushes the podium, to have their picture taken with President Sanders. He works a thinning crowd, the smile on cruise control now, the cries of delight a touch automatic, until at 10:40 P.M., grey with fatigue, he finally runs out of hands to shake, and deeds to laud.

"Words matter," he had told me many hours before, when I asked his core philosophy of college administration. "Feelings matter. Why, here in South Carolina"—he was back in storytelling mode—"a tiresome debate rages: does the Confederate flag, which still flies above our state capitol, represent heritage or hate, tolerance or slavery? Debates like that can suck all the oxygen out of a room. Do you know, the other day, as I was leaving the President's House, I saw a co-worker standing on the sidewalk in front of frat row, softly crying. It was Dorothy, one of the custodians who cleans up residence halls at night. Dorothy is a single mother who works at close to minimum wage to support herself and her children. She is cheerful, uncomplaining, and bears her many burdens privately. 'What's the matter?' I said, expecting to hear of financial crisis, or serious illness.

"I was wrong. She pointed at the Confederate flag flying over a fraternity house. She loved the students, she said, she didn't mind at all cleaning up their messes, but the flag made her think they hated her. I went to the house, and said, 'Men, I'm sorry, but I've got to ask you to take down that flag.'" They stiffened visibly. I was in for the diatribe. It's part of our heritage. We have a right. 'Exactly why should we take it down?' the frat president inquired coolly. 'Because it makes Dorothy cry,' I said. I explained my encounter. 'Oh,' said the frat head. 'We didn't mean to make Dorothy cry.' They discussed it that night. The next day the flag came down. Perhaps it will go back up tomorrow or next year or in four years, when all the fraternity boys now at the college have graduated. But for one moment they understood that what matters is not the right to display, but to think of the person to whom you display. They used imagination to let unselfishness prevail. On campus or off, that's the best idea that anyone has ever had."

Sanders maneuvers the Infiniti off the sidewalk beside the college gym, waving to constituents as he drives away. Even in the dark, glimpsed for an instant under a streetlight, he can spot and call them. The kid who came to school with one pair of shoes. The girl who is going to be a social worker. The alumnus who has not missed a College of Charleston basketball game in twenty years.

"Was that true, that Dorothy story?" I ask him. "Or was it one of your parables?"

"True story," he answers, sighing. "All too true." In less than nine hours, he will be back at the mahogany desk in Randolph Hall, to deal with the NCAA accreditation teams, to greet the novelist Anne Rivers Siddons, who is visiting from Atlanta, to handle the aftermath of the throat-slashing, to sit through impassioned student debate over cocktail versus long dresses at the graduation-week formal. The gold car moves slowly toward the President's House, down narrow, dark eighteenth-century streets perfumed with honeysuckle, past silent classrooms and noisy dorms.

SUMMER:
Eternity's Eye

A few summers back I went to Alaska on a Princeton alumni cruise, working my passage as a faculty lecturer. At first the excursion line balked at the client list. They'd never sailed with so many people born before 1910. Don't worry, the alumni office said. Really. At Sitka, seventy-five adventurers went aboard—with multiple sclerosis, with heart disease, in wheelchairs, on borrowed time. They tore through the assigned readings, and demanded more. To inspect icebergs and salmon runs, they inched without complaint into bobbing black-rubber Zodiac rafts, then rose at five to scan for grizzlies and eagles and killer whales till staff naturalists begged for quarter. Many alums still drank like their college selves; the young bartender grew wild-eyed at the requests for Rob Roys and Gibsons, Sazeracs and brandy Manhattans. And during the last day's trivia quiz the alumni threw themselves into competition with a true ferocity that hinted, for just a moment, why their days on Pacific carriers or Wall Street had worked out, on the whole, so very well.

One overcast morning, as the boat threaded past coast ranges

246 | BRIGHT COLLEGE YEARS

and spruce islands, the Princetonians gathered at the prow to dedicate an orange-and-black cruise flag. (One of the wives, who always traveled with a supply of fabric in the school colors, had run it up in her cabin overnight.) Intrigued, the crew gathered, too. A deckhand on indefinite leave from Cal State–Fresno poked me in the back. "What's their motto mean?" he murmured, watching *"Dei sub numine viget"* catch and hold the Arctic wind.

"'Emulated, but never equaled,'" said a retired industrialist, from the depths of his ski jacket. "Or, if you prefer, 'God went to Princeton.'" As all around us humpback whales surfaced, drew breath, and fell away again under the dark water, an Episcopal vestryman from Maryland intoned the Prayer for Princeton:

"O eternal God, endow our university with grace and wisdom. Give inspiration to those who teach, understanding to those who learn, vision to its trustees and administrators, courage and loving service to those who bear her name. Amen."

Many alumni prayed along with him, robustly; they, too, knew the text by heart. The deckhand, shocked, poked me again.

"These people *pray* to their *school?*"

"It's hard to explain," I said.

We docked for dinner at a village called Petersburg. Once its fishermen used glacier ice to keep the halibut catch fresh all the way to Boston; now their children survive by serving tourists Dolly Varden trout and seaweed pickle. The Sons of Norway dining hall boasted a decrepit upright piano. Before dessert was done, the aged Tigers gathered around it, and began to sing. Oh, how they sang: under a deep orange moon, far into the Alaskan summer night, they caroled college music I had believed extinct, songs to the faculty, and songs to the security guards—the proctors—and a song for the president, then chorus on chorus, perfectly harmonized, of "Going Back to Nassau Hall."

Their spouses stood with them, silent. Only Princetonians may sing the college songs. "Definitely first wives," whispered a Smith graduate beside me, reaching for more chocolate cake, watching the tired, straight-backed women smile and smile. "But you can still just see how they all must have looked at Princeton's senior prom, in the spring of 'thirty-nine.'"

If you want to observe this vanishing species in its native habitat, the Ivy League schools in late May or early June are an excellent bet, for that is when such alumni migrate back to their ancestral campuses for the ritual of Reunions. At Oxford, a college reunion is called a Gaudy (a nod to *Antony and Cleopatra:* "Let's have one other gaudy night"). At Cambridge, the gathering of the classes is, unromantically, Alumni Weekend. Most American campuses have adopted the British model, sponsoring five-, ten-, twenty-, or forty-year alumni assemblies. But in the alumni-relations and development-fund world, Princeton graduates are famed as steadfast to the point of mania. Princeton is the world's only school to stage a full-out all-class rendezvous extravaganza every single year. Alumni come to Reunions on stretchers, or in casts. Engineering graduates have sent agonized regrets ("detained out of town on business") from the Skylab space station. Some reunion years are more important than others. A twenty-fifth or a fortieth brings such pressure for bonding that four class members in five may return.

Princeton alumni are not the nation's most financially loyal (52 percent of Dartmouth and Duke graduates write checks each year; Notre Dame, 47 percent; Lehigh, 46 percent; Princeton, 43 percent; Yale, Clark, and Rice, 42 percent; the University of Alabama, 39 percent), but its sixty-five thousand alumni make the pilgrimage back to campus in greater numbers than any other collegiate tribe. Princeton's median class—the midpoint of the long alumni line running back to 1746 and forward to 1996—is the Class of 1970. Since I had been thinking about my own campus summer of 1970, I decided to watch their Twenty-Fifth Reunions proceed.

You never know who anyone is, in the town of Princeton. The kid devouring pizza in front of Woolworth's will soon run a Middle Eastern country. The gaunt man wearing tennies all winter turns out to be a Nobel laureate. Central Princeton is one street and two stoplights, strong on cashmere and china outlets, low on bookshops and bakeries and hardware stores. This is a cautious, sedate, inturning suburb, except in August, when (if car windows are left open) its desperate gardeners toss enormous sacks of zucchini into your back seat, and flee. Princeton has always been a company town. The Continental Congress met briefly at the college, but soon moved to Washington in search of better climate. Gilded Age magnates and their mansions made the village a fresh-air retreat between New York and Philadelphia. By the 1950s, Princeton had a necklace of sod farms and research parks. Now heavy trucks rumble through night and day, hypermalls drain the four-block downtown, and churches run food pantries for area needy—some of them despairing middle managers who can make their house payments, or feed their families, but not both.

Reunions swells the town's population by a third. For three kinetic days and two rowdy nights, ten thousand alumni roam about, trying hard to step in the same river twice. Their wardrobes are a hundred shades of orange: tangerine and marigold, popsicle and peach, rust and bittersweet and the scarlet of blood oranges. Some old grads try to remember names of campus buildings, or to recover, haltingly, the local patois. ("I left my JP at the Woo before taking the dinky to the city.") In the TigerNet tent, hundreds send free E-mail to absent friends. In side-street coffee bars, activist graduates busily print "Slave Owner" over Washington's portrait on all their one-dollar bills. Some alumni hurry to the bookstore and order hand-knotted Tibetan tiger rugs ($600), tiger-face needlepoint kits, tiger-striped earmuffs, or orange-and-black leash and collar sets. ("At last, your dog can have that authentic Princeton look!") Others circle the marble vestibule of eighteenth-century Nassau Hall, searching the rosters of Princeton's service dead for names they know. As is the custom on many campuses, the wars are listed, but not the sides. Union, Confederate, German, Allied: all are alumni in the end.

Princeton taxi drivers love Reunions, none more than the ex-policeman who once went onto campus as an undercover drug agent. ("I had long hair, if you can believe it, and of course I weighed a lot less then.") Now he reminisces with his middle-aged fares about epic busts and confrontations. At the cab-stand crosswalk, two blond '69ers gaze gloomily about. "When we were here, the university was so stuffy and repressive. There were hardly any women, or blacks, or Jews." A small dark woman in a jogging suit turns. "Did you ever consider just transferring to Rutgers?" Both men suddenly look as though they have swallowed a pin, the WASP tic of extreme disapproval. Outside a French restaurant, a student I have not seen since his sophomore year listens to his father rant. "A hundred and thirty thousand goddamn dollars, and he can't even get honors as a goddamn history major!" The son stands rigidly silent, in his eyes old pain, and new rage. A Hispanic alumna from the Seventies, elegant in a beige silk shorts suit, beams at the laughing corporate lawyers somersaulting under Gothic archways. "Drink up, troglodytes," she says, encouragingly. "Twenty more years, boys, and then it's over, women and minorities will overwhelm every campus in America—but this next generation is going to be a dilly." "You think?" I say. She offers a small cool smile.

"I found the Ivy League highly instructive. You can be lunch, or you can turn carnivorous, too. Grudging acceptance is not enough. Not at these prices." All over town, knots of people walk and talk, summoning their pasts. "To me, the characteristic sound of elite higher education will always be people sobbing in the bathrooms," says an Eighties grad, staring up at her old dorm-room window. What else does she remember? Foot-hollowed stone. Magnolias luminous under spring rain. Boys carrying orchid corsages in clear plastic boxes. Mandatory swim tests, so that the cream of American youth could survive any repeat of the *Titanic*. Saturday-night sidewalks littered with Champagne corks. Snowy Sundays in a college common room, firelight warming the brass chandeliers, the heavy Jacobean furniture, the faded Kashmir carpets. Any great classes, or wonderful professors who changed her life? "Maybe. Not really. I was too freaked for security and success to notice."

Three-fourths of the alumni are, of course, not here. Some are unsentimental about their undergraduate years, others repelled by a togetherness so insistent that it has its own local verb form, to reune. This school has always specialized in team players and energetic well-rounded extroverts, with a strong leavening of Southerners, socialites, and engineers. Meditative loners, grouses one self-described meditative loner, "are tolerated, but not fed."

Yet still they come, even the artistes, by train, by bus, by car, by private plane. A professor stands, hands in pockets, watching the crowds, then quotes George Macdonald: "'There are places you can go into, and places you can go out of, but the one place, if you do but find it, where you may go in and out both, is home.'"

In giving-office parlance, Reunions is a long-term development event. To fund-raisers, higher education is a system for breeding loyalists who send nice things: checks, yes, but also dinosaur skeletons for the campus museum, Meissen for the president's house, and clear title to the Montana ranches and Caribbean islands that make such good biological research stations. Converting raw adolescents into institutional stakeholders is never easy; keeping them allied over the years is harder still. Alumni everywhere feel they, ultimately, own a campus, a conviction as disconcerting to command-and-control administrations as the sensation of being dispossessed and superseded can be to graduates who have faithfully donated for decades.

The National Alumni Forum has not penetrated Princeton. It does not need to. When electricity was installed in the college library, in the early 1900s, Princeton alumni mourned for years the loss of gaslight's lovely play on gilded bindings. Many campus trees are labeled with neat ceramic plates (popping off now, because no one remembered trees also grow in diameter). A good number were inaccurate to begin with, but attempts to improve or change brought wails of rage. Old jokes are favored, too: "How many Princetonians does it take to change a lightbulb? Six—one to do the work, five to talk about how good the old lightbulb was." During Reunions, every hour is scheduled: alumni soccer matches, milk-punch brunches, seminars on East Asian telecommunications, all-faith prayer breakfasts. Not repeated is the previous year's open session on What's Wrong with Princeton, What's Right, which featured administrators, faculty, a trustee, and students fielding interrogation from four hundred agitated graduates.

Half our alumni are loyal, the premise ran, the rest disgruntled or disaffected; discuss. The queries flew, frantic with love and abandonment.

"President Dodds always told us, 'Come back as often as you can. This place is yours,'" cried a 1940s alum, referring to a long-gone campus executive. "He who enters a university walks on hallowed ground," called another old grad, "but our faculty spend too much time away. Mencken said professors don't belong in government and industry—they should resume teaching sophomores how to hate their fathers."

"Mencken also thought college football would be much more interesting if the faculty played, instead of the undergrads," a public-policy student beside me said, softly.

How much corporate money are you taking? It's risen rather quickly; about 15 percent of the budget, in fact. What about the moral decadence of the faculty? Next question. This university ruthlessly stresses research over teaching, a Fifties alum declared. Actually, countered a university vice president, the average size of discussion sections is eleven people. Students onstage moaned, made faces, turned thumbs down. "Try sixteen people!" "Eighteen!" "I know someone who had thirty-two."

"I find this discussion thrilling, a real tribute to the spirit of our school," said the v.p. staunchly. "Please remember, part of the campus experience is learning to be creative in taking advantage of its many resources."

"Down with vice presidents!" called a '65 behind me.

"*You're* a vice president," his wife observed.

"Too true." He thought a moment. "Death to improvident administrators!"

But Princeton is not improvident. It is old, patient, knowing, and very, very rich. A Yale political scientist recently argued that six schools will survive in the long run as the cream of American higher education—Harvard, Chicago, Stanford,

Columbia, Duke, and New York University. Princeton does not like such talk. Its endowment is over $4 billion now, more than the GNP of some small nations. The student debating society, Whig-Clio, has begun arguing a new topic: Should Princeton Secede? An enterprising undergraduate calculated that Princeton has enough money to fund itself till 3050, without raising another cent. One of my former students finds this worrying. "*Countries* don't last that long," she told me, pacing restlessly along the short walkway between computer science building and university archives. "The Roman *Empire* didn't last that long. A school should be subject to natural forces, a live growing thing." But (like Harvard, Stanford, Texas, Yale) Princeton means to be immortal.

A last voice at the alumni forum was a woman from the Class of 1980. "Of my twelve female entry mates, eleven went on for graduate work. Twelve of twelve say they would not send their daughters to Princeton. This school wants women only as statistics. It does nothing to prepare them for the inability to have it all."

Other female Princetonians, consulted, thought first in checkbook terms. "My Ivy education meant prestige, and access to power," said a St. Louis executive. "But I also helped bear the emotional and psychological brunt of bringing higher education into the twentieth century. A fair trade, but not one that inspires gratitude."

"I will give," countered a political scientist. "My family is not well-off. Endowed scholarships kept me in school. Good teachers, women and men both, transformed my life. Returning the favor, with interest, seems only right."

That men and women give very differently to colleges is a depth charge higher education never expected. Campus fundraising is largely run by, and structured for, male graduates, and its core assumptions remain pure Jane Austen: male alumni are expected to make money, female graduates to marry it. Development offices have always found women most interesting, fiscally speaking, after widowhood or inheritance gave them donatable goods: stocks and bonds, office buildings, oil wells, decent Manets. For decades, college giving offices tracked every variable but gender. Age, religion, ethnicity, income, marital status yes, sex no.

But by 2002, nearly 60 percent of college students will be women. Female college graduates now control record wealth, particularly asset wealth; they hold as much corporate stock as men, more cash, more real estate, more bonds, far less debt. Nearly twice as many women as men have earned bachelor's degrees since 1960, yet female donations bunch at the bottom and top ends of the giving scale. Women give more of the $10–$250 donations ("nominal gifts," in the language of philanthropy), while more men occupy the crucial mid-range, supplying "major gifts" of five and six figures; at the "ultimate gift" level, women reappear, but not in force.

What, if anything, do women owe an alma mater? In development lore, men are emotional, sentimental, competitive donors. ("What did Bob give? Fine, put me down for twice that.") Women are logical, and picky. Men like to back showy causes; women are more willing to make anonymous gifts, or support undramatic needs like new wiring and handicapped ramps. Men give to preserve, women to change.

"There are two ways to raise funds, irrational and rational," observes a former Bowdoin president. "With male alums you often go out drinking till all hours to extract some whopping donation. I found that morally dubious—and hard on my liver. Women don't respond to rah-rah. They want facts. They want accountability. Administrators can really resent that."

Back in the Sixties, the major objection to coeducation at formerly all-male schools, especially Eastern schools, was financial, not sexual: "They won't give like the men do." (To avoid reducing the absolute number of male alumni, many schools simply enlarged total class size.) Fears of disloyalty live on. In 1987, trustees of the University of North Carolina at Chapel Hill tried to restrict female enrollment on the specific grounds that women graduates are unreliable donors. And so some are: alumni of Catholic women's colleges are the most fiscally loyal, closely followed by graduates of secular single-sex colleges like Wellesley, then, a distant ambivalent third, women from coed schools.

Why don't women give? Why women *won't* give may be the better question. Nearly all American campuses, these days, maintain a room where fifty or a hundred student and faculty volunteers sit and dial, murmuring about money late into the night, heads bent over lists of alumni in Mankato, Bahrain, Vancouver, Bangor, Omaha, Encino. Phone-a-thons are the low-rent, low-tech way to tap alumni; gifts from these cold calls average seventy dollars, and the reasons for turndowns are consistent. Men refuse from resentment:

"I won't give, because my degree hasn't gotten me a good job."

"I'm unhappy with your letting gays into ROTC."

"I don't care if we won the Rose Bowl, I still say the football team is going to hell."

"I hate the ideas you teach now. Clean up your act, and I'll reconsider."

Women, from exhaustion at trying to maintain the balanced life:

"I'm a single mother now. It's all I can do to pay health and car insurance."

"My husband just got downsized. I loved the U, but life is tight right now."

"I'm having a baby. You'll get tuition money in eighteen years."

"I'm unemployed now, I'm so sorry, I got a great cheap education and know I should give, but I need shoes for the kids more. Call it realpolitik. I was a philosophy major, can you believe it? I can't either. Oh, God, campus seems so long ago."

Two historians of philanthropy, Sondra Shaw and Martha Taylor, have analyzed the constellation of struggles and doubts that shape women's campus giving. Many older alumnae have made no money decisions beyond household budgets or local volunteerism (what researcher Taylor dubs the Supermarket & Bake Sale Mentality). They see the future as alien and threatening, are adept at evasion. "I've got to ask my son." "I don't think my accountant will let me." Among older women graduates who have worked, "Look out for yourself first" is a fiercely repeated mantra. (Women of all ages worry about money far more than men do; a collective terror of bagladydom makes their fiscal attitudes very like those of first-generation immigrants, or Depression-era Americans.)

The Bastion of Males argument often motivates self-made women, who at midlife think twice about underwriting schools that patronized or discouraged them at twenty. Donations, to these alumnae, mean leverage for change, and immunity to say things universities don't want to hear. "Why are women not being groomed for the inner circle?" "Why are there no women on your priorities committee?" Says one well-off Penn graduate, now in real estate: "Tenure more women, then we'll talk. Maybe." A group of 1950s Radcliffe alumnae agree; they are asking about forty thousand members of Harvard-Radcliffe to put all campus donations into an escrow account until Harvard puts more women on tenure. Nationally, women hold about 20 percent of the tenure spots on arts and science faculties. At Harvard, it's half that. The professional schools are even less inspiring: 8.9 percent of the faculty at Harvard Law School are women; at the Business School, 6.5 percent. (Consider us in context, the university retorts. At Stanford and Columbia, women made up 13 percent of tenured faculty, at Michigan 10 percent, at Princeton 12 percent. Lighten up. We're in the middle of a $2 billion fundraising campaign. We know, the women say. We know.)

"You'd Better Ask Me, Too" is a category of reaction strongest among midlife women in a two-career marriage. Few in this group find it amusing to be ignored as prospects for major donations while their husbands are separately wooed. A woman may give $400 to her old school, discover her husband sent $1,500 to his, and go ballistic: That's my money, too, you know! Women under forty mostly exhibit the New Career mentality: "It's my money, and I deserve to keep it." Many suspect college philanthropy remains at heart a boys-only game. Many send plenty of checks to campus as it is, all to repay student loans ("Give my school *more* money? Don't make me laugh.").

A great many alumnae perceive their time on campus as a business transaction: no bitterness, but also no bonding. "Women's giving combines two great mysteries, sex and power," observes Janet Holmgren McKay, president of all-female Mills College in Oakland, California. "We are about to find out if women will use their fiscal clout to hold schools accountable, on many levels. Money not only talks in higher education, it also confers the right to question, to stipulate, to withhold."

Yet the urge to make life easier for those on the way up is powerful, too. Persuading women to donate to higher education means invoking a powerful sexual politics: Should you bolster traditionally "female fields"—the liberal arts, education, the social sciences? Or be like Clare Boothe Luce, who never took a science class, but willed $70 million to advance women as professors of science and engineering? Old-fashioned campus priorities can enrage, especially when development offices tout a winning men's team as reason enough to send a check. ("I'm not putting my money in some sports sinkhole," says one Minnesota Ph.D.) Stanford recently mailed varsity letters to over two thousand female graduates between forty and sixty, competitive college athletes from a time when only men were allowed to letter in a sport. "Bittersweet," said one recipient, a former basketball player, now a psychologist in private practice.

Increasingly, too, women want the ethics of college giving discussed. Fund-raising is often courtship and flattery to the target's face, followed by predatory language behind doors—going in for the kill, putting the finger on a donor. But more and more alumnae who give desire not stroking but results. Make annual grants to specific programs, as the giant foundations do, say former administrators. Don't endow professorial chairs, give new faculty salary lines instead. Give for storm windows, not general funds. Make stringent conditions. Ask to see receipts.

Even at schools coed a century and more, female giving remains fraught, and the auguries mixed. Most Ivies must wait another quarter century before the first classes with high percentages of women mature into big-money prospects. Princeton, last of the Ivy League to let in females, will wait longest. For all the schools that resisted coeducation, it is an anxious time. Women, a Harvard fund-raiser once told me, fretfully, have such long memories.

•   •   •

As freshmen, the Class of 1970 knew only the old confident collegiate world. But by senior year, most were doing their best to conform to a new campus zeitgeist, dizzy with freedoms, electric with rage. Cambodia-invasion protests shut down many Princeton classes in the spring of 1970. The local chapter of SDS booed a visiting Nixon cabinet officer to silence. Walter Lippmann was voted an honorary doctorate at graduation; so was Bob Dylan. "Oh, you were *bad*," writes their former admissions dean in the official Twenty-fifth Reunion Book, a dignified hardcover opus with an epigram from George Bernard Shaw: "Reminiscences make me feel so deliciously aged and sad."

The average '70, their Reunions survey finds, is a doctor or lawyer. Almost none have known discrimination in the workplace, and interrupting a career to raise children mystifies them, too; such tradeoffs are the province of wives. Their sex lives are cooling, their politics drifting right, and they are surprised by their own happiness. 'Seventy is a distinctly well-off class, even by the local, skewed, standard. One in four owns a house with a swimming pool, some are multimillionaires, one is Steve Forbes. Twenty-one of their classmates are dead: by suicide, by drowning, by helicopter crash. Of cancer. Of a brain tumor. In San Francisco, following a long illness.

For their Reunions book, each class member writes an essay. Some send poetry ("Let us exchange business cards/like snow . . ."), others haltingly record ("What do you mean, 'please type'? We should submit on disk, or uplink over the Net!") eight hundred thirty-one lives after diplomas. Yoga pilgrimages. Paratrooper training. Surf kayaking. Piano lessons at thirty-nine. Research on hamster sex. Early retirement, in order to fly-fish.

My favorite food is pickled herring, my favorite wine Margaux.

My life is filled with blessings I can't enjoy.

I have built nearly one thousand houses and condos in the Killington, Vermont, area.

I'm still a middle-class, left-wing, humanistic, music/writing kind of guy.

I have learned to scrutinize desire. My unemployment checks from my last job as a used-car salesman are drawing to a close.

I can't believe my kid is a preppie.

I don't gator too much these days.

Friends are wrinkling.

May 1970 was nine thousand days ago. I've slept through the equivalent of three thousand of them and—why not tell the truth?—frittered away another three thousand.

Happily single.

Happily remarried.

Three kids, and two *wonderful* pot-bellied pigs.

See you at Reunions. See you in the P-rade. To social scientists, Ivy League bonding rituals are disconcerting in the extreme. While most college alumni bulletins incorporate the dignified gossip of class news, Harvard, Yale, and Princeton most frequently provide glossy magazines thick with class notes, an obsessive group autobiography that begins at the door of the first-year dorm and ends at the tomb, class on class marching to the cliff edge, and beyond. You cannot defect, you cannot renege; hate the place, transfer, purge it from your résumé, tear up your fund-drive envelopes, Alumni Records does not care. *Tu es Princetonensis in aeternum,* forever and ever, world without end, from Aaron Burr and Lyle Menendez to John F. Kennedy, who left due to illness in his first year but is still, by local reckoning, Princeton '39.

And Princeton has the P-rade, capstone of Reunions. Since just after the Civil War, alumni have traveled thousands of miles for this sloppy, lavish parade, which winds through Princeton's suave leafy campus, led always by the twenty-fifth-anniversary returnees. Each class, oldest to youngest, cheers on its predecessors and then—memento mori—joins the march. The Class of '70, assembling for their historic hour, peer disapprovingly at a Louise Nevelson sculpture on the library lawn ("*That's* new"), then study their marching orders ("Quite frankly, I liked the *old* P-rade route better"). At last they head off, straggling and disorganized—not a generation good at ceremony—escorted on their long walk by indulgent wives or embarrassed gawky sons. A few in '70 lean on canes, several have serious paunches, many are grey-haired. Some openly weep. Others wave official class pith helmets at the administration offices they tried to sack a quarter-century before. One member of '70 detours his preadolescent daughter to the big Henry Moore oval near Nassau Hall.

"If you look at this sculpture sideways," he says proudly, "it looks *just like* the profile of Richard Nixon." "Who's Richard Nixon?" she inquires. Silently, they rejoin the line.

Seated in an orange-and-black golf cart, the oldest returning graduate, Class of 1917, dozes on the Nassau Hall lawn. For Reunions, he often takes the bus from New York to Princeton, an hour's tiring ride. But when the marshals in their velvet Renaissance caps bustle up, and the P-rade jerks once more into motion, applause revives him. He remembers to wave his tiger-headed Old Guard cane, and sometimes calls out jokes and catchwords to faces only he can see. He is one hundred years old, and for this moment he has outlasted thousands of men. Some in his cohort went down with the Lafayette Escadrille, others lost everything in the Depression; he is still here.

A golf cart carries one returning member from The Class of '20, and one widow. The Class of 1922 is the first that can totter, three ancients poking each other with walking sticks. All hearing aids and cataracts, '23 feebly whirl plush tiger tails. A sole returnee of '26 is eased along the walkway, borne up by middle-aged grandchildren.

A bunch of '89ers, mellow with milk punch, try to cross the parade route but fall back, alarmed: the 1930s classes are going by. "Sweet Jesus," says a rotund stock analyst, "that's us in 2039." The Class of 1935 is a fine fit corps of eighty-year-olds, even essaying a soft-shoe now and then, but on their heels comes a wave of sound: "Sis! Boom! Bah! '36, '36, '36!"

The watchers whistle and cheer. For two hours, theirs is again an all-Princeton universe, comradely, silk-lined, vivid with memories of bright college years. Here and there are faces I last saw in Alaska, moving toward the very front of the P-rade now, but still singing. A white-haired wife gently holds her husband's shoulders so he can watch classmates go by; his left side is useless from a stroke, his head lolls, but he has made it back. The Class of '44 swings past in lederhosen, the Allentown, Pa., high school band thumping out "In the Mood." The Classes of '45 and '48 have enough energy to leap to the sidelines and kiss classmates' wives. Genetics and exercise tell now: some GI Bill–era grads look fifty, others eighty. The '49ers all play kazoos, nearly drowning out the Dixieland band that follows. The classes of the Fifties pass next, into the shadow of a Tudor archway, out again into the sunlit library plaza. Many of the marching men struggle with overexcited Labradors, or grandchildren in tiger-striped face paint.

A band of Colonial re-enactors go by, then a coach-and-four, then a regiment of kilted bagpipers. A video crew from Brussels hurries along the spectator lines, valiantly recording the local rites. A lost '57 walks past on his hands; '64 bops, ponderously, to "Louie Louie," '65 waves blowups of freshman photos, all flattops and bow ties. The graduate school alums, break-dancing to a steel band with nerdly verve, shout, "We are *geeks!* Yay, *geeks!*" By '73, coeducation begins in earnest; '75 wanders past in tie-dye; '79 escorts a small, resentful, but very real tiger, panting in the early-summer heat. Plumed pirate hats, orange and black yin-yang blazers, a vintage Bugatti, more bobbing signs: We Look Better Naked. Friends Don't Let Friends Go to Yale.

Only from the late Seventies on do races and genders mingle unself-consciously, and now come the first sightings of gay Princetonians and their lovers hand in hand, of confident brown-skinned yuppies pushing Aprica strollers. Among the Eighties classes, I spot people I once taught, heading unaccountably toward middle age: getting bald, hoisting kids, comparing sunscreens. The only thing more unnerving than knowing your peers are running the world is realizing that your ex-students are, too.

Last of all walk the graduating seniors, chanting: "We want jobs! We want jobs!" Down the years, along the snaking line of marchers, floats the reply: "You can have ours! You can have ours!"

Quietly, amid all this festivity, another gathering occurs. Since 1976, some three dozen alumni—executives, copywriters, carpenters, scientists—have convened each Reunions in an oak-paneled seminar room to read together a canto from Dante's *Divine Comedy*. Robert Hollander, chair of the comparative literature department (wearing his Class of '55 official jacket, a bold and fetching orange plaid) provides footnotes and directs conversation, mainly by getting out of the way. His former students do the rest, in an ardent collective rush to imbibe, in one afternoon, enough high poetry to last them another twelve months. Year flows into year at these conversations, June after June comes round, the readers at the table a little greyer, a little heavier. After the first minutes, no one notices.

"I work in an Inferno," says Stephen Chanock, a Washington, D.C., pediatric oncologist (Class of '78). "After a day of nine-year-old cancer patients, it's very consoling to have Dante in your head. Every day, for me, is Canto Three—confused voices and cries out of darkness, bravery, despair, the immense relief of letting go."

"I come back to revitalize my brain," says Charlene Cosman '73, who oversees accounting for a chain of drive-through convenience stores on Long Island. "Actually, I want to make sure I still *have* a brain." She sometimes brings a plastic bust of Dante (adorned with a snappy orange bowtie) to these meetings, standing it near the chalkboard. The assembled Dantisti applaud.

"Time runs differently in Paradise," Hollander explains, his finger on this year's canto, *Paradiso* I, lines 1–36. "The voyage has not begun, the voyage is already complete. You can understand, or you can remember, but not both."

Dante, his Reunions fans contend, was mostly wasted on their younger selves. Hollander made many of them memorize the poem's first forty lines: *"Nel mezzo del cammin di nostra vita/Mi ritrovai per una selva oscura . . ."* "Midway upon the journey of our life, I found myself within a dark wood, where the straight way was lost." The cadence comes back to them unexpectedly, in the shower, on the train, in boring meetings, at crossroads of every kind.

"Remember *Purgatorio* XIX?" says one Dante veteran, and

others nod; it was the Reunions selection a few years back, in which just before dawn (the hour of true dreams) the sleeping poet envisions a crone, hideous and malignant, who suddenly changes into an alluring woman. She is, she claims, a Siren, one who lures humanity to destruction. But the Siren is routed, five lines on, by a second mysterious female, described only with the enigmatic phrase *"una donna santa e presta."*

"'A lady, holy and alert,'" Hollander repeats. "All right, folks, now that you've brought it up, who is the second woman?" Six centuries of Dante commentary are available on the Internet now, but in this instance tradition complicates, not clarifies. Two early scholars identified the mystery lady as Truth, but fifteen later experts violently disagree: she is the active life, the light of discernment, the goddess of wisdom; she is philosophy, reason, solicitude, grace. The Dantisti stare in silence at the page, wisely refusing to meet their teacher's eye. Just like old times: Don't call on me. My roommate ate my homework. Could you repeat the question?

"Think about the Siren," Hollander urges. He hunches over the long walnut table, eyes crossed, fingers scrabbling at his grey regimental mustache. "She's ugly, vile, the horrid embodiment of cupidity—" (Far down the line of faces, an investment banker flinches, looks about, and bends again to the text.) Mr. Hollander's theatrics trigger argument, but the voices in the room stay tentative at first, worried, self-conscious.

But then from the notebooks of memory, scraps of knowledge begin to float up, and link: the sex of angels, the etymology of Demosthenes' lisp, the name of Mohammed's second son, and slowly the group assembles an untidy heap of clues to the lady's identity. They vote: the mystery woman of *Purgatorio* XIX is probably—surprise—Beatrice, Dante's earthly muse and celestial guide. Someone moans. "What have you got against Beatrice?" Mr. Hollander asks, with mock testiness. "She's an airhead," mutters a voice near the window.

Their ninety minutes are over, but the Dantisti sit tight, wistfully advancing a few more counter-theories, some final subthemes. Why, someone asks, are gays the nicest people in Hell? Hollander looks up, smiling, from his worn and annotated text.

"In the *Purgatorio*," he says, "Dante goes out of his way to show us lovers, gay and straight, sharing the solemn kiss of peace. He always surprises. How much affection do we have on this campus today, between gays and straights, for all that we claim to be members of one community? Dante's version is touching, shocking, profoundly decent; for all our modernity, he is the better adjusted. Their requests, after all, are so few. Say a paternoster for me. Say a poem for me. Pray for me, remember me. It's all anyone wants."

At a quarter to six, Mr. Hollander pleads for adjournment. ("Peanuts! The Glenlivet! Num, num! Out the door and to your right, first floor of Maclean House, see you there, and I will tell you how, for my sins, I am working on a movie version of the *Divine Comedy*.") Pausing at the door with an armload of sherry and bitter lemon, he stares after the dispersing Dantisti.

"I'm proud of them. That was good. You know, once in Rome I stood in a locker room and admitted what I do for a living. My tennis partner, an Italian businessman, was enchanted. He began to recite. And echoing from every locker-room corner, voice after voice took up a passage from *Inferno*. A roomful of voices, eighteen lines of bloody perfect recitation. They all thought it very natural. I was damn near in tears." We begin to walk down the uneven slate sidewalk, Hollander musing still.

"I used to write poetry myself, but Dante killed it off. At

twenty-seven, you see, I had an epiphany. I was sitting in Butler Library up at Columbia, bored with graduate work and not
very good at it. I picked up a scholarly journal, read an article
on meaning in Dante, and time stopped. I remember gazing at
the tennis courts below, watching the geometric paths of the
ball, and thinking, 'So this is how it works.'"

He looks across the wide lawns behind Nassau Hall. In
courtyard after courtyard, the evening parties are tuning up,
swing for the '30s classes; classic rock for the '60s people;
swing again at the '80s reunion tents. Hollander was an undergraduate here before he was a professor; except for research leaves in the Roman and Florentine archives, he has
watched this same view, this one patch of ground, for forty-
four years.

"Many a spring I've had violent fantasies of leaving this
place. Every fall, I'm back. The siren's song of teaching is aw-
fully strong, even in an unlettered age. And every June, people
come from around the world to spend an hour with me on the
utterly impractical. It restores my instinct that some things, like
poetry, really are worth knowing in your bones."

He watches the last of his old students move off. Some take
the long way there, some idle near a striped canvas pavilion
where soft jazz plays. In the silvery light, the faces dim and are
lost, and then the retreating figures grow vague, too. Soon all
that floats back to us are the voices, disappearing, disappearing
under the darkening trees.

After Reunions weekend, graduation soon follows. The seniors have recovered, more or less, from the rigors of thesis
season, when many did not sleep or shower or change clothes
for days; when local copy shops kept drivers on call to rush the
tardy to departmental offices, bound final projects in hand. Seniors with job offers and seniors with firm plans to flounder
and drift stand kissing in the blue twilight, or wander alone,

touching walls and window ledges, feeling already like ghosts in a familiar place.

Backstage, administrative high season grinds on. An alumni officer trots past, wild-eyed; 126 E-mail and voicemail messages await him. The dean who must tell parents that their kid isn't graduating, not this year, walks slowly across campus, looking worried and tired. A development officer strolls past, triumphant. The revolutionaries of '70 have become the first twenty-fifth-reunion class ever to raise $4 million for Alumni Giving.

All graduations mean strategic worries—guests with wheelchairs and students with seeing-eye dogs; the ovolactovegetarian dignitaries, the Portapotties, the pickpockets. Worst duty of all, on any campus, can be convincing faculty members to turn out for a graduation procession. ("I loathe medieval drag," is a common response.) Princeton produces four dozen professors in full regalia, though several admit to T-shirts and shorts beneath. Waiting their cue, they circle the tall chapel-courtyard sundial crowned with a stone pelican tearing open her breast to nourish nestlings with her heart's blood—a favorite medieval image of communion, of charity, of sacrifice, of the teaching life. The mace bearer lifts his burden. "It's *showtime!*" murmurs a scientist, and two by two they march away, looking learned and grave.

Increasingly, graduation dress varies at U.S. campuses. At Northern Arizona University, many Indian seniors accept their diplomas in buckskin dresses or fringed boots. At the University of Hawaii, leis blaze above the academic black. African-American graduates may decide to wear kente-cloth stoles, splendidly striped in red and black and gold and green. Adhesive-tape messages—usually "Hi Mom" or "Send Money"—top thousands of mortarboards each year. At Henry Cogswell College in Washington State, the graduating class, all fourteen of them, fit nicely into a freight elevator; at the University of Texas–Austin, graduates must rise stadium section by stadium section. At Eastern Kentucky recently, seniors petitioned the dean for permission to wear fire helmets and police caps with their graduation robes, to signal their new careers. No way, the dean replied.

Few schools give out actual diplomas at graduation, merely an embossed leather cover, proxy for the document to arrive in the mail once parking tickets and library fines are paid. Some diplomas really are sheepskin, some artificial vellum, a few white plastic. Diplomas render every graduate a walking advertisement for a college, but a campus is not responsible should its product prove defective. The credential is by name and by nature twofold, di-ploma, sealed back upon itself.

At Princeton's graduation, degrees, honors, awards, ceremonial gestures, all are done. The Latin salutatorian has delivered an impassioned greeting. The crib sheets tucked in each senior's program have done their work—*hic ridete, hic plaudite, hic vociferamini Veni, vidi, vici!*—and those being graduated have all laughed, applauded, or cheered on cue, a mild scholarly conjuring trick, to impress the relatives. In front of Nassau Hall the lawn is a wilderness of crumpled tissues and half-empty soda cans. The party has migrated to the president's garden, for punch and strawberries and videoed farewells. A grounds crew loads podiums and risers into vans, rewinds orange-and-black bunting, rakes straight the tender trampled grass. High above, the sycamores are in full commencement foliage, and a warm south wind sweeps across America's first campus, bringing the sound of moving leaves that Emily Dickinson (Mount Holyoke '47) called the river in the tree. It is true summer now, but not for long. At hundreds of U.S. colleges and universities, Dear Advisor letters are already arriving from the newest undergraduates—mailed across town, across a state, across an ocean. Fall term is fourteen weeks away.

> Dear Advisor: Can I take Norwegian?

> Dear Advisor: Can I take Urdu?

> I don't want any math. I like cooking.

> My key interests include urban planning, optometry, animal training, and toxic waste. Just thought you should know.

> I want to take physics because of the many interesting real-life applications involved, i.e., car and plane crashes.

> My driving, obsessive interest is human biology. Also T'ai Chi.

> All I care about is water polo. No morning classes, please.

> I love history, but fear majoring in it will limit my career options exceedingly. I need at least $80,000 a year to be happy.

> Do you have any courses in social unrest? Please sign me up for all.

> I have a wide array of interests to go with my diverse personality. Should I major in English?

> I think George Kennan is the ideal human.

> I want to avoid science, literature, and all foreign languages.

> I want to experience a philosophy or a sociology. There are none in Florida.

I think a law career would definitely constitute a viable input to my life.

I don't care what I take so long as it can be applied to me.

I wish to learn greatness at the university.

Index